AMERICA AFIRE

ALSO BY BERNARD A. WEISBERGER

*

Reporters for the Union

They Gathered at the River

The American Newspaperman

The Age of Steam and Steel

Reaching for Empire

The Dream Maker

The WPA Guide to the USA

Cold War, Cold Peace

Many People, One Nation

The LaFollettes of Wisconsin

BERNARD A. WEISBERGER

AMERICA AFIRE

Jefferson, Adams,

and the Revolutionary Election

of 1800

WILLIAM MORROW

An Imprint of HarperCollins*Publishers*

For Ken Cameron

HarperCollins books may be purchased for educational, business, or sales
promotional use. For information please write: Special Markets Department,
HarperCollins Publishers Inc., 10 East 53rd Street, New York, NY 10022.

FIRST EDITION

Designed by Kate Nichols

Printed on acid-free paper

Library of Congress Cataloging-in-Publication Data has been applied for.

ISBN 0-380-97763-X

00 01 02 03 04 QW 10 9 8 7 6 5 4 3 2 1

Contents

PART III
WAR ABROAD, POLITICS AT HOME, 1793–1796

PART IV
TOWARD DISUNION, 1797–1800

PART V
CAMPAIGN AND CONSCIENCE, 1800–1801

Washington, D.C., Inauguration Day, 1801

IT WAS 4:00 A.M. on March 4—still dark and wintry cold in Washington—when a fat old man of sixty-five, without retinue or fanfare, settled his sleepy bones into a public stagecoach. Ahead lay a jouncing fourteen-hour trip to Baltimore, forty-plus miles away, the first stop on a long trip to Quincy, on the outskirts of Boston.[1] He was still officially the president of the United States and would be until Thomas Jefferson was sworn in at noon. But in reality, the unheralded departure marked the finish of his presidency and of thirty years at the center of history. In gloom, chill, and apparent stealth, John Adams was ending his public career.

Historians have not been kind to Adams for his predawn flight a mere eight hours before the installation of the man who had beaten him in the 1800 election. It was "a case of plain bad manners" according to one scholar.[2] Others claim that he crept sullenly out of town, cheating the public of the ceremony of transition, because he would not suffer the humiliation of watching the winner claim the prize. A typical show of Adams's cranky temperament, these critics suggest, and an ungracious contrast to his own swearing-in of 1797, when he was decked out in a brocade suit and a ceremonial sword and Jefferson, the loser in the previous year's election, looked on. But in fact, Jefferson had no choice on that occasion—he had just been sworn in as vice president.

Adams was indeed angry in those final days, though not necessarily at Jefferson, his old partner in the Revolution though they were currently political enemies. Shortly before March 4, for example, he had courteously reminded the president-elect that he need spend no money on transportation, since two taxpayer-owned carriages and seven horses would be at his disposal in the stables of the presidential residence. Jefferson in turn had paid a civil good-bye call to sip tea and nibble cake with Abigail Adams, a dear friend for many years.[3] In a later exchange of letters, the now recently ex-president wished the new incumbent "a quiet and prosperous administration,"[4] though after that there would be an eleven-year chill before more letters passed between them.

Adams, meanwhile, claimed to look forward to retirement. It was already an established tradition set by George Washington, in imitation of the legendary Roman landowner-general Cincinnatus, that the good citizen of a republic did not seek high office, accepted it only when requested by the people, and gladly gave it up as soon as duty allowed in order to return to his acres. Adams, too, informed a friend that "the remainder of my days will probably be spent in the labor of agriculture [at Peacefield, his eighty-acre farm near Quincy] and the amusements of literature in both of which I have always taken more delight than in any public office."[5] But underneath his optimism was the sting of rejection by his fellow Americans, which is exactly what defeat in a reelection campaign amounts to. Adams felt it all the more keenly because he was convinced, as usual, that his official actions—no matter how unpopular—had been not only well-intentioned but unalterably right.

Worse than his sense of public ingratitude was the conviction that the country as a whole was on a downslide. After only a restless two weeks back at Peacefield, he poured out his feelings in a letter to his former secretary of the navy. "A group of foreign liars," he fumed, "encouraged by a few ambitious native gentlemen, have discomfited the education, the talents, the virtues and the property of the country. The reason is, we have no Americans in America."[6]

No Americans in America? And after only a quarter century of independence? Could this be the view of John Adams, one of the republic's most important founders? Granted, he had always harbored a deep distrust of human nature, inherited from ancestors who believed in original sin, and he had suffered the recent affronts of a divisive and losing campaign. Still, it was only a short time ago, as history went, that he had been proud to stand as vice president beside George Washington during the first, happy inauguration under the new, unifying Constitution. What had turned his optimism to bitterness? How could such bright beginnings become so dismal for him so soon?

The answer may have been just outside the coach window, through which Adams could see the crude and unfinished "seat of government" where he and the Congress had worked and lived in partly completed buildings for the last few months. Washington, D.C., was founded with high aspirations toward becoming the capital of a model classical republic founded on virtue. And it had immediately encountered the gritty realities of local politics, private ambition, and outright greed. Its brief history almost duplicated in miniature that of the infant nation. Both were aspiring but unfinished works. The cartoon image of either could have been a half-chiseled marble statue up to its knees in mud.

✳

WITH RARE EXCEPTIONS, the capital cities of other nations were established by the accidents of history. They were already market towns or gathering places before becoming seats of the mighty. The capital of the United States, however, was created from scratch by a political horse trade. The Constitution (Article I, Section 8) provided for a district no more than ten miles square for the "seat of government," over which Congress would exercise exclusive jurisdiction. It was to be created by a state or states voluntarily yielding some territory. A perfectly adequate existing city like Philadelphia, the temporary capital after 1790, would not do because Pennsylvania might thereby exert too much influence on the federal establishment within its boundaries. Constitution or no Constitution, states still kept a wary eye on one another.

When the First Congress, sitting in New York in 1790, began to debate the actual site of the future District of Columbia, sectional jealousy came into play. Southern members, supported by Jefferson, then secretary of state, were especially eager for a location close to them. Alexander Hamilton, heading the Treasury Department, hoped to firm up the national credit by getting the federal government to "assume" the war debts of the states and guarantee their payment. At an arranged dinner party, the two leaders struck a deal—Southern votes for "assumption" in exchange for Northern endorsement of a Potomac River capital to which the government would move in 1800. After surveys, the District was marked off where an eastern branch, the Anacostia, flowed into the Potomac between the small towns of Georgetown and Alexandria. It was an almost totally uninhabited area, heavily wooded, with gentle elevations and some riverbank tidal marshes. The choice gave great pleasure to President Washington, whose Mt. Vernon home was nearby, and for whom the capital itself eventuallly was named.

The next step was to move from deal to design. The assignment of planning a worthy federal city was given by Washington himself to a thirty-six-year-old engineer and architect, Major Pierre-Charles L'Enfant, a French-born Revolutionary War veteran who had come over to join the Americans in their fight for liberty and stayed. His credentials included survival through the winter at Valley Forge and capture by the British at Charleston, plus some postwar decorative and artistic commissions. L'Enfant's father had been a painter employed by the king of France, which may well have influenced the son's thinking. The major wanted to make Washington "proportioned to the greatness which the Capital of a powerful Empire ought to manifest."[7] He laid out a scheme of wide radial boulevards that would provide beautiful "vistas," superimposed on a rectangular grid of streets, with open plazas at major intersections suitable for public buildings that would be republican temples; for statues, parks, gardens, even "five grand fountains." The "transverse avenues" would be as much as 160 feet wide, more than one third the length of a football field, and the grand, mile-long boulevard connecting the "Congress House" and the "President's palace"— today's Pennsylvania Avenue—was planned to be 400 feet wide, with tree-lined walks along a broad carriageway.[8] There was an unmistakable resemblance to the overpowering royal palace and grounds that Louis XIV had created at Versailles. L'Enfant's ambitions assumed that the same kind of lavish funding and unquestioned authority would be at his command. It was a fatal mistake.

Who would pay for all this grandeur? Not Congress. Senators and representatives were not interested in burdening the taxpayers of their states. Maryland and Virginia between them lent some $200,000 to the United States, but the three commissioners named by the president in 1791 to supervise the development would have to rely on private investment. The plan was to get the District's landowners to deed half their holdings to the federal government. After surveying, lots would be sold at public auction. The reasonable presumption was that the value of the lots would soar as population and business poured in. The United States would pay construction costs out of its receipts, and when it needed land from the private half for public purposes, it would compensate at a fixed low price of about sixty-seven dollars an acre.

But nothing went right. The first public auction was a resounding flop despite considerable boosting by President Washington himself. So were the second and the third, selling only handfuls of lots. No one seemed willing to bet on the future of Washington. Meanwhile, Major L'Enfant and the landowners were at odds. They were outraged that his spacious avenues and squares would require them to sell large quantities of good real estate at the official instead of the market price, and he was equally determined that their greed should not spoil his design with incorrectly placed or ugly structures. He even had one private home that encroached on Pennsylvania Avenue torn down, and he plunged ahead with his projects regardless of the lack of money and the restraining orders of the commissioners. Washington finally had to fire him early in 1792. He had a checkered later career and in his impoverished old age could be found around the Capitol, a tall figure, dignified but threadbare, trying to badger Congress into awarding him some $95,000 for his services rather than the $2,500 they offered.

L'Enfant's replacement was Andrew Ellicott, who had already been engaged in making surveys, and who had briefly used as his assistant a gifted and self-taught free black astronomer, mathematician, and maker of clocks and almanacs named Benjamin Banneker. Banneker's presence establishes one strong foundation for the important role, from the very start, of African-Americans in the history of the District of Columbia. Another is that because laborers were hard to attract in the 1790s due to a shortage of affordable housing, much of the labor on the first public buildings of the land of the free was done by slaves rented from local owners.

Ellicott and a changing cast of commissioners soldiered on as best they could, trying to get started on the "President's Mansion," designed to look like an eighteenth-century English country gentleman's home, and the Capitol, which was supposed to have two pillared wings and a central structure topped by a dome in Roman-pantheon style. But money was still scarce, so in 1794 the commissioners decided to let speculative investors have their try. They sold six thousand lots—on credit—to a syndicate headed by Robert Morris that promised to pour dollars into private developments and to give the commissioners a monthly stipend. Morris's reputation seemed safe enough. He was the former superintendent of finance during the Revolution, a signer of the Declaration of Independence, a delegate to the Constitutional Convention, a onetime Pennsylvania senator, and reputedly the richest man in America. But much of his fortune was tied up in other speculations, and after building a few costly houses and pricing modest-income buyers out of the market, Morris and his partners went broke in 1797, and he himself wound up in debtors' prison. The commissioners were left with worthless promissory notes and a continuing need to scrounge for loans.

The result of this saga was predictable. By June 1800, when 126 officers and clerks of the federal government and their two boatloads of official records arrived for business, Washington was nowhere near ready.[9] A brick building for the Treasury Department stood near the presidential residence but was finished only on the outside. The uncompleted home of the State and War Departments stood nearby, surrounded by piles of brick, lumber, and rubble. There were a few decent (and expensive) houses scattered just west of these government buildings, a few more for officers at the Anacostia Navy Yard, and a great many shanties housing workmen. When the congressmen arrived up in November, only one wing of the Capitol had been completed. It was in a clearing amid the trees on Jenkins Hill, around which a straggle of boardinghouses awaited their residents.

The nation's leaders were not cheered by what they found. Albert Gallatin, soon to be secretary of the Treasury, wrote home that the "local situation is far from being pleasant or even convenient." Around the Capitol, in addition to the overcrowded boardinghouses, were "one tailor, one shoemaker, one printer, a washing woman," one shop each for the sale of groceries, stationery, and dry goods, "and an oyster house."[10] When the 106 representatives and 32 senators went to make an official session-opening call on President Adams at his "mansion," they had trouble traveling up still unpaved Pennsylvania Avenue, littered with stumps and bushes and dismally muddy. They made a brave show of it anyway, in "hackney coaches from Baltimore . . . preceded by the sergeant at arms with the mace, on horseback."[11]

The Executive Residence—not yet called the White House—was not much better. Abigail Adams had recently arrived after a trip in which her carriage got lost in the dense woods surrounding the capital. She was appalled at the conditions. "[N]ot one room or chamber is finished," she reported to her sister; no servants' bells, not enough firewood delivered despite the fact that it was so damp within that it was "habitable [only] by fires in every part, thirteen of which we are obliged to keep daily, or sleep in wet and damp places." She had to hang the laundry in "the great audience room." Outside there was "not the least fence, yard, or other convenience."[12] She admitted to some pleasant views of the river and to possibilities of handsomeness in the upstairs drawing room, but she was clearly suffering the shock of transplantation from Philadelphia, as were the government workers, who must have felt a sense of exile. Philadelphia was a civilized place with learned societies, libraries, museums, concert halls, a university, a hospital, lighted streets. Washington had none of these. The outgoing Treasury secretary, Oliver Wolcott, sniffed with disdain: "There is no industry, society, or business. . . . [A] few . . . gentlemen live in great splendor; but most of the inhabitants are low people . . . [who] live like fishes, by eating each other."[13]

In time there would be kinder assessments. That first winter a social life did develop around receptions by the "old families" of former planters who stayed in the area. A small middle class of resident professional men shared services in the town's lone church with the congressional transients, or weekly concerts by the six-member Marine Band. A democratic camaraderie was nourished in the boardinghouses. At Conrad's, for example, only a couple of blocks from the Capitol, Vice President Jefferson sat willingly among thirty other boarders at the far end of the dinner table from the fireplace—though he was allowed a private drawing room for conferences.

All the same, the census of 1800 clearly showed the city of Washington to be a backwater, with only 109 brick houses (to 267 of wood) and a total population of 2,464 whites—fewer than in Georgetown or Alexandria—623 slaves, and 123 "Free Negroes." As an experiment in capital-building, Washington, D.C., seemed on the edge of failure.[14]

✳

MANY TIMES in the ten-year struggle to make Washington, D.C., a second Rome it must have seemed that the new republic itself was a failure. Through the 1790s harmony gave way to savage quarrels over the country's future direction. Idealism plummeted in the face of harsh realities. Partisan rancor festered and erupted in riots, repressive laws, and vicious slanders. The 1800 election that climaxed the apparent death-spiral was only settled at the last minute by the House of Representatives in one stormy, intrigue-ridden February week.

Yet for that very reason, the inauguration day of March 4, 1801, was a triumph simply because it passed in peace. And John Adams was one of the day's heroes. If he did not linger to watch Jefferson take the oath, the reason was quite possibly simple uncertainty as to what was proper. This situation was truly new. At his own inaugural, Adams had inherited the blessing, the policies, and the cabinet of the Washington administration. Now, after losing only the fourth presidential election in the nation's history—and only the second seriously contested one—he was yielding the office to the head of an opposition political party—a brand-new creation in itself—who had radically different ideas and plans for America. A thoroughgoing, genuine transfer of power by popular vote had taken place. Adams, whether consciously or not, was setting a stunning precedent—freely handing over his high office to his political antagonists. His predawn exodus occurred only because 4:00 A.M. was the coach's regular hour of departure. He, John Adams, until that moment the leader of the nation, would leave the capital as a private citizen on a public conveyance.

Six hours later President-Elect Thomas Jefferson followed through with equal, and more consciously chosen, "republican" simplicity. At 10:00 A.M., a militia company from little Alexandria gathered in front of his living quarters on New Jersey Avenue, just southeast of the unfinished Capitol. When he was dressed and ready, Jefferson left his room and walked the short distance to the circular Senate Chamber, which had already been his working "home" for three months. Walking with him was a group of congressional friends and local dignitaries including two members of the outgoing cabinet. A party of the militia officers and marshals from the District marched ahead, and a salute from Washington's volunteer artillery company boomed out as he entered the building. Other than those martial touches, the inaugural "parade" was nothing more than a small cluster of civilians, the president-to-be included, trudging quietly uphill on a March morning.

That low-keyed transfer of the reins of government was a new development in the tortured, centuries-old history of dynasties violently changing hands. It was a victory for the idea of popular self-government itself, which at the time was practiced almost nowhere in the world outside the United States. And it was all the more remarkable coming on the heels of those contentious 1790s, when on numerous occasions the American experiment seemed almost certain to crash and burn just as conservatives everywhere predicted. How that turmoil arose, and how the crucial election of 1800 preserved the Revolution and the infant American republic, is the story that the following pages will unfold.

PART I

DISCORDS

OF AN UNFINISHED

NATION

CHAPTER 1

Philadelphia, Summer
1787

IN THE SUMMER OF 1788, a classic statement in defense of the Constitution argued that a "well-constructed Union," meaning a tightly knit nation rather than the existing loose "Confederation" of states, had one powerful advantage, namely, "its tendency to break and control the violence of faction." A faction, the writer said, was a number of citizens "actuated by some common impulse of passion, or of interest, adverse to the rights of other citizens, or to the permanent and aggregate interests of the community." And all "popular governments" showed an alarming "propensity to this dangerous vice."[1]

When the Constitutional Convention ended its business on September 17, 1787, it had failed to subdue the vice, and as a result, the "violence of faction" would nearly destroy the new Union in only thirteen short years.

To say as much is not to condemn but to understand. So pervasive is our reverence for the Constitution that we easily overlook its shaky and literally sweaty origins. It is the handiwork of daily meetings among a few dozen men in heavy clothes, cooped up six days a week for most of four months in a stifling Pennsylvania State House with windows shut tight against the swarming flies of a neighboring livery stable. In a moment of enthusiasm Thomas Jefferson called them "an assembly of demigods,"[2] no doubt thinking particularly of delegates George Washington and Benjamin Franklin. But far from carrying the stamp of divine inspiration, the "grand convention" of 1787 was bound by human limitations. Its fifty-five members shared a commitment to a stronger nation but were also pleading the special interests of the individual states and classes they represented. The debates, especially among a talented few, were amazingly learned and civil. But there were also moments of hot temper and sulky deadlock, and at least twice there were threatened walkouts when only compromise staved off a breakup. Three of the most active framers never did sign the finished Constitution. So the delegates were far from believing that they were setting down holy writ for the ages. Nor did their fellow Americans think so. It took three quarters of a year to win ratification of the document in the needed minimum of nine states, and that was with promises of early amendments. Even then victory was barely squeezed out in crucial Virginia and New York. The last holdout, Rhode Island, which never even took part in the convention, did not join the Union until May 1790.

The Constitution, in the 1790s, was still considered a fragile work-in-progress—more a provisional outline than a charter for the ages. It didn't yet have the emotional power to unite people automatically behind it. And it showed early signs of misjudgments and of business unfinished. First of all, since they shared a general coolness toward "democracy," the framers failed to foresee the growth of a drive toward more widespread participation in "popular governments." Second, they never anticipated that "factions" could embrace whole sections of the new Union, or that there might be large-scale permanent coalitions of "factions" in the form of political parties. And of course they could not know that the new ship of state would be launched into a wrenching tempest of international warfare caused by a French Revolution that was soon to begin.

All of these developments unleashed the passions of special interest and thwarted the hopes of immediately setting up a national government dedicated purely to the "permanent and aggregate interests of the community." One result was that the machinery of succession to the presidency would be out of date in the very first election after the most popular man in the country had stepped down from power, and seriously dysfunctional by the time of the second. The seeds of the crisis of 1800 were planted in 1787 in Philadelphia. The Constitutional Convention set the stage for the drama and introduced some of the cast. One delegate, South Carolina's Charles Cotesworth Pinckney, would become Adams's running mate. Two others would be far more significant players—James Madison and Alexander Hamilton, friends in 1787, intense foes thirteen years later. The whole story of the nation during that interval reflected their unraveling alliance. Madison was so much at the heart of the convention that he has been called the Father of the Constitution. Hamilton had only one highlighted moment, but it was enough to foreshadow a career whose impact on America's future may have been the most lasting of all.

⚹

BY 1800, Madison was a chief planner for the new Republican Party, which backed Jefferson for president. It strongly supported states' rights, and history remembers Madison in part for his eloquent defense of that stance. But when he arrived in Philadelphia early in May 1787, days before the scheduled opening session, Madison was still a nationalist and with good reason. He came fresh from months in New York City as a frustrated member of the one-house Congress created by the 1781 Articles of Confederation.

The Articles proclaimed a "firm league of friendship" among thirteen explicitly sovereign states. Each one sent a delegation—chosen by its legislature—to the Confederation Congress, and each delegation, regardless of the state's size, was entitled to one vote. The league carried the name of the United States of America, but "United" was a fiction. The raising of armies, the collection of taxes, and the exercise of Congress's few powers depended entirely on the voluntary cooperation of the states. Any important decision required the concurrence of nine, a sure recipe for allowing minority obstruction. There was no likely prospect for such a "nation" to grow or be taken seriously in the world, or even stay free for long.

✳

MADISON WANTED a new government with its own elected officials, courts, currency, and real power to fight wars, conduct diplomacy,
and regulate trade. So did other nationalists around the country, who
collectively had pushed the Confederation Congress into calling the
convention in order to "revise" the Articles. But Madison was on the
ground first, organizing the Virginia delegation for the coming debates
and drafting most of the nationalization plan that it would present the
moment actual business got under way.

He was an unlikely-looking revolutionary. At thirty-five, he was
short, balding in front, and so shy that fellow delegates sometimes had
to ask him to speak up when he held the floor. His father was a mid-
dling-sized planter who sent his bookish boy to private schools and
then, in 1769, to Princeton, where James exhausted himself completing
the four-year course in two years. He returned home and sank into a
year of depression, deprived of the scholarly surroundings he loved and
not really interested in running his plantation, Montpelier. Then the
revolutionary crisis rescued him from his breakdown. Completely committed to the cause, he was elected at various times to Virginia's state
legislature and state constitutional convention and, when the war
ended, to the Confederation Congress. It was there that he made
friends with Alexander Hamilton, a young army veteran with a rising
law practice, a growing family, and a way of thinking nationally instead
of provincially that chimed in perfectly with Madison's own feelings. It
was there, too, in 1783, that he got engaged to the sixteen-year-old
daughter of a fellow congressman. She later broke it off and broke his
heart. It took eleven more years before he could bring himself to propose to another woman, Dolley Payne Todd.

Madison spent a good deal of time in retreat at Montpelier, reading
voraciously in "rare and valuable books," picked up for him in Paris by
his friend Jefferson, on the nature and history of "confederacies."[3] By
1787, he was probably the country's leading expert on the subject. At
the convention someone took note that Madison "blends together the
profound politician with the scholar . . . [and] always comes forward the
best informed man of any point in the debate."[4]

But behind that professorial façade was an unswerving determination to be in control. Madison kept a private record of the proceedings to have available for his use in later debates. He took a seat at a front table where nothing could escape his notice and scribbled detailed notes that he polished night after night in his boardinghouse in the moments between committee meetings—and he was one of the busiest of all the delegates. They mounted up to hundreds of handwritten pages, an almost verbatim transcript of the proceedings. He kept them private during his lifetime, which ended in 1836, by which time he had outlived all other members of the convention. If his purpose was to avoid embarrassing other delegates by linking them to positions that they later abandoned, his own dramatic postconvention shift toward decentralization made him one of the chief beneficiaries of his own discretion.

*

THE OPENING WEEKS of the convention rang with a clash between the interests of large states and small ones. It was an issue that turned out to be less crucial than expected once the Constitution was adopted, but it nearly shipwrecked the whole effort at the start. The gathering began in harmony on May 25 during a spring downpour, eleven days late for lack of a quorum. The delegates immediately chose George Washington as presiding officer by acclamation. Washington turned the gavel over to a pro tem chairman, as he would every morning of the working sessions, and retired to Virginia's table where he sat, dignified and silent, until adjournment. The second day was devoted to adopting rules.

On the third day, Virginia's governor, Edmund Randolph—tall, handsome, melodious-voiced, and only thirty-three—read off the proposed resolutions of Madison's Virginia Plan to a silent and probably shocked audience. The plan called for a two-house national legislature, representation in both to be by population or wealth—good-bye to the one-state, one-vote equality that protected Delaware, with a population of about 50,000, from the voting power of Virginia and Pennsylvania, with 885,000 people between them. The new legislature would have power to make all laws necessary for the "harmony of the United States," to veto any conflicting state laws, and to use "the force of the Union" against any state that did not "fulfill its duty." It would also elect a national executive with "general authority" to carry out its mandates and a national judiciary whose judges would serve "during good behavior," meaning for life, unless impeached.

The next morning, the radical nature of these ideas was recognized. A flurry of discussion made it plain that the coercive Virginia Plan went far beyond the "revision" of the Articles of Confederation authorized by the call to the convention. In response Edmund Randolph added a forthright preamble: "Resolved that a *national* government ought to be established consisting of a *supreme* legislative, executive and judiciary." It was carried with the approval of six of the eight states whose delegates voted—a big surprise considering the convention itself operated on the one-state, one-vote principle. (If a delegation was tied, the state was counted as not voting.)[5] From that moment on, the convention was a runaway body, drafting an entirely new Constitution, with the opening momentum on the nationalist side.

But the small states had not given up, and they hit back hard early in June. Working for them was a time-consuming but indispensable rule that allowed any decision already made to be reopened, so that the whole structure of new government might be freshly reexamined as each piece was added. No defeat was final until the ultimate adjournment. Gunning Bedford, Delaware's fat and emotional attorney general, accused Pennsylvania and Virginia of promoting a system designed to give them "enormous and monstrous influence."[6] In truth, those two states plus Massachusetts and New York included more than half of the entire three million free inhabitants of the United States that summer. William Paterson of New Jersey swore that he would rather "submit to a monarch, to a despot" than sit in a legislature with votes apportioned by head count,[7] and he offered an alternative small-state plan that made a few changes in the Confederation government but left untouched the state-sovereignty formula that made it so ineffective.

At this point the issue of democratic fairness, which *would* remain central in the politics of the 1800 campaign, came to the fore. Madison and his large-state allies wanted to know why a small number of Americans living in New Jersey or Delaware should have an equal share of power with three, four, or eight times as many Americans in a larger state. They would not budge from their first position. But to their dismay, the volatile convention now voted for reconsideration of Paterson's *and* Randolph's resolutions. That was how things stood on Monday June 18 when Hamilton, one of New York's three delegates, took the floor to denounce both plans as inadequate.

✵

STILL A YOUNG MAN—either thirty or thirty-two that June[8]—Hamilton stirred passions among his contemporaries as surely as he has continued to ignite argument among historians, biographers, and readers down to the present moment. He is impossible to capture in a single image. He was a self-made man who beat the odds in a society where birth and rank still mattered; a foreign-born and rootless adventurer who more or less blueprinted the modern American nation; a brilliant advocate, financial planner, organizer, and administrator; and in the end a very human being who was scheming, unfaithful, quarrelsome, vainglorious, and fatally rash.

His origins on the island of Nevis in the British West Indies are both romantic and sordid. His mother, Rachel Faucett, had fled there from the nearby Danish-owned island of St. Croix and from a husband who later divorced her in absentia—justifiably or not—for having "given herself up to whoring with everyone." At the time of Alexander's birth, she was living with James Hamilton, the apparently disowned son of an aristocratic Scottish family, who was trying incompetently to survive as a businessman. She had already borne him another child. The couple later moved back to St. Croix and broke up. He disappeared into poverty. She died of a fever in 1768, leaving her two bastard, orphan boys to the kindness of strangers.

For Alexander, not yet fourteen, these strangers included Nicholas Cruger, who gave him a clerk's job in the import-export business he ran with a New York partner. As in most things he later undertook, Hamilton quickly proved brilliant at it. Intense reading overcame a spotty basic education and made him a clear writer with a huge fund of information about the markets, materials, and currencies of the Caribbean trade. By the time Alexander was sixteen, Cruger could travel for months and confidently leave him in charge of things. The experience gave Hamilton a hardheaded view of a West Indian world in which sugar planters grew rich on the sweat of brutally worked slaves, and mercantile profits went to sharp and aggressive risk takers. It was not a world big enough for his nonmercantile ambitions. To a young friend he lamented "the groveling and condition of a clerk . . . to which my fortune, etc. condemns me," and wished for a war "to exalt my station."[9]

He got his war soon enough, along with a cause and a country. In 1773 local St. Croix worthies chipped in to send the local prodigy to King's College (later Columbia) in New York for more education. Soon he had connected himself with the resistance movement against Britain and was writing deftly argued anonymous pamphlets for the revolutionaries. When fighting broke out he left Columbia—probably its most distinguished dropout—to become an artillery officer in the state forces, and throughout 1776 he saw active service in Washington's hard-pressed little army. Once again his talents, observed by admiring older men, led to advancement. He was appointed to Washington's staff, with the rank of lieutenant colonel, early in 1777. He was twenty-two at most.

There he stayed until 1781 as something like a private secretary to the commander in chief, flung into the thick of Washington's constant struggles to get money, manpower, and supplies from a quarrelsome and headless Continental Congress. The general became another protector and patron, relying on the gifted young man to draft letters, orders, and messages or negotiate with other commanders and political figures. That confidence had a powerful influence on history when Washington, as first president, named Hamilton the first secretary of the Treasury. In the meantime, Hamilton's acquired status and connections allowed him to take a huge upward step in social rank by marrying Elizabeth Schuyler, daughter of one of New York's richest and most powerful landholders. After the war Hamilton, like thousands of other American citizen-warriors, took off his uniform and rejoined civil society. He taught himself law in five months and began a shining career at the New York bar and in local politics. But he was never, like his in-laws, a true New Yorker. His sense of America as one nation was not di-luted by home-born state loyalties. What he felt for states was contempt, fed by memories of watching soldiers shiver and starve be-cause the state-dominated Continental Congress refused to create a central government competent to clothe and feed them. In fact, while still on Washington's staff he wrote in confidence to a friend suggesting that a convention was needed to create a "coercive union" that could "destroy all ideas of state attachments in the army." Such a statement in public would have been political suicide. A shrewd French intelli-gence agent was later to write to Paris that Hamilton, for all his gifts, had "too little prudence. . . . In his desire to control everything, he misses his aim."[10]

When he rose to speak that June morning in 1787 Hamilton was once again imprudent and risked throwing away the pro-nationalist influence he had been building for several years. He may have been overirritated by the resistance of the small states, or frustrated by the fact that in New York's three-man delegation he was helplessly outvoted by two anti-nationalists. In any case, the speech lasted all day (a fellow delegate noted of Hamilton, "There is no skimming over the surface of a subject with him"),[11] and its highlights, including Anglophilia, distrust of voters, and a wish for a kind of centralized "republican monarchy," were guar-anteed to alienate and infuriate moderates. They would have no imme-diate impact in Philadelphia, but later they would become building blocks in the political thought of the Federalist Party.

Hamilton saw society as a theater of perpetual conflict rather than cooperation for security. "Men love power," he said. "Give all power to the many, they will oppress the few. Give all power to the few, they will oppress the many." A hereditary elite and a hereditary monarch, he be-lieved, with vested interests in stability were the best guarantee against the turmoil of war between classes. He admitted to thinking privately that "the British government was the best in the world," and the House of Lords "a most noble institution." But Americans, alas, would never accept a monarchy. Nor would public opinion allow the American states, despite their uselessness and "the ambition of their demagogues," to be eliminated. So Hamilton's own "sketch" for a new United States government would concede something to the necessity of maintaining "republican" institutions and states—but as little as possible.

He proposed an assembly directly elected by the people every three years—that was the "republican" part. But there would be a senate with lifetime members and a lifetime chief executive or "governor," both named by "electors" a step removed from popular choice. There would be a lifetime judiciary, too. The "governor" could veto acts of the assembly and senate. States would stay in existence, but *their* governors would be appointed for life by the national government, and they would have power to veto any state laws contrary to "the Constitution of the United States."[12]

No one interrupted Colonel Hamilton's discourse, and no one paid the slightest attention to his plan thereafter. It simply died. Less than a week later he left the convention for all of July and all but one day of August. But he did return for the last eleven days prior to signing and showed the positive side of his complex personality by working prodigiously for the adoption and success of a finished Constitution that fell far short of his desires.

✹

CRITICAL WEEKS followed Hamilton's departure as the convention froze in stalemate over the question of majority influence versus minority protection in the national legislature. Luckily, another convention rule kept the proceedings secret so that the fight did not spill over and embroil the whole country before the finished work could be presented. And a fight it was. On June 29, in a fierce exchange, a sweating Gunning Bedford shouted at the large-state delegations, *"I do not, gentlemen, trust you,"* and warned that if the rights of the lesser states were trampled, they would "find some foreign ally of more honor and good faith, who will take them by the hand and do them justice." There it was—spoken aloud—the hovering fear that would haunt the coming decade, that the new nation would break up and each feeble part would become the puppet of a powerful foreign patron.[13] That peril finally drove even the most stubborn to yield. After some close votes, a near breakup, and a timely recess for offstage negotiation, the convention adopted the compromise suggestion of Connecticut's Roger Sherman. Much to Madison's disappointment, it gave half a loaf to each side— seats in the lower House of Representatives would be based on population; state equality would rein in the more "aristocratic" Senate.

After a breath-stopping moment when Randolph appeared on the verge of leading a large-state exodus, the convention resumed. The large-versus-small-state issue more or less vanished, or rather was transferred to other fault lines in the nation. These appeared as soon as the time came to allot actual numbers of seats to each state in the lower house. In the debates over that thorny point, Madison struck to the heart of the matter. "The states," he said, were "divided into different interests, not only by their different size, but by . . . the effects of their having or not having slaves. These . . . concur in forming the great division . . . in the United States."[14] He was a good prophet. The split that mattered would be between north and south. Tiny Delaware would in time find itself allied with Virginia, and little Rhode Island with Massachusetts, not simply over slavery, as Madison's words seemed to suggest, but over economic and social differences that would create special *sectional* interests.

Soon there would be a third section. One-legged Gouverneur Morris of the Pennsylvania delegation, whose aristocratic wit and eloquence often enlivened the debates, took note that the westward movement would create new states, which would, in population and votes, soon exceed the rest of the country and "ruin the Atlantic interests." Morris, a lifelong urbanite in New York, Philadelphia, and Paris, wanted to exclude future majorities from the "remote wilderness" by limiting the number of new states that could be admitted. So did others from the "maritime states," especially New England. But the convention eventually agreed with the realistic views of Pennsylvania's James Wilson and Virginia's George Mason that "whether we will or no," the people of the West would "speedily revolt from the Union if . . . not in all respects placed on an equal footing."[15] The door was left open, but the threat of western revolt would haunt the first twenty years of the republic's life. Isolated, undeveloped, and with urgent special needs, the

West would for some time act as a force "adverse to the . . . aggregate interests" of the United States as a whole.

In 1787, however, the main sectional battle was between the North and South over counting slaves as part of the population. Doing so would considerably increase the South's legislative representation, much to the disadvantage and resentment of the North. Though slave-holding was still legal (but dying out) in the northern states, the numbers were insignificant—about fifty thousand, one tenth of the half million in the South. Gouverneur Morris undoubtedly reflected universal northern sentiment when he said that the people of Pennsylvania would "never agree to a representation of Negroes." But North Carolina's William Davie likewise expressed general southern opinion when he announced that if the convention voted to exclude slaves from the head count altogether, "the business was at an end."[16]

The delegates got past that hurdle only by agreeing to use "the whole number of free persons" and "three fifths of all other persons"—the euphemism for slaves used throughout the completed Constitution—as the basis of representation. (It was the formula already agreed on to determine how much each state owed the Confederation treasury.) But the issue erupted again when the question of regulating or taxing importation of slaves arose. Morris set off rhetorical fireworks by denouncing the "nefarious" institution. But he knew perfectly well that there was simply no chance of putting a cap on slave imports and expecting the southern states to adopt the Constitution. As John Rutledge of South Carolina put it, southerners would "never be such fools as to give up so important an interest."[17] Once more faced with a choice between collapse and compromise, the delegates accepted compromise. The right to import slaves was guaranteed until 1808. And so slavery became the ticking bomb of the "more perfect Union" that the Constitution created.

The quarrels over slavery and the admission of western states were warning flags. The convention settled the issue of local versus central authority by the brilliant concept of "federalism"—of national and state governments exercising separate powers, some concurrently and some exclusively. But against the splintering potential of sectionalism there was no structural defense within the Constitution's provisions. Within a

short while an extraconstitutional device would appear with a partial solution (and new problems), namely, the national political party looking
for followers in every section. But the surprise birth of that same party
system threw a wrench into the already complicated machinery that the
convention had devised for choosing presidents. The ambiguities of the
delegates on that matter led straight to the near blowup of 1800, though
no one had any inkling of that in 1787.

*

"THE CONVENTION . . . [was] perplexed with no part of the plan
so much," Pennsylvania delegate James Wilson later explained.[18] The
dilemma was embedded in the larger question of what kind of "national
executive" to create. Delegates wanted no part of an autocratic ruler like
some of the high-handed colonial governors they remembered, appointed by a faraway king. But they had also experimented with weak
or committee-type executives under some of the new state constitutions
and the Articles of Confederation, and the fruit was sour—runaway legislatures controlled by a single interest, or paralyzed legislatures torn
among factions, with no firm leadership to restrain or guide them. Where
was the "balance" so dear to eighteenth-century artists and thinkers?
Finding it was, in one scholar's words, a little like playing three-dimen-
sional chess.[19] Moving any piece changed the patterns of the entire
board. Take a simple matter like the executive's length of term. Too
short, and it would be impossible for him to build support for his programs. But too long a time in office might let him hand out enough patronage to dominate the legislature with a solid cadre of grateful yes
men. What about his eligibility for reelection? A president confined to
one term would always be a transient, on-the-job learner with limited influence. But if allowed to run again, he might forever be campaigning,
perhaps winning time after time to become a lifelong despot. So any
change in the duration or number of terms required "balancing" by
adding or subtracting from the actual powers of the office.

The mode of election fit into this pattern. To whom should the
chief executive owe his job? The people at large? There was little sentiment for that. Most members agreed with Elbridge Gerry that unin-

formed and propertyless commoners could easily become "the dupes of pretended patriots." Like other businessmen, he was afraid of "the levelling spirit."[20] It could lead to high wealth taxes or the legislative annulment of debts. Popular choice would be, in George Mason's words, like asking a blind man to choose colors. Scots-born James Wilson, more inclined to trust in democracy, suggested a compromise, namely, the popular choice of "electors," who would meet on a given day to cast their ballots.[21] The convention at first, however, heavily favored choice of the chief executive by the legislature.

That, however, raised serious issues about the separation of powers. It might well make the president a pawn of Congress, or a conniver who bought his job with promised favors to members. So in late July they went back to the drawing board and discussed a flurry of propositions. Election by the state governors or by electors named by the state governors. Election by the legislature from a list, submitted by the voters, of each state's "best citizens." First-time election by the national legislature and any subsequent reelection by state legislatures. Finally, in desperation, a bizarre new idea from Wilson, which he admitted to be "undigested," namely, a lottery in the national legislature. Every member would draw a "ball" from a jar; a given number—say, fifteen—of these balls would be gilded, and those with the gilded balls would retire at once (so that no one had time to bargain with them) and make the choice.[22]

As late as August the draft Constitution was still calling for Congress to name the president for a single, nonrenewable seven-year term. But the unsatisfied delegates recommitted the issue to a final committee massaging that designed the presidency as it is now known, including a complicated method of choice that utilized Wilson's "electors" and tried to satisfy everyone. Each state would determine for itself the method of choosing a number of electors equal to its congressional delegation. Then the electors, who could not be members of Congress or national officeholders, would meet in their state capitals and vote for two persons, at least one of whom was *not* from their own states. Then they would send their marked ballots to the seat of government to be counted in the presence of Congress, and dissolve. The highest vote-getter won the presidency, and the runner-up became vice president. If no candidate had a majority, which was expected to happen often, or if there was a tie, the Senate would pick a winner from the top contenders.

The framers, by now weary, homesick, and faced with mounting board bills and backlogs of personal business, made one last change. They gave the job of settling a tie or a failure to achieve a majority, originally assigned to the "aristocratic" Senate, which was then chosen by state legislatures, to the more popularly based House. In those cases, however, the House would use a one-state, one-vote formula, a sop to the small states. The Senate could still pick the vice president if there was no clear second-place choice. There was no serious consideration of what the vice president should actually do, other than be available. The whole office had an air of last-minute improvisation about it. Finally, a job was assigned—to preside over the Senate, but without a vote except to break ties. George Mason objected to this intrusion of an "executive" official into legislative business, but Roger Sherman gently noted that otherwise the poor man would be "without employment."[23]

There was indeed some logic in having the man most preferred by electors nationwide backed up in case of disaster by the second most-admired. No one at all foresaw that the number one and number two choices might represent two organized bodies of voters with bitterly antagonistic views. The two chosen men, the thinking went, would agree on what was in the overall national interest and could be interchangeable.

✷

ON SEPTEMBER 17, 1787, the Constitution was finally signed by thirty-eight of the men who had taken part in the unprecedented experiment of actually inventing a new government for themselves, whose rules and principles fitted into a few pages of parchment. For all their limitations, they had shown a collective genius in their willingness to stick to fundamentals, compromise when necessary, and trust in the future. No one illustrated that better than Hamilton, the only signer from New York, who correctly said that no one's ideas were "more remote" from the finished document than his, but it was the best available and to refuse a signature (as did Gerry, Mason, and Randolph) would do "infinite mischief."[24] Then he stood behind his own words by returning to New York and joining with his friends Madison and John Jay to write, under enormous time pressure, eighty-five articles for the city's weekly newspapers, over the joint signature "the Federalist." Published in book form the next spring, they remain an incomparably lucid and compelling exposition of the Constitution's philosophy and workings. They helped win the critical battle for ratification in New York and wherever else they were read.

The pro-ratification forces actually performed a feat of slogan stealing. At the start of the convention the term *federal* was taken to apply to the existing and still widely cherished "confederation" of sovereign states. By calling the new arrangement of divided sovereignty a "federal" system and themselves federalists, the Constitution's defenders avoided the negative implications of the term *national*. But there was no question that the Constitution was a victory for nationalism. The United States Congress now had absolutely exclusive power to maintain armies and navies, sign treaties, regulate interstate and foreign commerce, and issue money. Above all, state courts would be bound to recognize the Constitution as "the *supreme* law of the land."[25]

Of course, victory was not total. The states kept great areas of independence, and there was room for strenuous disagreement on where the fence should be raised around the powers of the national government. All the same, there was a strong sense that emerged from the Constitutional Convention of an "American people" unlike any other and with a special part to play in history, a confidence both arrogant and touching. We were "singular," said young Charles Pinckney, in having "fewer distinctions of fortune and less of rank than among the inhabitants of every other nation." A failure to complete the convention's work, Elbridge Gerry warned, would "disappoint not only America but the world." George Mason said much the same in a letter home—he hated being away, but the work he was doing would have influence "upon the happiness or misery of millions yet unborn." And Gouverneur Morris was already boasting about "the splendor and dignity of the American Empire."[26] But time would soon prove that there were special problems in making a single, self-governing political community out of the many differing inhabitants of an "American Empire."

CHAPTER 2

The Nation in 1790

THE DELICATE BALANCES of the Constitution were brilliantly crafted, but the framers could not anticipate all the new kinds of weights that would be thrown into their newly made scales. They balanced the powers of state and nation through federalism; they balanced the "democratic," "aristocratic," and "monarchical" elements of government in the House, Senate, and presidency; and they balanced executive, legislative, and judicial powers with devices like the veto, the override, and lifetime tenure for judges. They assumed that these mechanical adjustments would of themselves handle the contrasting wishes of different classes and regions without perpetuating the "factionalism" that they detested.

They were wrong. The conflicts that had paralyzed the Confederation government of the 1780s persisted (though with changes) in the 1790s. Just how they translated themselves into wracking struggles between organized parties by 1800 will be shown in the coming chapters. But the narrative will be clearer for a review of what those differences were. Paradoxically, they sprang from the very diversity and vastness of the young United States—two facts of life that were sources both of trouble and of potential strength.

✳

PURELY IN TERMS of size, the infant United States was already an empire. In the enormous sea of space included within its 1790 boundaries—approximately 889,000 square miles—Spain, Great Britain, and France (not counting their overseas possessions) could have drowned, for altogether they totaled only a little over 500,000 square miles.[1] America's dominion was marked out on three sides by water—on the east by the Atlantic, on the west by the Mississippi, and on the north by the Great Lakes and the St. Lawrence River. Only on the south was the republic landlocked. The southern boundary of Georgia was extended westward to the Mississippi, cutting off access to the Gulf of Mexico and to the seas beyond. The great gateway to the Gulf, the port of New Orleans at the Mississippi's mouth, also remained in the hands of Spain, which in 1763 had gotten it from France as spoils of war in one of those constant transfers of imperial outposts between European kings—without the local populations being consulted in any way—that marked the great eighteenth-century chess game of war and diplomacy.

But size alone did not equal nationhood. Only settlement and cohesion could do that, and settlement was just what was lacking. Millions of virgin acres were considered open to the plow (no one paying much attention to the rights or claims of the resident Indian peoples), but in all that great expanse of mountain, forest, and river the population density was fewer than five per square mile. The 3,929,000 residents counted in the first census almost all dwelt within a serpentine coastal strip running from Maine to Georgia, about a thousand miles long and rarely more than a couple of hundred miles wide. That was the actual "United States" in which political action would take place. The two distinctive sections, North and South, that were already emerging were not quite equally balanced. Slightly over a million people lived in New England, then comprising four states, and slightly under a million in New York, Pennsylvania, and New Jersey. Of this total population of some 1,968,00 in "the North," all but 67,000 were white and free. In "the South," which embraced the remaining six states, there was a total population of 1,961,000—but 657,000 of these were slaves.[2] So the South, even with a slave counted in the census as three fifths of a person, was at a small but palpable disadvantage in representatives.

✳

THE CONFLICTS of interest that would have to be solved by political horse trading arose in part from economic geography. To begin with, there was New England, whose wealth was, to paraphrase a psalm that her preachers often quoted, founded upon the seas.[3] Long, bitter winters and rocky soils did not allow hardworking Yankee farmers to produce much beyond what they needed to feed and clothe themselves, and many were already moving westward. But the region did have a long coastline, abundant forests, plenty of skilled marine carpenters to turn trees into stout little vessels, and an unfailing supply of strong-nerved men to sail them anywhere in the world in search of codfish, whales, or cargoes of any kind to carry at a profit—silks and teas from China, furs from the Pacific Northwest, or groaning black men and women kidnapped, enslaved, and marketed like cattle in Africa. Most of the maritime fortunes of New England had been earned during colonial times in prosaic trips to the West Indies carrying rice, salted fish, lumber, hay, and horses for the sugar plantations. Or to Europe with holds full of West Indian molasses, Pennsylvania wheat, Virginia tobacco, or South Carolina indigo to make rich blue textile dyes. Or between British America's own Atlantic ports with rum, hardware, glass, fruit, books, furniture, textiles, and whatever colonists needed or could afford to import. When business thrived the heavy winners were wealthy mercantile families, but their prosperity spread downward to all those involved in commerce, from sea captains and lawyers to deckhands and dockworkers.

The enemies of New England's maritime welfare were not only storms and market fluctuations but the "mercantilist" policies then common, under which nations tried to confine commerce exclusively to ships owned by their own citizens. The "carrying trade" between the ports of Spain and her New World possessions, for example, was denied to ships that did not fly Spanish flags (though there were plenty of exceptions and evasions). This was British doctrine, too, but in the colo-

nial period American ships were considered British and had no problem. With independence, Americans suddenly became "foreigners" to
whom the vital commerce with the British West Indies was legally
closed. That was an ironic twist to freedom—a former door to prosperity slammed in the faces of the Revolution's victors.

What New England needed above all from the new United States
government was a foreign policy that would reopen those doors and negotiate new trading opportunities with other powers as well. In addition, Yankee fishing vessels, which had freely hauled in catches off the
coasts of Canada after that became a British possession in 1763, were
now shut out. That situation, too, cried aloud for remedy in Yankee
minds.

*

THE MID-ATLANTIC STATES shared some of these commercial
and shipping concerns. In New York and Philadelphia they had two of
the country's busiest ports. But their prosperous farms, which provided
huge quantities of food for home and foreign markets, created a separate agricultural interest that had a good deal in common with the plantation South. Looking to both the sea and the soil for their well-being,
Pennsylvania, New Jersey, and New York were "middle states" in more
ways than mere location on a map.

The South was a truly agrarian section. The backbone of its wealth
for over a century had been overseas sales of plantation-grown crops.
For Maryland, Virginia, and North Carolina, tobacco was the foundation
stone of society and politics. In South Carolina and Georgia, the last
colony to be founded (in 1732), rice and indigo were also major exports.
The needs of the large landowners who made up the southern elite
were explicit. Their overall agenda for the national government was
limited. They wanted no interference with slavery. They wanted foreign markets kept open, but it wasn't important to them whose ships
carried the goods—the cheaper the cargo rates the better. As heavy con-
sumers of imported goods, especially from Great Britain, southern
planters wanted nothing that would artificially raise import prices—no
tariffs to protect any Americans looking to challenge British dominance

in manufacturing. No bounties or subsidies to give American shipping a competitive edge. And no financial moves to stimulate investment that would put more money in the pockets of bankers and shareholders.

Southern planters and their political spokesmen—even those who favored the new Constitution—distrusted central power, especially when exercised in favor of the creditor class. This attitude had its roots in a long history of indebtedness. Tobacco planters in particular consigned their annual crops to British "factors" who sold them at the market price, used the proceeds to buy whatever British-made goods the planter had ordered, deducted their own fees and commissions, and sent back any leftover money. As often as not there was a negative balance, which the factor carried on his books as an interest-bearing loan secured by next year's harvest. Southern growers lived well and serenely amid stacks of unpaid bills. Like the English landed gentry whom they emulated, they thought such encumbrances were simply part of a gentleman's existence. But they hated business "speculators" on either side of the Atlantic, whom they suspected of manipulating prices and interest rates to the planters' disadvantage.

True, the planters themselves often speculated in land, but that was considered a respectable road to riches, the expression of a faith that more of God's earth would soon be under wholesome cultivation and that prices per acre would rise along with civilization.

✳

THERE WAS hardly a distinctive "West" in 1790 except for a bulge of trans-Appalachian settlement that would create the new states of Kentucky and Tennessee within half a dozen years.[4] It embraced frontier "communities" of scattered families subsisting in rough log huts on small patches of land hacked by hand out of the wilderness, where corn grew between the stumps and hogs ran wild. Their needs were few but urgent—military support, cheap land, markets for the furs they trapped and their cornmeal and pork, and above all, improvements in transportation that would connect them to those markets and pump the blood of development into their sparse existence.

But it is a mistake to assume that frontierlike conditions existed only in the remotest parts of the country. Once a traveler made his way inland from the Atlantic coast for more than several days in any state from New Hampshire to Georgia, he encountered a more egalitarian but cruder way of life—smaller farms, fewer professional men and merchants in the scattered towns, fewer amenities, more homespun clothing and homemade furniture, and more reliance on self, family, and neighbors for help with everything from childbirth to barn raising. The people of this backcountry, like those on the outer margins of settlement, also needed security, credit, markets, and improved transportation. They all had behind them a lengthy record of political, and in a few cases even armed, battles with the "aristocrats" of the coastal or tidewater regions who controlled the provincial and later the state governments. They were determined to get more land of their own, more seats in the legislatures, a better share of tax revenues, more courts and schools—everything that their growing numbers deserved. It was the troublemaking potential of these needy outsiders that had frightened conservatives in 1787 and drawn them into the effort to create the Constitution.

In addition to the issues dividing North and South, frontier and tidewater, the "middling sort" of people and the wealthy, there were other differences among Americans that added to the complexity of the political picture. Though the country's basic institutions had their roots in the religious, political, and economic life of seventeenth-century England, heavy immigration had already added new colors to the rainbow pattern of American society. In 1782 a French-born settler in rural New York, Michel-Guillaume Jean de Crèvecoeur, boasted that the American was a "new man," part of a "strange mixture of blood which you will find in no other country."[5] At least some two hundred thousand German-born or German-descended men and women lived in places as far apart as New York's Mohawk Valley and western North Carolina, though the major concentration in Pennsylvania had already created the term "Pennsylvania Dutch" (a corruption of *Deutsch*, German). The other heavy immigration of the 1700s came from the northern counties of Ireland. These "Scots-Irish," who gravitated heavily to the frontiers, though technically "British," were culturally speaking a stubborn, independent-minded breed of their own, A third major addition to the population—though a politically powerless one—consisted of the thousands of Africans who arrived in chains.

There were small but important urban pockets of French Protestant Huguenot families whose grandparents and great-grandparents had been thrown·out of France a century earlier. There were Jews likewise driven from Europe, many of them involved in international trade through family-owned businesses with networks of cousins and in-laws abroad. There were small numbers of Dutchmen and Swedes descended from very early settlements. None of these groups was strenuously "ethnic," but in the 1790s they often were at odds with their neighbors over religious matters. God was worshipped with admirable freedom in many ways, but some of them got more official backing than others. Congregationalism was a state-supported faith in parts of New England, and in some southern states the Episcopal, formerly the Anglican, church received tax revenues. Various state religious tests restricted officeholding and voting to Protestants or at least to Christians or to professors of faith in the Bible. Even where legal constraints were absent, the social and economic preeminence of Episcopalians and Congregationalists was a challenge to Jews, Dutch Reformed worshippers, Moravians, Lutherans, Mennonites, Catholics, Methodists, and Baptists. Some of these denominations, in particular Methodism, a recent import to America, had strong foundations among rural farmers and urban commoners—apprentices without the capital to start their own shops, day laborers, farmworkers, domestic servants, and others long shut out of decision making.

The hopes of such groups to rise in life fueled plenty of local political blazes in township and county elections for officials who ran such nuts-and-bolts operations of government as repairing roads and checking scales. Wider coalitions had occasionally been forged behind candidates for colonywide or statewide offices. But was there a possibility of creating nationwide groups organized for political action? Could there be an interlink between "outs" and "ins" in, say, North Carolina and New Hampshire that would unite them behind a single presidential hopeful? In 1790 the outlook was not promising because of the sheer physical difficulties of communication.

✻

IN THE 1790s the obstacles to simply transmitting a message were daunting. The only way for a politician, lawyer, or businessman in Boston to make contact with another in New York, Philadelphia, or Charleston was to send him a letter, written by hand with a sharpened quill (steel-point pens were half a century in the future) on heavy rag paper with homemade ink. Copies, if needed, had to be written out one by one. Devices like the letter press, which squeezed a damp sheet of paper over an original and took a faint impression, were slow, cumbersome, and rare. Secretaries were available only to the very highest officials. Almost every man in public life spent hours each day writing dozens of letters. The monuments of the most outstanding Founding Fathers are millions of words bound in thick volumes of collected works.

Mail contact was slow and costly. Congress didn't get around to creating the U.S. Post Office until 1792; an old system inherited from colonial days did set up post offices but could not work immediate improvements in the roads that linked them. Postage was paid for by the recipient. The 1792 act set rates ranging from six cents on a single-page letter going up to 30 miles to twenty-five cents on one traveling more than 450 miles, steep tariffs for those days. To save money (and paper), writers often filled up both sides of a sheet, then turned it at right angles and continued to write across their existing script. Then they folded the paper (no envelopes), sealed it with wax, and took it to the nearest post office.[6] From there it was confided to a "contractor," who ran a stage or wagon line.

Then came a long wait between sendoff and delivery. Forty miles a day, which meant about a week between Boston and New York, or a little under three days between New York and Philadelphia, was considered good time and depended on kind weather. But it was easier on the bones to do business by correspondence than to travel oneself. American coaches in 1790 were little more than wagons with transverse benches set on poor substitutes for springs. At every rut or rock, passengers swayed or bounced, and so did the baggage and mailbags piled around their feet. Rain poured in through imperfectly curtained side windows, made mud holes from which the coach had to be lifted by wet, filthy, and unhappy passengers, and brought long halts at streams too swollen to cross. The traveler arriving at a stopover in the late evening just had time to swallow cold leftovers and sleep for a few hours until wakened in darkness for an early start. And that was in the settled part of the country. In the West the even cruder roads were strewn with stumps and rocks that could overturn vehicles and maim and kill the unlucky. Water transportation was preferable, but sloops and schooners on the rivers could travel slowly upstream only to the first falls or shallows, and coastal vessels could be long delayed by contrary winds.

All these handicaps combined to make meetings hard to arrange between leaders in neighboring counties, let alone distant cities. Weeks of advance notice were needed. The political impact of such hardships was important. Quick adaptation to a changing scene was impossible. Misunderstandings, as for example among electors on a party's choice of candidates, could not be clarified overnight. Building a united leadership or an electoral "machine" would be tough and slow. It would have to begin within cities, where taverns and boardinghouses offered fire, lamps, writing facilities, and good cheer to small numbers of conferees around a friendly table. Connecting local caucuses in a wider network was the next, hard step.

Large-scale gatherings of voters were no light undertaking, either. There were some, held in churches, town halls (especially in New England), or other buildings big enough for audiences of several hundred, where the speeches could flow like wine and resolutions be passed by shouted acclamation. But genuinely "mass" public meetings, indoors or out, had to await the coming of large auditoriums, streetlights, transportation—a whole supporting network of urban services later taken for granted.

The press offered a way of transmitting political messages, but its reach was limited. There were some ninety newspapers in the whole country, most of them weeklies. Almost all had the same format of a single large sheet folded down the middle to create four pages. They were produced by the most literally "hands-on" technology. A tray of hand-set type covering two pages was inked by handheld rollers, then the paper was pressed against it by a heavy block of wood or metal screwed into place by a grunting printer or his apprentice. A day's work gave a press run of four or five hundred, the total circulation of the issue. But readership was wider than that, as papers were passed hand to hand, kept available in taverns, and mailed to country subscribers. Most of the pages were taken up with advertisements, announcements of local interest, official proclamations, and a small amount of news in eye-straining small print. But room could be left for public debates, usually in letters written under classical pseudonyms—"Publius," "Seneca," or "Cato" supposedly bringing the wisdom of antiquity to bear on current events. The trouble was that the writers easily forgot classical restraint. The record will show, as it unfolds, that the press was run by men more given to shouts and tantrums than to virtuous moderation.

✳

POLITICAL ARGUMENTS were addressed to the eyes and ears of a small electorate, though exactly how small is debatable. On the eve of the Revolution most colonies gave the vote to white, Christian, adult, propertied males. When the states became independent, there was a tendency in their new constitutions to lighten the property qualifications, so that by 1790, in most places, the taxpaying owner of any house or lot could meet them. More, however, was occasionally required for officeholding—and as for the idea of admitting people who owned nothing but themselves to the polling places, its hour had not struck. As John Adams said, "Very few men who have no property have any judgment of their own." Women were, of course, universally considered (by men) "not to have a sufficient acquired discretion to cast ballots," as a minister explained, because their domestic duties kept them from that "promiscuous intercourse with the world which is necessary to qualify them for electors."[7] But for men the newly relaxed rules meant that, according to scholarly estimates, 50 to 80 percent of them, depending on locality, had suffrage rights in 1789. The same researchers judge, however, that only 10 to 40 percent of this eligible electorate actually voted.

The turnout in colonial times had been on a very small scale, partly because many offices were appointive, partly because of the time-consuming grind to get to the scattered polling places, and partly because even qualified voters had a tendency to leave such matters in the hands of their presumed betters, the wealthy and professional classes. This "politics of deference" was broken into by the generally antiauthoritarian sentiments released during the Revolution. A 1793 get-out-the-vote handbill in New York appealed to prospective new voters with a reminder that "the pedantic lawyer, the wealthy merchant and the lordly landholder have already had their interests sufficiently attended to." Around the same time, someone in Virginia's House of Burgesses took note that members were "not quite so well dressed, nor so politely educated, nor so highly born as [in] some Assemblies we have formerly seen."[8] These anticipatory flashes of democratic lightning on the horizon, however, were still rare.

The process of getting nominated and elected was loose and informal. An interested bidder for an office, especially an influential citizen, simply made his desire known to a number of his friends and clients by post or word of mouth. Often that was enough in lightly populated districts. As the voting rolls got larger, more organization came into play. There were caucuses in the state assemblies, or meetings of interest groups where agreement was reached on a slate of names for different offices. These were circulated in handbills or newspaper stories. Once the word got out to like-minded voters, candidates promoted themselves by personal contact according to their energies and means. One tradition dating back to colonial days was to treat the electorate. George Washington, running for Virginia's state legislature in 1757, provided 391 supporters on election day with 28 gallons of rum, 50 gallons of rum punch, 34 gallons of wine, and 46 gallons of beer.[9]

Unsurprisingly, then, election days could be boisterous and irregular. They were sometimes held on short notice, with polling places set up in taverns, courthouses, and even churches and private homes. Voting was still done largely by voice, the voter stepping up to the election judges and declaring his preference to the cheers and groans of onlookers. Paper ballots were just beginning to appear, some with already printed slates, but these, too, were requested aloud from the poll clerks in a very public exposure of a voter's choice. Secret and unintimidated ballots were a long way in the future. The vote count itself ran on a loose schedule and might not be announced for days. The principle of self-government was regarded with solemnity, but the actual recording of the people's choice took place in an atmosphere that ranged from casual to rowdy.

✻

POPULAR ENTHUSIASM for politics is a good thing overall, a healthy sign that voters think they have a stake and a significant voice in government. In 1790 it was a warning of coming challenges to rule-by-gentlemen. The machinery to direct those feelings into safe and peaceful channels, however, had yet to be built and tested, and the process would be turbulent. But prospects were favorable at the start because the first presidential election, two years earlier, had taken place in the sunshine of a great and popular name respected everywhere. The American overture to national politics was a beguiling and deceptive hymn of unanimous welcome to George Washington.

PART II

PERSONALITIES, PLACES, AND DOMESTIC DISCORD, 1789–1794

CHAPTER 3

Washington's Hopeful
First Term

NOTHING in the experience of the American people, wearied by years of war and turmoil, was better calculated to lift their spirits than the mingled pageantry and solemnity of the approach to George Washington's first swearing-in. It was a dazzling show that climaxed a mercifully short election season. On November 1, 1788, the expiring Confederation Congress set the first Wednesday in January 1789 as the date by which the states should name presidential electors. Most states put the choice up to their legislatures in some form, and only three allowed a direct and complete popular vote. Then the electors were to meet in their state capitals and vote on the first Wednesday in February, and their ballots were to be counted in a joint session of Congress exactly four weeks later, on March 4. That final date was optimistic, for when it came only eight senators of the expected twenty-two and thirteen of an authorized fifty-nine representatives had made it to New York. There was no quorum. Only a month later, on April 6, could the temporary presiding officer of the Senate finally announce that George Washington was the unanimous choice of all sixty-nine electors and therefore the president-elect. A committee of notification was dispatched to Mount Vernon, and on April 16 Washington left, bidding farewell "from an aching heart" to all his "affectionate friends and kind neighbors."[1]

It took him a full week to cover the distance to New York City, the nation's original capital. He tried to be on the road by 5:30 A.M. and travel throughout each day. But at every major stop—Baltimore, Wilmington, Philadelphia, Trenton, New Brunswick—there would be welcoming delegations, honor guards flanking Washington's coach (when he did not choose to dismount and show himself to the crowds on horseback), official receptions and banquets, speeches and toasts that required response. Cannons boomed, bells rang, and bridges were draped with wreaths. White-robed women sang welcoming odes and strewed flowers, banners fluttered, and fireworks blazed. On the final leg, he proceeded from Elizabeth, New Jersey, to lower Manhattan on a crimson-canopied barge propelled by uniformed oarsmen, followed by a flotilla of colorfully bedecked small craft. "All ranks and professions," ran one newspaper account, "expressed their feelings in loud acclamations, and with rapture hailed the arrival of the Father of His Country."[2] A week later, dressed in a suit of Connecticut-made brown broadcloth, his hair powdered, silver buckles gleaming at his shoetops and a dress sword at his side, he took the oath of office on the portico of Federal Hall on Wall Street. In his twenty-minute address to Congress, drafted by his respected friend James Madison, he expressed hope that the members would allow "no local pledges or attachments, no separate views nor party animosities" to mar their devotion to the general good. He ended with thanks to "that Almighty Being who rules over the Universe" for allowing the American people the opportunity of "deciding with unparalleled unanimity on a form of Government."[3] Then he walked a few hundred yards to St. Paul's Chapel for a religious service, followed by more fireworks. In all, it was an imposing and unifying spectacle.

Everyone believed then that "devotion to the general good" and "unparalleled unanimity" would be permanent. Many would cling to that faith during the ensuing eleven years, in the teeth of steadily mounting evidence to the contrary. But Washington's behavior makes it easy to understand in retrospect. The president played his part like the great leader he was, enduring the delays and the verbiage with the same patience he had shown during his long, silent days of confinement at the Constitutional Convention. The strong national government established there was now in formal existence, but until it was visibly personified to those whom it governed, especially those who had opposed the Constitution, its roots were insecure. Washington understood the power of symbol and precedent to anchor institutions in the important realm of popular ideals. The term "role model" had not been invented yet, but he had been one for most of his fifty-seven years, practicing conspicuous self-discipline, consistency, simplicity, and devotion to the public weal like the Roman republican heroes then paraded as examples before every schoolboy. Every action that he took from 1789 onward would add a brush stroke to the presidential image, and he was determined that it should be one of a man clothed with honor and receiving the homage appropriate to the representative of all the people, yet not exalted too far above them.

It was not easy to find the balance, as Vice President John Adams learned when Washington first entered the Senate Chamber. Nervously, Adams asked the advice of the senators on whether they should stand or sit for the occasion (they stood) and particularly what his own ceremonial role should be. Pennsylvania senator William Maclay impatiently confided to his diary a hostile portrait of Adams as a pudgy, petty-minded egotist fussing about his own dignity. But there were truly perplexing ambiguities about the vice president's job. Was he a "shadow president," the man who might at any instant have to fill Washington's shoes and so should emulate his style? Or merely the nonvoting nonentity who held the gavel? A troubled Adams stumbled over his few words of formal greeting and rekindled Maclay's democratic irritability the next day when he proposed that the Senate journal record the chamber's thanks for Washington's "most gracious speech," as if Washington had addressed them from a throne. Adams compounded the offense in a subsequent debate on whether the president should be addressed by a formal title. His choice was "His Highness, the President of the United States of America and Protector of Their Liberties." But both houses ultimately agreed that "To the President of the United

States" would do very well, though Adams grumbled that the un-adorned word *President* suggested the head of a fire company or cricket club.[4]

Maclay, already an irritable controversialist, was unfair to Adams, and popular history has tended to perpetuate his unflattering portrait. Adams deserved better. He had already given his prime years to the service of the republic, had important work still ahead of him, and was a man well worth knowing.

✳

YOUNG JOHN ADAMS wanted to stay a farmer for life, but his father determined otherwise and insisted on his attending college. Father did know best in this case because the love of reading that John acquired at Harvard quickly awakened an ambition that could never have been sat-isfied by a life behind the plow in rustic Braintree, Massachusetts. "I am not ashamed to own," said twenty-year-old John, "that a prospect of an immortality in the memories of all the worthy, to the end of time, would be a high gratification to my wishes."[5] He chose the law as the path to fame rather than the ministry that his father preferred, and in a prospering and worldly Massachusetts far from its Puritan beginnings, that was a sound decision. By the time he was thirty, in 1765, he was a successful member of the Boston bar, profitably handling a large variety of commercial and other cases of that major seaport. He was also a new-lywed, devotedly married for a year to Abigail Smith, a spirited and out-spoken minister's daughter from Weymouth. By 1773, John, growing stouter and financially more comfortable, was the owner of a brick house in Boston as well as the Braintree farm he had inherited from his father. Like other women of the time, Abigail, left alone for long peri-ods by her busy mate, worked at raising the daughter and three sons she had borne in nine years of marriage. (A fifth child, a daughter, had died when a year old.)

Those same years of 1765 to 1773—from the Stamp Act to the Boston Tea Party—precisely spanned the growing crisis over Britain's attempts to tighten the administration of her American colonies and collect the taxes that she felt were her due. Along with other members of the professional and middle classes stung by the new policies, John Adams became deeply involved in the resistance that was particularly tumultuous in Boston, whose large population of workers grew restless when thrown into the streets by the economic ups and downs of the struggle. He joined committees, helped to write petitions and remonstrances, shared in boycotts, and published essays pleading the cause of his fellow Yankees. Life was an endless round of meetings, travel, and candlelit hours without sleep at the writing desk, all piled on top of his legal work, taking a toll on his health and family life.

There was resolute conviction behind this effort, but also vestiges of that youthful quest for "immortality" so easily sidetracked in the more mundane hunt for professional success. Adams soon found himself in office, despite a professed distaste for politics, as a member of the Massachusetts provincial legislature and then as a delegate to the first Continental Congress, chosen in the spring of 1774 to coordinate the activities of the thirteen colonies in the argument with the still supposedly respected mother country. When he set out by coach for Philadelphia on a hot August afternoon, he had no idea that he was for all practical purposes saying good-bye to Boston, where he would never again live or practice regularly, and beginning an entire new life.

By the time Congress reconvened in May 1775, after a winter adjournment, blood had been spilled at the battles of Lexington and Concord. What had been an assembly of peaceful protest began to transform itself, uncertainly and reluctantly at first, into the governing body of a national revolution. No one was more active in pushing the transition than John Adams. He left a major imprint on that Second Continental Congress. He pushed successfully for the selection of Virginia delegate George Washington to command the Continental Army, he labored to keep it supplied, and more and more he became a leader in the growing group of those ready to declare independence. His friend from the Pennsylvania delegation, Dr. Benjamin Rush, said that he was looked on as "the first man in the House."[6]

If so, it was due to competence rather than personal appeal. Adams was not cut out for the back scratching and deal making of good legislative managers. He was self-righteous, contentious, and opinionated, and he knew it. To his diary he lamented: "Oh! That I could wear out of my mind every mean and base affectation; conquer my natural pride and self-conceit, expect no more deference from my fellows than I deserve, acquire . . . meekness and humility."[7] His opponents would have heartily endorsed that wish. What they did not know was that the private Adams was a different man. He was capable of great warmth that he freely expressed to Abigail and to friends like Washington, Jefferson, and Benjamin Rush, and on the other hand he was as critical of himself—offstage—as any foe. His diary was filled with frequent denunciation of his vanity ("my cardinal vice and cardinal folly") and, amazingly, sloth, which would "be the ruin of my schemes."[8] The truth was quite otherwise. It was Adams's enormous diligence that earned him eminence. In courtroom and assembly hall, men listened to him not because his arguments were beautifully phrased but because of their evidence and logic. And if Adams was not universally liked, he was respected as a workhorse. Between 1775 and 1777 he sat on ninety committees covering every aspect of wartime finance and administration and was chairman of twenty-five of them.[9]

Undaunted by early difficulties and reverses, Adams was a true believer in a united America. He told a friend in 1774 that he would "swim or sink, live or die, survive or perish with my country." Not Massachusetts, not New England, but "my country."[10] He held nothing back. The years in Congress meant the sacrifice of his practice and income, a heavy burden for a man with a family. Even heavier were the long periods of separation from Abigail, whom he addressed as his "Dear Friend" in letters that would arrive in a post rider's bag or a sailing vessel weeks after they were written. The two were virtually in separate worlds, she managing the children and the farm alone in the confusion and upheaval of revolution and he, except for brief leaves of absence, consumed by the relentless grind of duty.

At the end of 1777 he was given a vital diplomatic assignment—to join Benjamin Franklin and Arthur Lee in Paris as one of Congress's three commissioners to France, which had recognized the United States. It was not a mission to be accepted lightly. A North Atlantic crossing under sail meant three to six weeks of isolation, seasickness, monotony, and very real danger of either death by shipwreck or capture by a British warship, which would mean prison and perhaps death. But winning France's full material and military support was crucial. Adams accepted and, as it turned out, had to make the voyage not once but twice. He left early in 1778, taking ten-year-old son John Quincy along for company and education. In Paris he shared quarters with the aged Benjamin Franklin, whose genial enjoyment of late hours, good company, and attractive women put him off. So did Franklin's homespun-philosopher role playing and excessive deference, as Adams saw it, to the French government. Adams dodged involvement in bitter quarrels between Franklin and Lee and sensibly recommended to Congress that there should be only a single American minister to France. Congress agreed but named Franklin to the post, leaving Adams, now without a mission, no choice but to turn around after some eight months and come home. He arrived in August 1779 for a joyful reunion with Abigail. But only two months later he was asked to go overseas again. The British were putting out peace feelers, and his assignment, which there was no question of his refusing, was to conclude a treaty if they should prove genuine.

Even in that brief autumn at home there was no rest. Braintree named him a delegate to the convention that was writing a state constitution for Massachusetts, to be submitted to the voters for ratification. He was elated at the idea. He wrote that this was "a time when the greatest law-givers of antiquity would have wished to have lived. How few of the human race have ever enjoyed an opportunity of making an election of government for themselves or their children?"[11] His draft version, much of which was adopted, after he left, had a bill of rights and a system of checks and balances among a two-house legislature representing the lower (or at least middle) and upper classes, a strong executive independent of both, and an appointed judiciary.

This time he was gone for eight years, a period that had its share of frustrations but also of accomplishments and pleasures. When negotiations with British representatives in Paris lagged, he was posted to Amsterdam, where he won recognition of the United States and loans from Dutch bankers. Eventually he had to share his treaty-making assignment with Franklin and John Jay, but he helped make the final 1782 peace pact one that not only recognized the United States but pushed its boundaries to the Mississippi and the Great Lakes. Named the country's first minister to Great Britain, he had the special thrill of being civilly received by the king as free America's representative in May 1785, just a bit over ten years since the opening shots of the war were fired near his home.

By then, blunt "John Yankee," as Adams called himself, had become a seasoned and successful diplomat, even if he failed to win earnestly desired commercial treaties with Britain and European powers. He had also learned to enjoy the concerts, the theaters, the learned company, and the elegant dinners of Paris, London, and Amsterdam. In 1784 Abigail joined him, free at last from nine years of marriage by correspondence, and together they savored holidays in the English countryside. There were pleasant visits with other Americans abroad including Jefferson, the new U.S. minister in Paris. Now a widower in his forties, with two small daughters, the tall, loose-jointed southerner charmed Abigail and was in turn delighted to find himself at ease with a woman of wide reading and lively mind. Jefferson and Adams both followed the Constitutional Convention, which Adams called "the greatest single effort of national deliberation that the world has ever seen,"[12] through exchanges of letters with friends on the scene. Both approved the Constitution as written, with reservations. Adams, his foreign mission ended, arrived home in June 1788 just as it was ratified by the necessary nine states.

Pleasantly surprised to find himself now known and admired outside of Massachusetts, Adams allowed his name to be put in the running for the vice presidency—everyone knew the electors would award the first prize to Washington—and came in easily, far ahead of the nearest other contender. Adams knew that the job itself held little besides honor; and labeled it "the most insignificant office that ever the invention of man contrived."[13] But he thought of it as both a duty and a stepping stone. At a minimum it offered a few years of domestic stability, very precious to a man nearing sixty with grown children, after the constant shuttling of twenty years of revolutionary fervor and diplomatic postings.

✳

IT WAS, then, a simple case of nerves rather than obsequious mediocrity that explained Adams's inauguration day fluster over protocol. But it would echo disastrously against him in the 1796 and 1800 campaigns, when he was charged with seeking an American monarchy. Though the accusation was campaign hyperbole, it was not completely wild. Adams at fifty-five, like many middle-aged men, was becoming more conservative—especially after eight years out of the country. Great Britain's prosperity made her system of government, hereditary titles and all, look less repugnant than in 1776. Adams still distrusted "aristocracy," but he was more frightened of "mobs" like the armed and debt-ridden farmers of Shays's Rebellion in his own Massachusetts who had tried to shut down courthouses in 1787. He groused that the selfish rising generation had lost the patriotic virtue of sacrifice. He saw elections as huge opportunities for bribery and demagoguery and more than ever believed that a strong executive, free of election-time pressure, was needed to keep peace between rambunctious commoners and propertied elites. This yearning for a sort of republican sovereign never ripened—at least in Adams's case—into the open advocacy of an American king. But by itself it was enough to outrage those who had opposed the Constitution because they thought that even as it stood the presidency already allowed too many openings for "despotism" through its powers of veto, appointment, and command of the army. It was a lingering division of opinion that became one of the seeds of discord to come.

But in 1789 Washington delayed the sprouting of those seeds by actually behaving with a king's majesty while not losing the accessibility of a First Citizen. He briefly considered neither giving nor receiving invitations so as to save his time and energy but decided against that for two sound reasons. "The novelty of it," he later explained, "would be considered as an ostentatious show of mimicry of sovereignty; and secondly . . . so great a seclusion would have stopped the avenues to useful information from the many, and make me more dependent on that of the few." So he gave small, hourlong receptions once a week, at which he dressed with considerable formality, greeted the guests with bows (but no handshake), and took up a position with his back to the fireplace while the visitors formed a circle around the room. The president then exchanged a few words with each one in succession, proceeding counterclockwise.[14] When the circuit was complete, they all left except for a few who had invitations to dinner.

Insofar as his dealings with the Congress went, Washington worked his way through a series of encounters whose general outcome was that the Senate's power to "advise and consent" on appointments and treaties became confined to "consent," and the president did not appear in person to take part in any deliberations. Both sides found the arrangement convenient. It shielded the lawmakers against any undue influence from the presidential presence, and it protected Washington from sitting through time-consuming partisan squabbles. This above all was what he wanted to avoid. His inaugural address had called for "enlarged views . . . temperate consultations and . . . wise measures," none of which could be expected if the demons of faction were unloosed.[15] He hoped to set the tone by appointing as heads of the three major "executive departments" created by Congress men of proven merit drawn impartially from the northern, middle, and southern states. His secretary of war and longtime friend, Henry Knox, was from Massachusetts. Profane, outspoken, and fond of good living, Knox was a former bookseller turned artilleryman, noticeable in any gathering by virtue of his nearly three hundred pounds and two missing fingers (from a hunting accident). He would be in charge of an army of fewer than a thousand men. For the Treasury, Washington turned to New York and named his onetime aide-de-camp Alexander Hamilton. The Department of State might well have gone to another New Yorker, John Jay, who had been secretary for foreign affairs in the Confederation, but Washington tapped him instead for chief justice of the Supreme Court. The state post went to fellow Virginian Thomas Jefferson, then in Paris as ambassador to the French court and getting ready to come home on a leave of absence.

Entire shelves are filled with books that trace virtually the whole history of the United States to the fateful moment when Hamilton and Jefferson, who would become mortal (and immortal) antagonists, entered Washington's official family. But Jefferson did not actually join the cabinet until March 1790, meaning that the first significant breach between old allies was the one opening up between Secretary Hamilton and his onetime friend James Madison, now a leading member of the House of Representatives.

Madison was a representative somewhat by default, since his anti-Federalist rivals in Virginia's state legislature, led by Patrick Henry (of "give me liberty or give me death" fame) had blocked his possible election to the Senate. He ran for the House instead, but even in that larger body his experience and knowledge as a principal designer of the new government, and his intimacy with President Washington, gave him a commanding spot. His soft voice was listened to respectfully not only by the rest of the ten-man Virginia delegation but by a sizable number of the other representatives, so he was in a position to move his proposals quickly to the floor and eventually—but not always—see them pass. He set an agenda that reflected his strong nationalistic priorities.

The first was much like the president's, namely, to bring the still numerous anti-Federalists aboard as far as possible. Stamping out the traces of the battle over ratification was important. To this end he pushed, as a first order of business, for the consideration of the amendments that various states had demanded in exchange for joining a stronger Union. More than two hundred had been proposed, almost all aimed at restricting federal power, sometimes drastically. Madison had opposed such a "bill of rights" at the convention. It would involve time-wasting debate over hypothetical dangers, and worse, spelling out some already taken-for-granted rights might imply that the federal government could step on any others not specifically named. And practically speaking, it would mean nothing against a really determined majority. "Repeated violations of these *parchment barriers* have been committed . . . in every state," he wrote in October 1788.[16] But eight months later there were good political reasons to switch positions. "If we can make the Constitution better in the opinion of those who are opposed to it," he told his fellow members of Congress, "we act the part of wise and liberal men."[17] Madison got seventeen amendments through the House. The Senate whittled them down to twelve, which went out to the states at the end of September 1789. Ten got the necessary number of ratifications by March 4, 1791. Especially important in neutralizing anti-Federalist opposition were the Ninth and Tenth, which clearly state that the enumeration of certain rights in no way denies others retained by the people, and that all powers not specifically given to the United States by the Constitution are retained by the states.[18] These additions promptly rewarded Madison's skillful management, as hold-out states North Carolina and Rhode Island finally joined the eleven states already under the Constitution's umbrella.

On another important front, however, Madison and the spirit of unity were having trouble. On April 8, only two days after Congress at last got a quorum to do business, he introduced a bill providing for import and "tonnage" duties, the latter simply a flat tax on foreign shipping entering U.S. ports according to carrying capacity. The Treasury Department had not yet been created, but Madison was in a rush to get some revenue into the government's hands and the importing season was beginning. His modest proposed taxes on items like molasses, sugar, and tea, however, immediately brought members with other ideas to the floor. In one speaker's words, the tariff bill ought also "to encourage the productions of our country and to protect our infant manufactures." But a protective tariff produces no revenue if it works, its aim being to cut off competing imports. Madison's hope of early money was thwarted, since Federal Hall promptly echoed with demands for protection for Pennsylvania glass and iron, South Carolina hemp, Virginia coal, Maryland paper. These were stoutly and vociferously resisted by states and districts, especially in the South, that relied heavily on imported manufactures. The final version, containing both "revenue" and "protective" schedules, did not work its way through both houses until September 1789.

Madison's tonnage tax also was shorn of a discriminatory provision that he had inserted, which would have made the charges higher on British ships. His hope was to enhance America's diplomatic strength in disputes with Great Britain by reducing her heavy dependence on British-made goods and steering some import business to France. But trade with France was smaller, more specialized in luxury goods, and less profitable. Commercial interests in the North would have none of Madison's idea. It was defeated, and with it was lost a little of the spirit of conciliation among sections and interest groups that he was nursing.[19]

By September the Treasury Department was established and Madison was anticipating a fruitful collaboration with his old friend Hamilton, especially because while other executive-department heads answered only to the president, the law required the Treasury secretary to furnish reports and information directly to Congress, which had charge of raising and spending money. But Madison was swiftly disabused of happy expectations. Alexander Hamilton had some very distinct ideas of his own about fiscal policy, and he intended to use that mandatory link to the House not to help Madison but to build a following of his own.

Hamilton had disliked Madison's plan to discriminate against British shipping. His admiration for the British style of governing, which included a strong and quasi-independent minister of finance, had not waned. He thought that more, not less, trade with Great Britain would fatten the American treasury. When an unofficial emissary from London named George Beckwith arrived in New York to sound out prospects for Anglo-American commercial agreements, Hamilton expressed himself freely and undiplomatically, at least according to Beckwith's later report. He said that Madison was making a mistake. "The truth is," he added, "that although this gentleman is a clever man, he is very little acquainted with the world." And the undercutting went on. "I have always preferred a connexion with you," he told the Briton, "to that of any other country. *We think in English.*" Madison would not win, he promised, since the pro-British viewpoint was that of "the most enlightened men in this country . . . [and] of a great majority in the Senate."[20]

The Treasury appointment pleased Hamilton mightily, and he had no qualms about giving up a lucrative practice and growing influence in New York State politics in order to accept it. Having his way always appealed to him more than private riches or honors. His character problem was not greed but petulant impatience at frustration, and unscrupulousness in pushing opponents out of his path. His *Report on the Public Credit* of January 1790 crisply laid out the path to national solvency as he saw it. First and above all, the United States should pay off its fifty-five million dollars' worth of debts. It was a daunting sum at the time, especially for a still undeveloped country, but without a solid credit rating the new nation was going nowhere. The mechanism would be an exchange of old securities for new ones guaranteed by a "sinking fund," a share of the government's annual revenues earmarked by law for debt retirement. To this part of the overall plan, called "funding," Hamilton added a second element, "assumption," which meant that the Treasury should "assume" and repay an additional twenty-five million in the debts of the states, which had been incurred for the common purpose of victory. Hamilton's vision of a revitalized economy rested on other props, too—a national bank, a program of stimulus to manufactures, and new consumption taxes to supplement the revenue generated by tariffs, land sales, and postal receipts. But those he held back for the time being. Funding and assumption would be hard enough to sell.

The reason was that Hamilton's broad and clear long-range intention was not universally accepted. He wanted to attach the interests of the small but powerful lending classes to the nation and not the states. Moreover, looking beyond the time when the existing debt would be extinguished, he envisioned more federal borrowing. He insisted that a permanent debt, with interest and principal faithfully and promptly repaid, could be a national blessing. Wealthy and influential creditors would always care deeply about the fiscal health of the United States because it was linked to their own. Fully trusted and negotiable Treasury obligations could be an acceptable kind of currency, supplementing scarce gold and silver coin, and would also be collateral for private development loans. The debt would thereby be "capitalized"—the nation's pledges, in the right hands, would be available credit, encouraging investment and growth.

The trouble was that sound fiscal policy did not always spell out equal justice for all. No one disagreed that the twelve million or so owed to French and Dutch bankers should be paid off at par, or full face value. But the domestic debt was different. Much of it consisted of IOU's from the Continental and Confederation Congresses issued to suppliers of wartime goods and services or to soldiers in lieu of pay. In hard times, confidence in these pieces of paper had plummeted, dragging their face value down with it. Cash-strapped original holders had been forced to sell them at heavy discounts to men with deep pockets who bought them up in quantity. To redeem them in full would therefore greatly reward a small number of speculators.

Madison was among the first on his feet in House debate to point this out. Two years later Hamilton would claim to be surprised at the challenge. "When I accepted the office I now hold," he wrote to a friend, "it was under a full persuasion . . . I should have the support of Mr. Madison in the general course of my administration. . . . You will naturally imagine that it must have been a matter of surprize to me when I was apprized that it was [his] intention to oppose my plan. . . . [T]he change of opinion diminished my respect for the force of Mr. Madison's mind and the soundness of his judgment." He even professed to be shocked at "intimations . . . given to me that Mr. Madison, from a spirit of rivalship or some other cause had become personally unfriendly to me."[21] A widening gap had opened between the two ex-revolutionaries.

Madison's arguments carried weight. Others, too, questioned why a speculator who had bought a hundred-dollar certificate from a hard-pressed veteran for forty dollars should collect the full hundred, especially if he had done so only recently on the mere rumor of the funding plan. Stories were already circulating of swift vessels leaving New York and swift riders dashing for the interior, scooping up certificates at pennies on the dollar from gullible innocents who had not yet gotten the news. "My soul rises in indignation," a Georgia representative complained, "at the avaricious and moral turpitude displayed."[22] Madison put forward a compromise, a split payment plan that would divide the full value between original and second (or third or fourth) holders—sixty for the hypothetical speculator, forty for the veteran. But Hamilton countered that the job of tracing transactions would become a long nightmare of incomplete paperwork and upset the whole concept of restoring faith in a government that paid its obligations promptly and fully. His side had its moral case, too. The secondary buyers had laid out their money in good faith. Fisher Ames, a thirty-one-year-old Boston lawyer who was becoming one of Hamilton's major supporters in the House, asked if a government "established for the purpose of securing property" should, as its first act, be guilty of having "divested its citizens of seventy millions of money . . . justly due to individuals" who had contracted with it. He tweaked Madison with a reminder that Madison himself had "helped to frame the constitution . . . I hope that the love of his own work . . . will induce him to abandon a measure which tends so fatally to disappoint . . . the hopes of his country."[23]

The difference went deeper than mere dollars and cents. Hamilton already had an uncanny anticipation of a national economy in which encouragement to the investing classes, a numerical minority, would generate productivity that would enhance everyone's well-being—but it necessarily meant allowing room at the top for fortunes to be made by the few. Madison's viewpoint, conditioned by years of his agricultural region's indebtedness, was that a Hamiltonian system encouraged a demeaning scramble for money that sacrificed other virtues like civic cooperation. It also hurt true producers of tangible goods—farmers being his prime example—while it benefited men who got rich by essentially betting on and manipulating the prices of securities, mere pieces of paper. These were the speculators and "stockjobbers" of whom Madison's friend Dr. Benjamin Rush would write: "I sicken every time I contemplate the European Vices that [Hamilton's] gambling report will necessarily introduce into our infant republic."[24] The debate would resound through two centuries of American history and is still alive. In 1790 it was a portent of fights immediately ahead whose outcome was unpredictable.

It was Madison who lost the first round when his compromise was soundly outvoted in February and the "funding" portions of Hamilton's report were basically approved. It no doubt helped that many senators and representatives themselves held government certificates of debt. But the secretary had a harder time getting votes for assumption. Anti-Federalists still resisted anything that diminished the role of the states, even if it meant lifting financial burdens from their taxpayers. More important was another issue of fair treatment. Some states—Virginia chief among them—had already paid off all or most of their wartime debts. Others, like Massachusetts and South Carolina, had made little headway. Assumption meant that the federal government would be exacting money from Virginia citizens who had already dealt fairly with their own creditors, and paying it out on behalf of delinquent Massachusetts. In addition, there were complicated balances to be adjusted in deciding exactly what amounts would be assumed from each state. Madison was able to appeal to these resentments and ambiguities and beat Hamilton in a succession of votes on the matter. Spring dragged by in deadlock, and Hamilton chafed. Assumption was indispensable to the whole plan; creditors had to be guaranteed payment from one single, reliable source to build the confidence that he wanted. Thwarted and brooding, he was in a tight place when, on a June afternoon, he chanced to run into his cabinet colleague, secretary of state Jefferson, on the doorstep of the president's house. That was not an unusual happening. The entire federal establishment amounted to no more than a few hundred men living within a few square blocks of lower Manhattan, and they all knew and frequently encountered one another socially and officially. But this unplanned meeting had powerful long-run results.

✴

PRESIDENT WASHINGTON was recovering from a nearly fatal bout of pneumonia. It had been a sickly springtime in New York, with influenza prevalent. Hamilton himself was not well, Jefferson recollected some years later; he looked "sombre, haggard, and dejected beyond description. Even his dress [was] uncouth and neglected."[25] Hamilton spoke to him at some length, explaining that the assumption plan was absolutely crucial, "a sine qua non of a continuance of the Union," and if he did not have "credit enough to carry such a measure," he would resign. But since he and Jefferson were both members of the same administration and "its success was a common concern," perhaps they could help each other in getting support for their projects.

It was not at all surprising that Hamilton turned to Jefferson in this way. The two had only known each other personally for a few months and were not yet the Great Antagonists in history's pages. It is very misleading to read the past with a foreknowledge denied the participants. Jefferson in 1790 had yet to become the Sage of Monticello or the heroic statue in the rotunda of the Jefferson Memorial in Washington's tidal basin. What his contemporaries saw that year was a tall, loose-hung man in his midforties, his hair still reddish brown and worn long, the picture of a vigorous plantation owner hardened by years of outdoor exercise in the saddle. Former colleagues in the Virginia legislature and the Continental Congress remembered him less for legislative achievements than as a polished political writer. He was, of course, the author (with editorial input from others) of the Declaration of Independence—but that document hadn't yet assumed a semisacred character in the public mind. After 1776 Jefferson had gone on to become a controversial governor of Virginia who had the mortification of seeing the state invaded during his term (in 1781); from 1784 to 1789 he was in Paris, therefore an absentee during the battle for the Constitution, on which he took a detached and moderately critical position. Not an "original" Federalist, he actually had to be persuaded by Madison to accept his job in the new government.

Only close friends like Madison and John Adams knew the charm of Jefferson's company and the breadth of his learning as well as the contradictions that still make him, in one biographer's words, the "American Sphinx." A rich aristocrat (he owned as many as ten thousand acres, though he called himself simply a "farmer") who denounced aristocracy. A slaveowner (he had as many as two hundred) who wrote beautiful invocations to liberty. A preacher of rustic simplicity whose appetite for things like good books, fine furniture, choice wines, and scientific instruments kept him permanently in debt. A denouncer of cities who adored Paris. The list goes on. He was a diligent, systematic, and brilliant law student who did not like the rough-and-tumble of actual practice. Though he could focus his reading in several languages very narrowly when necessary, he was happiest ranging over a variety of fields like astronomy, architecture, legal and natural history, botany, or anthropology. His inventions—like the dumbwaiter or the swivel chair—were practical, but his political thought evoked abstract and unrealistic ideals—like a society in which all members actually were born equal, or a nation without cities, or a redistribution of property every generation. He spent the prime of his life grappling with the gritty duties of public office while yearning for the seclusion of his mountaintop home in Monticello, for his library, his violin, his writing desk.

On that 1790 afternoon of warm June breezes rich with dockside smells from the nearby Hudson River, he saw no reason not to accommodate Hamilton on the matter of assumption, about which he did not have strong feelings. "I am apt to suppose difficulties pretty nearly balanced on both sides, when I see honest and able men . . . equally divided in sentiment on a question," was his view.[26] The sun hadn't set yet on the idea, cherished by Washington, of an administration above faction, its members united in their notion of public good. So Jefferson invited Hamilton and Madison to a small dinner the next evening at the rented home where he lived alone, never having remarried since losing his wife in 1782. (He never would.) At that table, renowned for the fine cuisine Jefferson provided, a deal was struck. Madison would allow two Virginia representatives to switch votes and favor assumption. Meanwhile, Congress was choosing the "residence" of the permanent capital, with New York and Philadelphia strong contenders. Hamilton would persuade his friends to get behind a location on the Potomac, to please southern states. The vote of the Pennsylvania delegation was critical, and it was to be obtained by making Philadelphia the temporary capital for ten years, starting in December. The bargain was kept, and final versions of both the assumption and funding bills passed in August, thanks to Thomas Jefferson. By 1792, however, Jefferson told Washington that he had been fooled by Hamilton and "made a tool for forwarding his schemes, not then sufficiently understood."[27]

The story is so good that it seems a shame to add that sound recent scholarship suggests a less important role for Jefferson's hospitality. Actually it appears that a more complicated quadrille of horse trading and vote switching on both measures, assumption and residence, took place before they got their final shape.[28] One way or another, it would be the

last time that Hamilton, Madison, and Jefferson were to collaborate on
any significant matter.

✻

ON DECEMBER 6, 1790, the third and final session of the First
Congress met in a newly built Philadelphia courthouse converted to a
Federal Hall. It was now a lame-duck body, since the Second Congress
had already been elected but would not take office for another year.
The Senate was, as in New York, literally the "upper house," since its
chamber, handsomely carpeted and supplied with seats upholstered in
red leather, was on the second floor. Its sessions were still not open to
the public and would remain secret for another three years. Otherwise
its pretensions to aristocratic dignity, such as a larger salary than the six
dollars a day allowed representatives, or rules requiring messengers
from the House to bow on entry, had been defeated.

John Adams, in the chair, still was unreconciled to the insignificance of his office and still irked some senators by remorseless unre-
quested lectures on parliamentary precedents. He was really not as
inconsequential as he feared, since very close divisions on a number of
issues gave him frequent chances to break ties. In all he would wind
up casting a record thirty-one deciding votes in the eight years he
spent as vice president. But relative idleness galled him, especially
after the move to Philadelphia. Abigail, who had remained at his side
in a pleasant home in New York, now decided against the inconven-
ience and cost of a double residence and returned to Quincy, leaving
John to room in a boardinghouse and complain about "tedious days
and lonesome nights."[29] Even before her departure, however, his rest-
lessness had led him to compose some "anonymous" newspaper letters embodying his recent thoughts on government, and these would
shortly get him into trouble.

On the whole, Congress had reason for collective self-satisfaction as
it headed toward a March adjournment. It had set up the major executive departments plus the offices of postmaster general, attorney general, and the federal judiciary; provided for administering the public
lands; sent out the Bill of Rights to the states; and enacted the first two

parts of Hamilton's financial system. So far its internal disagreements had been relatively civil, and it had not drifted too far from the happy assessment of Fisher Ames during the spring of the previous year. "There is less party spirit, less . . . acrimony of pride . . . less personality, less intrigue, cabal, management or cunning than I ever saw in a public assembly."[30]

But then Alexander Hamilton revealed the third part of his design, the Bank of the United States, and a divide was crossed. It would be a long time—at least nine years—before anyone could again be cheered by an absence of "party spirit" in public affairs.

✳

THE TREASURY SECRETARY'S second report to Congress asked for a bill to charter what he frankly called a "national" bank. It would have an initial capital of ten million dollars accumulated by the sale of stock. The United States would hold one fifth of the shares and appoint five of its twenty-five directors. Private buyers would own the rest and name twenty directors. The bank would be the exclusive fiscal agent of the United States, paying its bills and collecting its revenues. It could issue banknotes of its own, receivable for debts provided they were redeemable in specie. These notes—plus its own stock, which would be negotiable—would further enlarge the supply of money for business growth. And the bank could engage in ordinary lending transactions, which, thanks to its holding of the government's deposits, could be on a generous scale.

The new bank would, in the words of a Maryland representative, "raise in this country a moneyed interest at the devotion of Government."[31] That was, of course, Hamilton's idea. Mutual devotion between capital and government was good for the country. But his bank would enrich its private stockholders, on whom it conferred a monopoly, and it would further centralize the power of the financial communities in the Northeast. On those two grounds alone it was anathema to congressmen from other parts of the nation. Hamilton had the votes to win fairly quick passage for the bill within a few weeks, but thirty-three of the thirty-nine "yeas" that he got in the House came from the North;

fifteen of the twenty "nays" were from the South. The victory was strictly sectional, another signpost on the short road to turmoil.

Madison was one of the strong objectors and let it be known clearly that he thought the bill not only pernicious but unconstitutional. When it reached Washington's desk, the president, aware of this objection, reflected on whether or not to exercise his veto for the first time. As was his habit, he turned for informed opinion not only to Madison but to his attorney general, Edmund Randolph (whose office then was merely part-time and advisory), and to Secretary Jefferson. Of the three Virginians, the first two had been strong nationalists at the Constitutional Convention, but both Madison and Randolph were now of a different mind. They said flatly that nowhere did Article I, Section 8, which listed the legislative powers, authorize Congress to charter a bank. What was more, it was dangerous to imply that so doing was just a part of the general power to tax and spend and establish a currency, or to make any laws "necessary and proper" for exercising any congressional function. Such a "latitude of interpretation," claimed Madison, was "condemned by the rule furnished by the Constitution itself," which exactly spelled out the powers it granted. And the brand new Ninth and Tenth Amendments reinforced the point by reserving any unmentioned or undelegated powers to the states and the people. Jefferson, in reporting his own view to Washington, vigorously concurred.

Washington weighed these words and then referred them to Hamilton for rejoinder. In a few days, climaxed by a nearly all-night writing session with his wife transcribing his scribbled draft, the compact and energetic secretary turned out a fifteen-thousand-word opinion defending an active role for the infant federal establishment, jabbing his points home with underlinings. "Every power vested in a Government," he wrote, "is in its nature *sovereign* and includes by *force* of the *term* a right to employ all the *means* requisite to the attainment of the *ends* of such power," provided they were not expressly denied by the Constitution or "not immoral or . . . contrary to the essential ends of political society."[32] The issue was clearly laid out for the president—broad or narrow construction of a Constitution on which the ink was hardly dry. On February 23, 1791, he made his choice and signed the bill. Soon thereafter another Hamilton project, an unpopular excise tax on distilled spirits, was approved.

For Jefferson and Madison these were bitter defeats. As they saw it, Hamilton was winning one battle after another in a drive to centralize control of the economy in the hands of a sectional minority fattened with the profits of dealings in paper—a minority that could be the nucleus of a new pro-British, promonarchical aristocracy, just as the antifederalists had warned. The "licentiousness of the tongues of speculators and Tories," Madison wrote to Jefferson in May, "far exceeded anything that was conceived." And Jefferson had already written to George Mason, who had refused to sign the Constitution and opposed its ratification, that the only way to correct "what is corrupt in our present form of government" was to vote in a larger "agricultural representation" in Congress, which would "put that interest above that of the stock-jobbers."[33]

Throughout the spring and summer of 1791, while the prices of government securities and Bank of the United States stock rose in step with increased tax collections, Jefferson and Madison continued to worry that Hamilton's operations, whatever their success, were damaging "republican" ideals. The two had not yet fleshed out their definition of the word and were nowhere near using it in conjunction with the still-suspect term "democratic." But their concern was pushing them to explore the political terrain, to see if there were groups in America that could be rallied under the flag of "republicanism" in the same way that the Federalists were marshaled behind wealth and rank. By November of that year, the results were beginning to be visible. The same Representative Ames who had found so little party spirit in the opening session of the First Congress had a different assessment of politics just before the start of the Second. "[T]ranquillity has smoothed the surface," he informed a friend, but "faction glows within like a coalpit."[34]

CHAPTER 4

The Curse of Faction

IN MAY 1791 the third springtime of George Washington's presidency rolled across the nation, where people were gradually accustoming themselves to the actual presence of federal officials like postmasters and revenue collectors. But relations between the leading figures of the administration were becoming more wintry. On the heels of Hamilton's triumph in the bank fight, Jefferson and Madison began what looked suspiciously like a program to build an organized opposition. They denied any deliberate intention to nourish factionalism, but all the same, political overtones pervaded seemingly nonpartisan activities—an innocent vacation trip together; the writing by Jefferson of an endorsement for a book by Madison; and the hiring of a writer, a college chum of Madison's, to a minor State Department post.

In mid-May, Jefferson came up from Philadelphia to join Madison in New York, and they set off together on a relaxed circular journey up the Hudson River to Albany, then eastward to Connecticut, south to Long Island, and back to Manhattan. On Lakes George and Champlain, beautiful at that time of year, they fished for trout and shot squirrels, while Jefferson made copious notes on the local plant life, collected specimens to try in the gardens of Monticello, and indulged in such touristlike behavior as writing his thirteen-year-old daughter, Polly, a letter on birch bark. They *were* tourists, in fact, two propertied southern gentlemen who took along their private servants, horses, and light carriage. They saw neat New England farms and towns and some sights to which slaveholders were unaccustomed, like the "free negro" who owned a thriving 250-acre New York State farm, which he ran with "white hirelings," and who, Madison noted with apparent surprise, was "intelligent, reads, writes, understands accounts, [and] is dextrous in his affairs."[1]

Some friends of Hamilton, however, were convinced that the "botanizing" tour was only cover for an expedition to recruit anti-Hamilton allies. One of these friends, an Albany lawyer named Robert Troup, warned the Treasury secretary that during Jefferson and Madison's brief stay in town, there was "every appearance of a passionate courtship" between them and a pair of Hamilton's bitter rivals in the laybrinthine world of New York state politics.[2] One was Robert Livingston, usually referred to as "Chancellor," the title of a judicial position he held. The other was the youthful new senator Aaron Burr, chosen by the legislature (as all senators were then) over the incumbent, Hamilton's father-in-law. There is no record of such a courtship or even any meetings between Burr, Livingston, and the Virginia travelers on that particular visit, nor of any political conversations during the rest of their jaunt.

But neither Madison nor Jefferson made a secret of their interest in learning about any northern leaders who might share their dissatisfaction with Hamilton's projects. Troup wasn't necessarily wrong. And while full-blown political warfare was still in the offing, there were decided political overtones in a publicly aired clash of opinion that had pitted Jefferson, somewhat to his embarrassment, against his friend Vice President Adams.

At the root of the debate was the French Revolution, then just two years old. It had not yet destroyed the French monarchy, for the king still ruled under a constitution. In fact, however, he was a virtual prisoner of the legislative assembly and of street mobs in Paris. The feudal privileges of the aristocracy and clergy had also been swept away. This swift earthquake that toppled ancient structures of power and privilege also shook conservative Americans like John Adams, whose vice presidential role unluckily gave him spare time to write a set of letters in fall 1790 to a newspaper, the *Gazette of the United States*. He put them in the form of "discourses" on the writings of a historian named Enrico Davila, who had lived nearly two centuries earlier, but they were really critical meditations on the upheavals rocking America's late ally, France. It was a mistake to sweep away distinctions of rank, he argued. Human nature included a *"passion for distinction . . .* for the notice and regard of . . . fellow mortals." These yearnings did not always produce admirable results—they were at the root of "avarice and ambition, vanity and pride, jealousy and envy . . . as well as the love of knowledge and desire of fame." But they couldn't be erased, and a realistic political system would see to it that they were "gratified and encouraged and arranged on the side of virtue." Furthermore, ordinary people took great vicarious satisfaction in identification with a leader surrounded by splendor and opulence, and it was best that he be hereditary, because rivalry between different candidates for the role only produced, in Adams's vigorous language, "slanders and libels first, mobs and seditions next, and civil war with all her hissing snakes, burning torches and haggard horrors." Finally, the easily inflamed imagination of Adams suggested, humanity was not perfectible, and unlimited faith in the progress of reason could lead to relativism that made "murder itself as indifferent as shooting a plover."[3]

These were unmistakably arguments for monarchy, aristocracy, and religious authority—though not necessarily in the United States. In any form, nonetheless, they were totally unpalatable to a freethinking republican like Jefferson. But he did not, by his own recollection, intend to get into a public debate with Adams over the *Discourses on Davila* until forced to by a chain of circumstances. In England, conservative thinker Edmund Burke had also published a set of critical *Reflections on the Revolution in France* and drawn return pro-Revolutionary fire from Thomas Paine in a steaming essay entitled *The Rights of Man*. Paine was a name well known in America, where he had lived from 1774 to 1787. A man of the working classes—a former corset maker and tax collector—he was a shirtsleeved radical democrat and religious agnostic endowed, years ahead of his time, with a mighty talent for reaching a mass audience. In 1776 he had written a bestselling pamphlet, *Common Sense*, that built popular momentum for independence with its blunt calls for independence from "the royal brute of Britain."

Early in 1791 a copy of *The Rights of Man* got into the hands of Madison, who passed it to Jefferson, a great admirer of Paine. Jefferson was supposed to hand it off to a Philadelphia printer for an American edition. He did so, with a covering note expressing his pleasure that at last "something . . . was to be publicly said against the political heresies which had of late sprung up among us." He insisted that he was totally surprised when the work appeared in booksellers' shops inside of a week, carrying his remark as an endorsement on the opening page. Every informed leader would understand that the "political heresies" were those of Adams, and Jefferson admitted as much to Madison but added: "[I] certainly never meant to step into a public newspaper with that in my mouth."[4] Then he wrote to Adams as well, saying that he never intended their disagreements to be anything but private. Adams answered graciously enough that the "friendship that has subsisted for fifteen years between us . . . ever has been and still is very dear to my heart"[5] and there was no real quarrel. But then both men awkwardly protested too much. Adams disclaimed authorship of letters in the Boston press, over the signature "Publicola," which were highly critical of Jefferson. He failed to add that they *were* the work of his twenty-three-year-old lawyer son, John Quincy, who had often been Jefferson's companion in Paris days. Jefferson responded with the fib that he really had not had Adams in mind as the source of the "political heresies." And neither man wrote to the other again for several years. The two rival candidates-to-be of 1800 had squared off openly for the first time.

✳

JEFFERSON HAD fewer qualms about attacking Hamilton, but since Hamilton was a fellow member of Washington's official family, it was better to let Madison be the point man. But Jefferson began to work behind the curtain and was soon covertly helping to set up a newspaper strenuously opposed to the Washington administration. Its editor was a colorful and contentious Princeton classmate of Madison's, Philip Freneau. Freneau was one of the first American writers to spread his efforts among journalism, literature, and politics as he tried simultaneously to make a living and find a megaphone for his opinions. The son of a New Jersey importer of Huguenot descent, he used his college years to sharpen a talent for verse in lampooning contests between literary clubs. In a serious vein he turned out (with future novelist Hugh Henry Brackenridge) a patriotic poem, "The Rising Glory of America," read at his graduation exercises in 1771. He was just nineteen.

Five years later, with the Revolution in progress, Freneau was still basically a talented young man with liberal political and religious ideas and no settled direction in life. He tried and dropped schoolteaching, then took a private secretary's job in the West Indies. On the voyage there he picked up a taste for the sea, learned the elements of skippering, and made some trips as a cargo supervisor. On one of these voyages his ship was captured by a British cruiser. Freneau was clapped into a stinking, overcrowded, and disease-ridden prison ship in New York Harbor, where he nearly died of starvation and fever before winning release. For the rest of his life hr nursed an unsparing if understandable Anglophobia.

In the 1780s, trying to support a young family, Freneau alternated between sea voyages and land-bound spells of writing poems and editorials for the New York press. Early in 1791 he let Madison know that he was thinking of starting his own weekly paper in New Jersey. Madison shared the news—and a better idea of his own—with Jefferson. Freneau's sentiments were admirably republican: Why not set up his paper in Philadelphia? There it would be a counterweight to pro-Hamilton voices in the capital city and could spread the good word through the country when distributed by mail. It was a shame for a man of Freneau's "talent and principles," Madison wrote, to be "burying himself in the obscurity he has chosen in New Jersey."[6] So the first step on giving a "republican" coalition a voice led to a poet's New Jersey farm. Jefferson, agreeing with Madison, offered Freneau, who was fluent in French, a job as a translator in the State Department, at a yearly salary of $250, and with duties so light "as not to interfere with any other calling,"[7] though he discreetly did not suggest what "any other calling" might be. No one could more sincerely disavow partisan purposes than Jefferson, or be more persistent in apparently pursuing them. After some hesitation that kept his sponsors on edge, Freneau accepted, and the first issue of the *National Gazette* appeared at the end of October 1791. Its out-of-town subscription list included names personally recruited by Jefferson and Madison.

Freneau was a great choice for a controversialist. He used language with the combined extravagance of a poetic satirist and a blunt sailor. He eased the *Gazette* into partisanship, however, by giving featured play to unsigned sober essays that Madison wrote on general economic and political themes like "Emigration" and "Money." Though their tone was academically detached, they brimmed with the suspicions that had been growing for months in Madison's mind. He spoke of how important it was to resist "the daring outrages committed by despotism" and of "arbitrary interpretations and insidious precedents" that would turn the carefully restricted government of the Union into "a government of unlimited discretion." He warned of the dangers in "unnecessary accumulations of debt of the Union," and of "pampering the spirit of speculation within and without the government," which would lead to "a government operated by corrupt influence; substituting the motive of private interest in place of public duty."[8] No names were named, but there was not much room to doubt that Hamilton's fiscal program and loose-construction doctrine were targets. Madison was much more sulphurous in private, describing the rush to buy shares of U.S. Bank stock as "a mere scramble for . . . public plunder . . . by those already loaded with the spoils." Such "stockjobbers" would become the "praetorian band [the name used for a Roman emperor's bodyguard] of the Government, at once its tool and its tyrant."[9]

This was the tone that would soon prevail and set the pot seething in anticipation of the approaching second presidential election. Jefferson and Madison were becoming convinced that Hamilton was leading the way toward the creation of a moneyed oligarchy, and perhaps they sincerely believed that an actual, titled nobility would come next. Far-fetched as it sounds with modern-day hindsight, the infant United States was almost alone in the world in its republicanism, and the idea of turning bankers and investors into barons and earls sounded like something that open Anglophiles might yet get around to. And if titles and lands were dealt out to the very rich, could monarchy be far behind? Realistically this was an unlikely prospect. The one possible candidate for an American king was Washington, and his attitude was unequivocally negative. "I am told that even respectable characters speak of a monarchical form of Government without horror," he wrote. "What a triumph for our enemies."[10] And neither Adams nor Hamilton ever actually dreamed of an American peerage—they simply claimed that the people themselves might seek one if and when the "excesses" of democracy became too unsettling, a good argument for conservatism. But in the steadily worsening "heats and tumults of conflicting parties,"[11] as Jefferson called them, charges of corrupt intentions and malicious motives began to fly. Powder trains were being laid.

Hamilton was naturally infuriated when Freneau stepped up the level of attack. "A public debt is a public evil," ran one piece at the end of April. "[S]chemes for throwing magnificent wealth into the undeserving hands of a favorite few . . . have opened the eyes of the people." Another blast, Freneau's own to judge by the imagery, called the secretary's proposal for funding the debt "a monster, from whose fetid bowels proceed monarchy, aristocracy and slavery."[12] Hamilton worried that public opinion might shift and endanger his whole plan for giving the government a solid financial base. Already he had suffered a defeat in the just-recessed Congress when a Madison-led voting bloc beat off his efforts for a program of federal incentives to establish manufactures.

He reacted with pseudonymous counterattacks in his own pet paper, the proadministration *Gazette of the United States* (where the *Discourses on Davila* had appeared). It was edited by John Fenno, a former Bostonian of middling years and conservative temperament, who had gone broke as an importer and moved to New York in 1789 to try the printing business. He set up a paper that would, in the words of one of his patrons, disseminate "favorable sentiments of the federal constitution, and its administration," and perhaps obtain "the patronage of Congress."[13] Hamilton indeed rewarded Fenno with printing contracts, and the printer faithfully followed the government to Philadelphia and put his pages at Hamilton's disposal.

The journalistic style of the 1790s made no bows to objectivity and allowed editors room for personal attacks, which readers apparently enjoyed. Freneau and Fenno were soon in a brisk slanderous cockfight. But Hamilton, who was pulling Fenno's strings, was after bigger game than Freneau. His sense of persecution required a more sinister villain: Thomas Jefferson.

✶

IN MAY Hamilton had exploded to a correspondent that he was "unequivocally convinced . . . that Mr. Madison, cooperating with Mr. Jefferson, is at the head of a faction decidedly hostile to me and my administration . . . actuated by views, in my judgment, subversive of the principles of good government and dangerous to the Union, peace, and happiness of the country."[14] Now in July, having been tipped off to Madison and Jefferson's connection with Freneau, he went public with his attack. Why, he asked in one letter to Fenno's paper, was Freneau getting a government salary? Was it for translations? Or "for *publications* . . . to vilify those to whom the voice of the people has committed the administration of our public affairs" and "to disturb the public peace" by "false insinuations"?[15] A few days later, writing as "an American" [a pseudonym that, like all those used by both sides, was easily penetrated by the small community of political insiders], he charged that Freneau had been brought to Philadelphia and set up with a sinecure at taxpayer expense in order to run a "paper more devoted to the views of a certain party, of which Mr. Jefferson is the head, than any to be found in this city."[16] Freneau responded with clamorous denials and even swore on affidavit that he had never, ever discussed the idea of a newspaper with Jefferson or gotten any remote hint of what to include in it from the secretary of state "or any of his friends." Jefferson also pleaded innocent, not in the press but in a letter to Washington. "I protest in the presence of heaven," he told the president, "that I never did by myself or any other, directly or indirectly, say a syllable, nor attempt any kind of influence."

No one was being completely truthful.

Washington was acutely dismayed that two members of his cabinet were clawing at each other in public. He wrote to both from Mount Vernon, where he had gone for the summer, and begged them to cease and desist from quarrels that were "harrowing and tearing our vitals" and threatening the whole country.[17] Each one responded in September with a more embittered defense. Jefferson said that he had never tried to meddle with any legislation promoted by the secretary of the Treasury except when he was "duped" into helping with assumption because at the time he hadn't understood Hamilton's complete scheme to "undermine and demolish the republic." He had kept his growing disagreements private—it was Hamilton who had attacked first in the press—and he would be glad to let the matter drop until his anticipated retirement from office early in the next year. After that he would not endure "the slanders of a man whose history, from the moment history can stoop to notice him, [was] a tissue of machinations against the liberty of the country which has not only received and given him bread, but heaped honors on his head."[18] Hamilton, too, claimed to be the victim. "I *know*," he wrote, "that I have been an object of uniform opposition from Mr. Jefferson from the first moment of his coming to . . . New York. . . . I *know*, from the most authentic sources, that I have been the frequent subject of the most unkind whispers and insinuating from the same quarter." He had held his tongue as "a silent sufferer of the injuries which were done me" until it was beyond doubt that "there was a formed party deliberately bent" on killing his measures, which would "subvert the government." Only then, he finished, did he consider it "a duty . . . to draw aside the veil from the principal actors."[19]

<hr>

HAMILTON'S PETULANT TONE probably owed much to the weariness of constant overwork and the strains of a hard few months. Congress had tabled his *Report on Manufactures*. A private consortium that he had organized called the Society for the Encouragement of Useful Manufactures, aimed at rounding up private capital to start factories in what would become Paterson, New Jersey, was languishing for lack of investment. One of its chief backers, William Duer, who was Hamilton's friend and former assistant in the Treasury Department, had gone broke in speculations involving bank stock and was in debtors' prison, amid accusations of having inside knowledge that were damaging to Hamilton's own reputation. And finally, while his wife was summering in Albany, the slim and elegantly dressed secretary was beginning an extramarital affair that would come back to haunt him in 1797, when party warfare had become even more murderous.

Hamilton might have concentrated his hostility on Madison, who was his most visible and dangerous threat in the House of Representatives. Their old partnership was in ruins. "The opinion I once entertained of the candour and simplicity and fairness of Mr. Madison's character," said Hamilton to a friend, "has . . . given way to a decided opinion that *it is one of a peculiarly artificial and complicated kind.*"[20] But Jefferson, whom he suspected of already having an eye on the presidency, seemed to goad him particularly. Their enforced steady association as Washington's department heads got them into frequent quarrels and invasions of each other's turf. As Treasury head, Hamilton was hoping to get a commercial pact with Great Britain that he thought would greatly benefit American trade. He detested Jefferson's pro-French and anti-British foreign policy and secretly was doing his best to undercut it. Jefferson, meanwhile, to promote his own preference for agriculture over industry, strayed into the area of fiscal policy that Hamilton thought was exclusively his own. A question of style was involved as well. Jefferson, born to assured social position, gave the appearance of greater breadth, more self-control and artfulness in pursuing his goals than did Hamilton, who had single-mindedly pushed his way to the top. When Jefferson and Adams ran against each other after the Washington administrations, it would be as temporarily estranged friends. But Jefferson and Hamilton, those two hugely gifted men, truly despised each other and seemed born to do so.

In September 1792, however, they still had one common cause— persuading Washington to run again. If he did not, a sectional and partisan battle would break out for which neither was ready. Jefferson's assessment to his chief was direct: "North and South will hang together if they have you to hang on." Hamilton likewise begged: "I pray God that you will determine to make a further sacrifice of your tranquility and happiness to the public good."[21] Washington previously had been outspoken about his plans to retire, but now, aware of the soundness of the advice he was getting, he said no more about quitting. That left the door open for his second unanimous election. There was an effort by the republicans, not quite yet jelled into a party, to combine behind New York's George Clinton for the second spot. But when the official count took place, John Adams had defeated that challenge, 77–50, although—another dark omen—he did not get a single electoral vote in three of the six southern states. There would be continuity at the top for four more years and at least a token show of unity because Washington persuaded both Hamilton and Jefferson to stay at their jobs.

Nonetheless, it was impossible not to see that in the second Washington administration, organized political resistance and the organized defense it provoked would be realities. The two-party system barely foreshadowed in 1791 was developing clear outlines in 1792. The dream of permanent consensus on the common good was dying fast. That in itself was not necessarily a bad thing. Genuine disagreements about the future direction that the nation should choose would need a mechanism for expression. A political party itself could be an agent of compromise, bringing diverse interests together under a broad umbrella. And two parties could be enough to accommodate the views of most Americans most of the time, and would do so successfully for most of the 208 years to come.

But that depended on a kind of "partisanship" that was not blind or passionate; that stopped short of accusing the other side of treason or of revolutionary intentions. One that did not, in Jefferson's words, create animosities that "raised a wall between those who differ in political sentiments."[22]

That lesson hadn't been learned yet, and because it had not, the young nation was about to enter a period of maximum danger of being torn apart by unexpected and not always controllable forces. And as if to provide some metaphor of the fragility of the American experiment in democracy, the capital city in 1793 was savaged by a plague of yellow jack.

✶

PHILADELPHIA WAS a jewel among America's few cities, a promise of what the future might hold for the nation. Local boosters even hoped that its attractions might persuade Congress to reconsider the decision to move on to the District of Columbia in 1800. Some fifty thousand Philadelphians enjoyed rare civic amenities—clean, paved, and lit streets lined with neat brick houses in the affluent neighborhood near the Delaware River, plus fire companies, charitable societies, circulating libraries, a "philosophical" society, a natural-history museum, a medical college, and a university. Many of these had been set up by the efforts of the recently deceased Benjamin Franklin, a citizen of the world who was proud to have it known that he was also the first citizen of Philadelphia. Philadelphia's cosmopolitan population of German, English, Irish, Scots-Irish, Huguenot, and Jewish ancestry worshiped and lived in peace. The city's legal and financial communities throve in the shadow of the Bank of the United States. An array of newspapers opened their columns to advertisements for musical and theatrical performances and the services of a rich variety of craftsmen, from dancing masters, pastry cooks, and coach makers through barbers, brewers, blacksmiths, saddlers, and dozens of others, evidence of a time when almost everything was made by hand and to order. Of course, as a port town, Philadelphia also had its working-class neighborhoods as well as its wharfside dives, whorehouses, and back alleys, where poverty and crime cohabited, but they did not mar the overall air of prosperous confidence.

Yet the great city was vulnerable to an often recurring plague of yellow fever, a weakness it shared with other Atlantic ports that were damp and hot in summertime and that were visited regularly by ships from the West Indies, where the disease was common. It was a horrible malady, quick-acting but cruel. It began with chills and a headache; then the skin and eyes became jaundiced, high fever set in, and the patient became incontinent and puked up great quantities of stale blood from internal hemorrhages, which gave the disease the name *vomito negro* in Spanish-speaking countries. Death came in two to eight days to as many as three out of four victims—or what was left of them.

Philadelphians knew what yellow fever could do, but none, including the distinguished cluster of resident doctors, knew how to arrest its irresistible spread. It was only in the early 1900s that U.S. Army doctor Walter Reed would prove the carrier to be a mosquito, *Aëdes egyptii*, that bred abundantly during warm weather in swamps, cesspools, cisterns, wet refuse heaps, anyplace with stagnant water. The female acquired the virus when biting an infected person in order to fill her belly with the blood that was her diet. She would regurgitate some of it in biting the source of her next meal, and that person's perilous blood in turn would be carried on to others by any number of feeding mosquitoes. In densely populated neighborhoods the multiplication of cases was explosive and increased until frost ended the mosquito-breeding season. The only salvation, if one could afford it, was flight, preferably to cool and open country.

The first cases were discovered in mid-August; by the third week the death toll was climbing, On September 1 Jefferson wrote to Madison back in Virginia that seventy had died already, but on the sixteenth alone sixty-seven people were buried, and eight days later ninety-six corpses went into the ground. Congress had already left town. Jefferson had recently moved to a country house on the banks of the Schuylkill River but would also depart soon because, he explained, "all my clerks have left me but one so that I cannot go on with business."[23] Pennsylvania's state legislature and governor departed, and finally so did President Washington. By October it scarcely mattered. Clerks were ill or simply not showing up, and in effect government—except for emergency administration of the stricken city—was suspended. Alexander Hamilton and his wife both caught the fever and survived, but when they tried to reenter their homes in New York City they were forced to await medical clearance in rural East Greenbush, outside of Albany.

The doctors argued publicly and fruitlessly about how the scourge spread and how to control it. It was carried by putrefaction in the air; it was carried in the clothes and effects of the victims; it was local in origin; it was brought in from outside; quarantine would help; quarantine was useless; this treatment worked; that one only worsened things. And the plague continued. Men and women were terrified of human contact. The few people who ventured out did so with homemade preventives for the infection—handkerchiefs soaked in vinegar to smell, pieces of tarred rope around their necks, garlic to chew. Fires were lit and guns discharged in the deserted streets to clear the air of suspected poisons. Newspapers shut down. Banks closed; shops were shuttered; delivery of food to markets was haphazard. Other communities sent relief shipments but barred their doors to refugees. Dying victims lay unattended in their stinking and soiled beds; dead bodies piled up awaiting burial. The capital of the United States was under siege by an enemy whom no treaty could placate and no force of arms expel.

By October those who remained in the city were either too poor to run or were bravely sticking it out to help others. There were villains, like the nurses (male and female) who charged enormous sums and then often robbed and deserted the sufferers. There were gougers and looters. And there were heroes, like the ministers and doctors who would not abandon those they served whatever the risk, who stayed out of gallant humanitarianism. Among these the most notable was the merchant Stephen Girard, the richest man in town, who along with businessman Peter Helm took over the administration of the pesthouse established by the city in a vacant private suburban estate called Bush Hill. Girard coordinated the delivery and distribution of food, blankets, and medicines, assigned tasks to nurses, cleanup personnel, messengers, and grave diggers, and in addition made rounds as a nurse, tending with his own hands to the foul-smelling, delirious patients.

Then there was the amazing Dr. Benjamin Rush, professor at the College of Physicians, who, depending on the point of view, was either a hero or a disaster. At the epicenter of a furious controversy over the "correct" treatment, Rush already had a history that illustrated many of the still-baffling paradoxes of the American character, and he would later play a small role in the political wars just ahead. Nearing fifty in 1793, Rush had gotten his boyhood education at the school of a famous Presbyterian revivalist, Samuel Finley, and never lost his loyalty to old-time religion. Yet he fell in love with science when he studied medicine in Edinburgh, and he embraced the certainties of an ardent believer in reason, with no sense of possible contradiction between dogmas. One part of his mind argued that "the world, from the progress of intellectual, moral and political truth, is becoming a more safe and agreeable abode," while another prompted him to write: "I have thought that all good Christians should *sit, walk, eat* and even *sleep* with one hand constantly lifted up in a praying attitude to the Father of mercies to avert his judgments from us."[24]

He belonged to a small and privileged elite of doctors trained in foreign universities and had married money, but much of his practice was in poor neighborhoods usually served only by unlettered quacks. A happy workaholic with minimal sleep needs, he churned out books, letters, and pamphlets by the ream yet had time to give attention to hundreds of adoring students and thirteen children of his own. He was an advocate of temperance, of abolishing slavery, of practical education for boys and girls alike, of gentle and patient treatment of the insane, of demystifying medicine by simplifying its language for students and speaking frankly with patients. A vigorous republican, he was a friend of Tom Paine, Jefferson, and Madison but also of John Adams and other Federalists. He was a signer of the Declaration of Independence and a member of the Pennsylvania convention that ratified the Constitution. In 1786 he wrote: "The American war is over; but this is far from being the case with the American revolution . . . nothing but the first act of the great drama is closed."[25] Change for the better was inevitable and welcome.

Yet open-minded as he seemed, Rush was unable to give an adversary credit for a good argument or a good character—there was no right to be wrong. Stubborn contentiousness brewed trouble for him during the Revolution, when he got himself fired from an army medical superintendency by quarreling furiously with his superiors. His obstinacy had another aspect, too. Rush was a keen and thorough observer and recorder of clinical symptoms; his works included respected descriptive treatises on certain maladies. But he also loved to theorize and would sacrifice the evidence of his own senses to defend a medical opinion arrived at by deduction. That was exactly what he did as the yellow fever raged through the neighborhoods.

Working his way through published descriptions of other yellow fever epidemics, Rush found some cases of people who recovered after being given massive doses of laxative. He tried it on some of his own critical patients and became convinced as through a revelation that this cleansing of the bowels was one part of the one, only, and infallible cure. The other was bloodletting. Medical wisdom of the day prescribed it as an occasional necessity to rid the body of toxins. But Rush went far beyond that. He was convinced that all supposedly distinct diseases were variations of a *single* central irritation of the entire nervous system due to an overexcited vascular apparatus. The "multiplication" of diseases, he urged, was "as repugnant to truth in medicine, as polytheism is to truth in religion."[26] By definition, therefore, bleeding—like purging—was guaranteed to restore health. But in his zeal, Rush believed that up to four fifths of the blood in the body could be removed without harm. Worse, he underestimated the blood volume of a human—about six quarts for an average adult male—and would let as much as a quart every two or three days go gushing into the basin from the vein his lancet opened. The additional loss of blood undoubtedly killed dozens of patients already depleted by internal hemorrhaging and the drastic purges. But Rush would not let doubt penetrate his system. He swore that he lost fewer than one patient in twenty and that his regimen would reduce yellow fever to the harmlessness of a common cold.

When other doctors disagreed, Rush blew up. He blamed them for prolonging the agony by rejecting his advice. "The principal mortality of the disease," he wrote to his wife, who was at her parents' home in New Jersey, "now is from the doctors. . . . Never before," he added, "did I witness such a mass of ignorance and wickedness as our profession has exhibited in the course of the current calamity." Soon he stood in detested isolation from much of the Philadelphia medical establishment.

But if he was stubborn, he was also brave. Sleepless, snatching mouthfuls of food when he could, Rush saw as many as 120 patients a day and beat off more who clutched at him and begged his help as he walked the somber streets. He came down with the fever himself but recovered, sturdily crediting his own treatment for his survival. Then he resumed his man-killing schedule. His visible courage as well as his persistent, if misguided, optimism at least helped to keep panic from spreading and deepening.

In the end, of course, nothing worked—neither bleeding nor purges, plasters or sweats, cold or hot baths, isolation, diet, herbal concoctions—nothing in the therapeutic repertory of the time, and the daily burial toll climbed to its peak of 119 on October 11. The president began to explore the possibilities of convening Congress in another temporary location, but at last the onset of cold weather brought relief. By October 26 deaths had fallen to thirteen; by November 10 the president himself reentered the capital, and by the first week in December the Third Congress was able to meet there safely.

The plague killed about four thousand people in its two-month reign of terror. There would be later epidemics but none so severe. The 1793 experience left behind a legacy of sad awareness that the most seemingly blessed locations in the country were still subject to powers and dominations not always within the control of reason. In its glory and promise Philadelphia in the 1790s typified American energy, achievement, and capacity to dream of a better society. And in its suffering Philadelphia forewarned that there would be inevitable dark days for even the most artfully designed systems of human coexistence.

Life resumed. So did politics as usual.

CHAPTER 5

Mr. Burr Launches
a Machine

THOUGH JOHN BECKLEY'S NAME is not familiar in history books, it should be, because he played a hugely important part in the young nation's march toward the electoral crisis in 1800. His relative anonymity is due to the fact that he was ahead of his time. Beckley was a first-class party manager and campaign organizer in an era when no such callings were recognized or thought respectable. He was a paradox—born in Virginia in 1757 to a titled Englishman but thoroughly anti-British and republican in sentiment. At William and Mary College he became one of the founding members of Phi Beta Kappa. Later, as the diligent and skillful clerk of various Virginia revolutionary committees and legislative bodies, he became a friend and ally of Jefferson and Madison and, with the latter's help, the first clerk of the U.S. House of Representatives. This insider role helped him to exercise impressive talents for collecting and passing along political intelligence, keeping contacts among like-minded leaders, composing and distributing pamphlets, and bringing voters to the polls. He put these skills wholeheartedly at the service of the defenders of republican purity against the schemes of "the Treasury," meaning Hamilton's Federalist followers.

As the story will later show, Beckley's help was crucial in winning key states for Jefferson both in 1796 and 1800. But he was already a partisan activist in September 1792 when he set off from Philadelphia on a mission to New York, carrying a letter from Dr. Benjamin Rush to Rush's friend, New York senator Aaron Burr. The effervescent doctor was asking Burr's help "in removing the monarchical rubbish of our government." Both he and Beckley had the upcoming election in mind. No one doubted that Washington would be chosen again, but there were hopes that if antiadministration electors would concentrate their second-choice ballots on one man, they could make him vice president instead of John Adams. A good choice for the role would be New York's popular governor, George Clinton. Both Beckley and Rush planned to get Burr's help in persuading Clinton to accept. And Beckley did return with Burr's assurance that he would do whatever was in his power to woo Clinton.[1]

But then a curious thing happened. Letters from other New Yorkers appeared to suggest that some of them would prefer Burr *himself* as the candidate. These were addressed to James Monroe, likewise a senator—from Virginia—engaged with Beckley in coordinating the rally of republican forces. Monroe, eventually to become the fifth president of the United States, was a friend of Madison and more especially of Jefferson, for Jefferson had been Monroe's private tutor in law nine years earlier when Monroe, barely in his twenties, was just out of the army with the rank of major and a battle wound to prove his mettle. Monroe, like Beckley and Jefferson, had attended William and Mary College, and he was on good personal terms with Senator Burr, who had been a fellow student of Madison at Princeton. All these connections suggested the possibility of a mid-Atlantic-state "old boy" clique in the making. Yet Monroe, though he was on cordial personal terms with Burr, reacted to his possible candidacy by making it very clear that he would not do.

"If Mr. Burr was in every way inexceptionable," Monroe wrote, "it would be impossible to have him elected. He is too young, if not in point of age, yet upon the public theater. . . . Some person of more advanced life and longer standing in public trust should be selected . . . particularly one who in consequence of such service had given unequivocal proofs of what his principles really were." It would be "disagreeable," Monroe wrote to Madison, to tell Burr that Virginia did not want him, "but this must be removed by the most soothing assurances of esteem on our parts."[2]

Monroe's letter revealed a good deal about how Aaron Burr was perceived by his 1792 contemporaries. At thirty-six, he was young indeed. He had not clearly shown what his "real principles" might be. And most important, some suspected him of underhandedly organizing the letter-writing campaign to replace Clinton's name on the ballot with his own. And yet, if he were to be turned down, his ego would require soothing and flattery to keep him cooperating with the embryonic Republican Party, because that cooperation would be critical. Aaron Burr had the political deftness of a Beckley and then some—but none of Beckley's willingness to leave the center stage to others. Hugely ambitious, vastly talented, always shadowed by criticism and suspicion, and never lacking for loyal friends and passionate enemies, Burr was an enigma in his own time and has teased historians, biographers, and novelists ever since. Whether a sinner or a victim, he was impossible to ignore or forget.

⚹

HE WAS almost exactly the age of Hamilton, with whom his name would be forever joined, and there were tantalizing similarities in their histories. Neither was born to wealth, but Burr, unlike Hamilton, had impressive connections. His father, a minister, was a cofounder of the College of New Jersey, which became better known later as Princeton. His mother was the daughter of Jonathan Edwards, one of the most distinguished churchmen in American history. Edwards is best remembered for a fire-and-brimstone revival sermon entitled "Sinners in the Hands of an Angry God," intended to terrify listeners into recognizing their natural wickedness and total dependence on God's grace to escape the eternal agony of hellfire. In fact he was no bellowing pulpit-pounder but rather a deep thinker and writer who struggled to reconcile reason and science with the belief in divine absolutism and mankind's helpless depravity. Burr inherited some of his grandfather's intellectual sharpness and none of his pained suspicion of worldly pleasure. He would spend most of his life living well—on borrowed money.

He was—again like Hamilton—orphaned at an early age and, with his older sister, raised by relatives. Precociously intelligent, he was admitted to Princeton at age thirteen and graduated in 1773. His campus contemporaries included Madison and Freneau. He began to study law in the Litchfield, Connecticut, office of his brother-in-law Tapping Reeve, twelve years his senior. Reeve would go on to found a private school of law at Litchfield whose graduates came to include a galaxy of distinguished justices and officeholders. But Aaron Burr had hardly gotten familiar with his first textbooks when war, patriotism, and the lure of adventure called him away to brave and controversial service. As a "cadet," still only nineteen, he endured the hunger and freezing cold of a December 1775 march to Quebec capped by a failed assault during a New Year's Eve blizzard. Burr just missed death by a blast of gunfire that killed General Richard Montgomery, at whose side he was advancing. But he did not, as later rumored, plunge back through the drifts carrying the commander's body on his shoulders.

In 1776 he was briefly on Washington's staff, but earned and heartily returned the general's lifelong dislike and was very quickly assigned elsewhere. There may be no truth to the story that Washington once caught him snooping through the mail on his desk, but it is on record that when a promotion to lieutenant colonel finally came through, Burr, whose estimate of his own abilities was never modest, wrote a blustering letter to the commander in chief saying, in effect: "What took you so long?" In the campaigns that followed his new posting, Burr overcame his boyish and diminutive appearance to emerge as a tough and competent officer, but by 1779, ill health due to the hardships of the field forced his resignation.

During his early service Burr had gotten himself a reputation as a flirtatious gallant, but midway through the war he fell seriously in love with a married woman ten years older than himself. She was Theodosia Prevost, living under suspicion in New Jersey as the presumed Tory wife of a long-absent British officer. When word came that James Prevost had died in the West Indies, Burr and the widow were wed in July 1782. He had just been admitted to practice law, after less than a year's tutoring by a New York attorney. He talked his way into a waiver of a minimum time-of-study requirement by pleading his army service. He was now beginning his profession with a wife and five stepchildren to support and a habit of generous spending. But as the war ended and the British left, a tangle of conflicting claims over Tory property surfaced. There was plenty of work for a small corps of New York City lawyers including ex-colonels Burr and Hamilton, and both of them quickly proved able to excel and to make a living in their new peacetime calling. Burr soon became the father of a daughter of his own, Theodosia, born in 1783. Alone of his children she would live to adulthood.

Unlike Hamilton, Burr did not show any interest in the politics of nation building. He was chosen to the state assembly in 1784 but gave the job little attention and stuck unobtrusively to local issues during his one-year term. He appeared to have no strong political convictions, expounded no theories of government, added nothing to the stacks of pamphlets generated by the groundbreaking debates of the 1780s on how free Americans could best rule themselves. This can be interpeted as either selfish opportunism, flexibly leaving all options for personal advancement open, or as a sensible and farsighted commitment to pragmatic compromise within an existing system, the very soul of democratic politics. Burr's historical critics and defenders endlessly argue both positions. In any case, he did not affront the general anti-Federalist sentiment in New York, which barely ratified the Constitution by three votes at the last minute. But with the new government in place in 1789, Burr suddenly entered political life with zest, and with intentions that were always slightly cloudy.

State politics were still in the mold set during colonial times, when the rich lands of the Hudson and lower Mohawk Valleys were carved into huge family estates sometimes embracing whole counties and more. Among them, clans like the Livingstons, Schuylers, De Lanceys, Van Rensselaers, Beekmans, and Morrises occupied most royal appointive offices and controlled the few that were elective through their influence on the small number of eligible voters. Joined by intermarriage with New York's wealthy merchants, they made up a potent conservative aristocracy. Alternately feuding and dealing with one another, controlling perquisites and patronage, they turned elections into contests between groups of personal followers. The close division over the Constitution in New York, for example, was driven not only by issues but by the fact that some of the "first families" were anti-Federalists who wanted no shrinkage in the state power that was in their hands, while others hoped that a strengthened federal government would protect them from "the mob" and open new opportunities to commerce.

That old order began to change during the Revolution. First, authority collapsed in many places in the state that were fought over savagely by American and British regulars, militiamen, Indians, Tories, and guerrillas. When peace finally came, frontier settlers took up land in the virgin western portions of the state. Tory estates were seized and redistributed. Tax support for the Episcopal (formerly Anglican) church ended, and an antislavery movement began to grow. Immigration increased, new businesses were established; new voters were harder to control. A democratic tide was rising, and few could ride it better than George Clinton, elected wartime governor for a three-year term under the new state constitution in 1777. Reelected again and again, he was, at age fifty, bidding for his fifth consecutive term in 1789. By then a popular and seasoned old "pol," Clinton had built a base among the "new" classes of independent farmers and middle-class businessmen while at the same time he used his own good family connections by marriage, plus his patronage, to maneuver for support from the highborn. He was almost impossible to beat.

Enter Aaron Burr and Alexander Hamilton, at that time acquainted only as fellow members of the New York bar. Hamilton was the better known and more influential both as the son-in-law of Philip Schuyler, who became one of New York's first two senators, and as leader of the state's Federalists. Their choice to oppose Clinton was Robert Yates, a friend of Burr's who had helped him get his license. So Burr supported Yates and found himself, on this one occasion, actually on the same side as Hamilton. Clinton won the election and, being the shrewd strategist that he was, held no grudges; he brought the gifted and popular young attorney into his own camp by naming Burr state attorney general. At the same time Clinton lured the powerful Livingston family away from their Federalist connections after Hamilton had already alienated them by denying them some expected patronage. So Burr now had the Livingstons and Clinton in his corner, and it quickly proved to be a crucial break. In 1790 one third of the Senate—including Senator Schuyler—came up for renewal. Clinton arranged to have Burr elected over Schuyler in the state legislature (which, in all states, chose senators until 1912), and then gave the vacated attorney generalship to a Livingston. A good deal of backroom conniving was involved. One furious Federalist complained of "twistings, combinations and maneuvers" that were "incredible." No one was more outraged than Hamilton, whose proud relative had been unceremoniously dumped by Burr and his "myrmidons," a term that literate voters in 1791 would immediately recognize as coming from the *Iliad* and meaning unquestioning followers of the warrior Achilles. From that moment on, the hostility of the secretary of the Treasury toward Burr would fester and swell to neurotic proportions.[3]

For Burr the victory was sweet in many ways. It elevated him from New York lawyer to national lawmaker, widened his contacts and aspirations, and also allowed him more freely to enjoy Philadelphia without the presence of his wife, whom illness kept at home during Senate sessions. She suffered from some kind of progressive, painful, and depressing disease, which, as she told her brother-in-law, drove her "as near a state of insanity as possible."[4] Like most spouses of public men at that time, she struggled to manage alone during Burr's absences while he peppered her with letters full of advice, written in ignorance of actual home situations. To her burdens were added three pregnancies within five years of Theodosia's birth. A girl was born in 1785 and died at the age of three, and there were two infants stillborn. But she appears to have remained devoted to Burr until the day she died in May 1794, and he wrote later that her life brought him "more happiness than all my successes," and her death "dealt me more pain than all sorrows combined."

Burr didn't remarry until, as an old man of seventy-seven, he captured a rich widow twenty years his junior, though rumor credited him with many liaisons in the interim. His large, dark eyes, high forehead, and clean-cut profile made him attractive to women, and to these charms were added good manners and sprightly conversation. "Honey trickles from his tongue," said one listener. Both sexes found him a charmer. As a New York Federalist businessman resignedly put it in a letter to Hamilton, "This person, C.B. [i.e., Colonel Burr] has an address not resistable by common clay."[5]

Unlike many so-called womanizers, however, Burr respected female minds, those of wife and daughter included. Rather than have little Theodosia become "a *mere* fashionable woman, with all the attendant frivolity and vacuity of mind," he wrote, "I would earnestly pray God to take her forthwith hence."[6] He chose tutors for her, drilled, directed, and quizzed her by post as she grew up, and had her reading Latin poetry and studying Greek grammar by the time she was ten—in addition to learning such parlor arts as playing the harp and piano. The child recognized and returned the love and dedication behind this pushing, and the unusual bond between the two as she grew into womanhood became one of the notable features of both their lives.

Educating Theodosia, entertaining the best of New York society, patronizing young artists like the portraitist John Vanderlyn, endorsing notes for old friends, and maintaining a Hudson riverside "country" home in what is now Manhattan's Greenwich Village all cost far more than even Burr's practice brought in. His letters were full of statements like: "I have been in hourly expectation of substantial relief in my pecuniary affairs," or "as to money matters, I am in the same state of impotent distress as heretofore . . . on every side good prospects, but not one . . . productive of a shilling."[7] Like many contemporaries, he speculated in western lands, used his political power to help his investments, and was often a bare step from arrest for debt. That might well have been the reason why he was forever suspected of nursing grandiose projects to enrich himself, and why he continued his pursuit of high office even without any strong ideological commitments.

Early in 1792 he let his name be floated for governor of New York and was even mentioned favorably by some Federalists as a man who could draw votes from all sides. But Alexander Hamilton firmly shut the door on that idea. The Federalists instead named the aristocratic-looking John Jay, an impeccable and universally respected lawyer-diplomat born to a wealthy merchant family of Huguenot descent. Jay, in his late forties, already had a solid career behind him. With Franklin and Adams he had negotiated the peace treaty ending the Revolution, headed the department of foreign affairs of the toothless Confederation government, written some of the essays in *The Federalist*, and become the first chief justice of the United States Supreme Court. Full of piety, goodwill, and civic responsibility, he was the model of the "wise man" who is always chosen as trustee, arbitrator, and consultant—the very antithesis of Aaron Burr.

But Burr did not run against Jay. The state's anti-Federalists needed someone stronger and named Clinton for a sixth term. Yet Burr wound up deciding the result. When the voting took place in the spring, Jay seemed to have won. However, the official vote counters found small, technical irregularities in the method by which ballots had been submitted in three counties, two of which Jay had carried. If those votes were thrown out, Clinton would win. The canvassers appealed to both New York senators for their opinions. Burr delivered a legal ruling against counting the disputed ballots. The canvassers accepted it, so Clinton remained governor and Burr was at the center of an apparent steal.

Federalists were left seething. Burr, swore one of them, "will prostitute talents, honesty & integrity . . . for the prosperity of a party."[8] No one was more vehement than Hamilton, who once more had seen Burr defeat a candidate he supported. When it seemed briefly possible that the nation's republicans might name the senator as their candidate for vice president that September, Hamilton was positively livid. Burr, he wrote to one friend, was "unprincipled, both as a public and a private man. . . . Embarrassed, as I understand, in his circumstances, with an extravagant family, bold, enterprising, and intriguing, I am mistaken if it be not his object to play the game of confusion, and I feel it to be a religious duty to oppose his career." Another letter declared that "as a public man, he is one of the worst sort—a friend to nothing but as it suits his interest and ambition. . . . 'Tis evident that he aims at putting himself at the head of what he calls the 'popular party,' as affording the best tools for an ambitious man to work with. . . . In a word, if we have an embryo Caesar in the United States, 'tis Burr."[9]

Most Federalists distrusted Burr almost that much, but the anti-Federalist opposition leaders were no less uncertain about his unsettled principles. No one ever seemed to be certain whether Burr was independent of party or simply ready to jump party lines whenever it would help him personally. Some believed him "unsettled in his politics and are afraid he will go over to the other side."[10] Others found in the charismatic New Yorker "traits of character which sooner or later will give us much trouble. He has an unequalled talent for . . . forming combinations of which he is always the centre."[11] Possibly to address such concerns, Burr, during his next four years in Congress, loyally fought floor battles on behalf of what was by then clearly emerging as the Republican (in some places called the Democratic-Republican) Party. But his efforts were not entirely rewarding. In 1796, to anticipate the story slightly, Jefferson was the Republican candidate to succeed Washington in the nation's third presidential contest. His supporters grappled again with the hard and still-unfamiliar job of getting agreement on a single figure to whom their electors' second votes should go. Burr worked diligently to round up backing for himself and came near to exhaustion visiting Republican politicians in states from New Hampshire to Virginia under those abysmal eighteenth-century traveling conditions. By September he was at least unofficially the running mate. But when the votes came in, they still reflected Republican misgivings. The final tallies gave John Adams the presidency with seventy-one electoral votes, made Thomas Jefferson his vice president with sixty-eight, and showed Thomas Pinckney, a Federalist, with fifty-nine. Burr lagged far, far behind with thirty. Not even half of those voting for Jefferson had made him the number-two choice. The major blow had come from Virginia, where Burr had only one vote as against twenty for Jefferson; Georgia and South Carolina, which went Republican, gave him no votes at all; and North Carolina provided six compared with eleven for Jefferson.

The 1796 election in New York State brought more bad news. A

Federalist majority was sent to the state legislature, which did not re-elect Burr to another senatorial term. At the start of 1797, at forty-one, he was back in private life, smarting at the memory of the injustices done him by the Virginians.

Then, in just three years of effort, he put himself in a position where they had to turn to him for help in the election of 1800. Burr, using all his skills and allure, built a primitive but recognizable prototype of a modern urban machine.

✴

THE KEY was building a base in the fast-changing, fast-growing city that was his home. According to later legend, his instrument was a kind of fraternal lodge known in 1797 as the Society of Tammany and Columbian Order in the City of New York, which he politicized and which was the origin of the notorious Tammany Hall that came to control New York's Democratic Party for a full century starting about 1860. That is mythology. The Society, founded in 1788 by an upholsterer named William Mooney, was originally nonpartisan and dedicated to promoting "the smile of charity, the chain of friendship and the flame of liberty."[12] Its members liked rituals and patriotic parades in which they dressed up as Indians. Its officers were called "sachems," and the "Long Room" in Martling's Tavern that served as its headquarters was known as "the Wigwam." Despite these apolitical beginnings, the Society, unlike more aristocratic associations, opened its doors to all, and gradually the ordinary workers who entered came to outnumber, then to alienate and drive away Federalist "braves."

Burr was never even a member or a recorded participant in any Society activities. But he was linked to Tammany through several of its key members who were part of a clique of admiring young men surrounding him, known as Burrites. They were partners in his political and business undertakings and sometimes in his scrapes with the law. The best-known, Matthew Davis, would eventually become Grand Sachem of Tammany and likewise Burr's devoted first biographer, managing to muddy the record further by losing or destroying much of his subject's correspondence. Burr farsightedly recognized the long-range political meaning of his influential friends in the Society of Tammany, namely, the possibility of mobilizing the faceless new thousands to swing elections. He saw to it that the Burrites controlled steering committees, organized and publicized meetings to name and support candidates, prepared lists of voters that included financial information and previous political records, canvassed door-to-door for funds, and made sure that the faithful got to the polls on election day.

Meanwhile, he was easily elected to the state assembly again for two successive terms and was able to advance his cause by several activities there. One was to amend state laws so as to allow individuals to form "tontines," that is, to chip in for group purchases of property, thereby automatically qualifying each member as a voter. Another spectacular stroke involved the creation of a "Republican" bank in New York. The city only had two banks, one of them a branch of the national Bank of the United States that Hamilton had created, and the other, purely local, the Bank of New York, also founded in 1791 under his leadership. Both naturally confined most of their lending operations to well-heeled Federalist applicants. Efforts to break the monopoly were routinely beaten back in the legislature. But Burr took advantage of the city's increasing need for a pure water supply to get a state charter in 1799 for the Manhattan Company, a private corporation formed to deliver water through a system of deep "uptown" wells, steam pumps, and wooden pipes, to homes at the populous lower end of the island. He slipped into the charter a provision that any surplus funds collected to raise working capital could be invested as the directors saw fit. Being friends of Burr, they saw fit to create the Bank of the Manhattan Company. So in addition to providing water to several hundred (eventually over two thousand) grateful residence owners, Burr now controlled a bank that offered low-interest mortgages and other loans to shopkeepers, craftsmen, proprietors of small businesses, and rising professional men, all of whom had lacked the connections to get credit from Federalist bankers.

By the beginning of 1800 Burr had gathered around him a bloc of New Yorkers whose gratitude he had earned and whose votes he could count on, the classic definition of a "boss." He was in an excellent position to send a slate of Republicans to the assembly in Albany in impending April elections. Their vote would be critical when that same assembly, in the fall, chose the state's presidential electors. Candidate Jefferson would need them badly, and he knew it; "All will depend on the [New York] city election, which is of 12 members," he reported to Monroe in January.[13] To secure the state, he would have to deal with Burr, whom his Virginian followers had treated so poorly four years earlier. To "the Colonel," that must have been a satisfying thought.

٭

BURR'S WELL-OILED Manhattan operation would to some degree serve as the template for other urban political machines, but they would not emerge until years later in a more citified America. It was possible for him to work his arts in New York as early as he did only because New York City already had a society of many strands that could be woven into different political patterns. For most of 1789 and 1790 it had enjoyed the distinction of being the capital both of of New York State and of the United States of America. Then the federal government moved to Philadelphia, and in 1797 the state capital, too, was relocated to Albany for the better convenience of the growing "upstate" population. By then it did not matter much to the city's self-image. New York might no longer be a political command post, but it was already on the way to becoming a financial, mercantile, manufacturing, and cultural capital. Its big-town profile, economic power, and special urban needs would become ingredients in the volatile political mixture of a diverse America still not comfortably united by 1800.

As a shipping center, New York was beginning to overtake (and would soon outstrip) Boston and Philadelphia. Between 1789 and 1801 the duties paid at the Federal Customs House overlooking the spacious, sail-dotted harbor rose from under $150,000 to some $5 million. The tonnage of vessels engaged in foreign trade shot from an approximate 19,000 to 146,000, and of those in the coastal trade from 5,000 to 34,000. In the same period the population roughly doubled from 33,000 to 65,000. Legions of carpenters, masons, glaziers, brickmakers, plasterers, blacksmiths, butchers, bakers, weavers, tailors, dyers, tinsmiths, tinkers, and potters—a Whitmanesque gallery of working people—toiled night and day to house and feed the growing multitude. Many services were performed by slaves, of which the whole state still had thousands.

New York lacked Boston's tradition of piety and uplift, though it had plenty of churches (seven built in the 1790s alone), and despite the presence of Columbia College, it was not yet up to Philadelphia's caliber as an intellectual center. But it had a strong sense of community responsibility to the poor and sick. In 1789 over six hundred paupers were dependent on the parish; the New York Hospital (ancestor of Bellevue) opened in 1791 and the New York Dispensary four years later. New York knew how to play as well as be serious, and there were ballrooms and theaters for the leisured. But the town's main preoccupation was already getting to be business. In "downtown" streets (lit after dark by oil lamps) men of affairs gathered to bargain and deal in places like the Tontine Coffee House, which—in 1792—became the site of a regular meeting of stockbrokers, though they did not formally become the New York Stock Exchange on Wall Street till early in the next century. Businessmen could also get news of markets and movements from as many as nine newspapers, copies of which were available to the diners and drinkers. Out-of-towners with transactions to complete could reach New York by a variety of stagecoaches, and the island city was well linked to its neighbors by regular sailing ferry service.

New York had its crude side, too. Wandering cows and pigs were still visible at public crossings, and dead dogs, cats, and rats were left to decompose in the gutters and vacant lots that turned into quagmires in rainy seasons. Along with open cesspools and damp cellars, these nursed a mosquito population that made New York yet another city vulnerable to yellow fever. An epidemic in 1795 took some 750 lives, and there was another in 1798, not as devastating as Philadelphia's but still with a death toll over 2,000.

The city's expansion northward was slowed by marshy ground near the East River and a large pond called "the Collect" that filled modern-day Foley Square, where the Federal Court House now stands. It was ringed with breweries, potteries, tanneries, and ropewalks, which used its water. New Yorkers boated and swam there in summertime and cut figures on ice skates during winter. Two often overlooked landmark events took place on the Collect. In 1795 a New Jersey engineer, John Stevens, ran a small steamboat with a screw propeller on its calm surface. In 1796 John Fitch, who had already been operating a steamboat of his own devising between Philadelphia and other towns on the Delaware River, did likewise. Neither man, however, was able to interest capitalists in providing development money, so the honor of becoming the recognized father of the steamboat went to Robert Fulton, who a full eleven years later—with investment backing—ran his paddle-wheeler the *Clermont* up the Hudson from New York to Albany in two days. By then the Collect had already been filled in and disappeared.

There was already a distinctive New York style. It was cosmopolitan, as might be expected in a place whose families, high and low, claimed Dutch, English, French, Irish, Sephardic and Ashkenazic Jewish, West Indian, and African ancestors. And it was also full-blooded and jazzy. John Bernard, an English actor who played New York in 1797, later recorded his memories. At breakfast in his boardinghouse he saw foreign visitors and transients from states as far west as Kentucky, as far north as Vermont, and as far south as South Carolina, elbowing one another as they raced to empty platters of fish, ham, beef, boiled fowl, eggs, pies, lobsters, and vegetables washed down with "tea, coffee, cider, sangaree and cherry brandy." Merchants left their homes at eight-thirty, and were on the wharves by midmorning shouting orders, dodging among crates and barrels, thumbing ledgers. Noon found them at the market, and at two they were "back again to the rolling, heaving, hallooing and scribbling." At four they went home to dress for dinner, at seven to the theater, and at eleven to supper with friends to "smoke cigars, gulp down brandy and sing, roar and shout . . . till 3 in the morning." Bernard concluded that it was simply the way New York functioned. "Thus the New Yorker," he wrote, "enjoyed his span of being to the full stretch of the tether, his violent exertions during the day counteracting the effects of his nocturnal relaxations."[14] Abigail Adams may have put the same thought in another way when faced with the unpalatable prospect, to her, of moving the vice presidential home to Philadelphia. "When all is done," she said, "it will not be Broadway."[15]

✴

TWO CENTURIES AFTER 1800, the metropolitan pattern already visible in New York would become the one most characteristic of the United States. But to Hamilton and Burr's generation there was another kind of smaller-scale "urbanism" taking shape that would also generate conflicting interests needing to be expressed and reconciled through political parties. The town of Albany, neither exactly "rural" nor "urban," was a showcase and headquarters for a briskly developing "inland commerce" not clearly anticipated in the architecture of the Constitution.

Albany, 150 miles upriver from New York, also lived by commerce—it had been founded by the Dutch as Fort Orange, a stockaded market where the Iroquois came to barter their furs for the white man's hardware and whiskey—but its 1790 traffic was different. Albany collected the lumber, grain, and other farm produce of the Mohawk Valley just west of it, and of Vermont to the east, and shipped them downriver to New York. There they were bought and shipped to Europe. In return, manufactured goods were sent upstream for redistribution to the interior. Everything was on the modest scale befitting a "city" of between 3,500 souls in 1790 and 5,350 ten years later. Business was on a cash or barter basis—there were no banks—and the "merchant marine" numbered some ninety ships, half of them locally owned. They were small sailboats, usually operated by a crew of four, which included a cook for the eight or ten passengers who traveled each way. The round trip, with stops for loading and unloading by wagon, could take two or three weeks or even more. Winter ice closed business down, so an owner could count on only about ten round trips a year at a profit per trip of about one hundred dollars. Of Albany's buildings that clung to rising heights on the west side of the lovely river, almost a third were stores, storehouses, and stables. Handling some manufactured goods like paper, processed tobacco, glass bottles, and leatherware made in neighboring towns gave the economy a little diversity.

It was a slow town. A visiting Frenchman said that hospitality was not "a prominent feature in the character of the inhabitants of Albany," who had a "dull and melancholy" look.[16] Aaron Burr, like other lawyers and legislators, regarded his time there as a kind of penance. He wrote to a young Frenchwoman: "You expect amusement from my letters—amusement from Albany! You have certainly lost your senses or your recollection—I eat breakfast and dinner & go to bed and attend court—this is the history of my life here."[17] Excitement of an unwelcome sort was provided by fires, to which the wooden structures were especially vulnerable. One in 1793 destroyed twenty-six houses. Three of the town's slave populace, two of them women, were found guilty of setting it and were hanged. In 1797 another blaze consumed five blocks and prompted the clergy to declare it a "judgment of God for the sins of the community" and call for a day of prayer.[18] There was not much opportunity for sin. A night watch of twenty-four men selected nightly and obliged to serve or pay six shillings patrolled the streets. And as late as 1803 there was only one "respectable" public house where men could lodge and exchange gossip and favors. An old-time resident recalled meeting Clinton, Burr, Hamilton, Livingston, and other notables there.

As against New York's imported fabrics, Albany proudly wore homespun. She was still another part of a new America swimming into focus on the eve of the incoming nineteenth century. The river town would be one of many small-to-middle-sized inland commercial centers that depended for survival on continued immigration and development. In Albany's case that specifically meant the steady creation of new farms in the virgin acres that stretched westward toward the Finger Lakes and the Genesee Valley. Other necessities were improved transportation, easy access to the capital required for new businesses, and loosening the grip of land-buying syndicates, some controlled by foreign investors, on huge tracts they were holding for speculation. These goals would be hard to achieve without breaking the power of the old families and the newer financial aristocracy that Hamilton was trying to create. So while some voters in the area around Albany supported federalism, there was a large core of voters ready to listen to Republican arguments. These were the source of George Clinton's power. Between his upstate following of middling farmers and entrepreneurs and Burr's downstate New York City working-class adherents there was a political marriage that would last for many years—long after both men were gone and the Federalist and Republican labels had been replaced by other party names.

Upstate and downstate, province and capital, coastland and upland all were labels that showed how class and regional issues were becoming solidified within every state. Each state had a differently "flavored" politics, but in all of them, broad-based political activity was becoming an unavoidable necessity. Politics was more than a mere survival tool, however. It was also a kind of entertainment, a collection of familiar rituals, and a bonding force among different social, ethnic, and religious groups. But its unifying qualities were offset when political argument was carried to dangerous and divisive extremes. Which force would triumph? The 1790s did not know, and with good reason often feared the worst.

Like national politics, the intrastate variety could be played with sharp elbows and threats of violence. But the major divisions in the country in the 1790s remained those separating the South, North, and West. They were reflected in many variations, and some of the most interesting and important were on display in three unofficial sectional "capitals," Charleston, Boston, and Pittsburgh.

CHAPTER 6

Wedges of Sectionalism

WHAT MADE MEN Federalists or Republicans in the 1790s? What did lofty abstractions like "government," "society," or "freedom" mean to those on each side? And how were those words linked to hard-edged, material interests to produce political passions? These were the questions in the air as Americans marched along the unfamiliar and risky road through the first few national elections, framing answers at each milepost event.

Some of the more intriguing responses came from Charleston, which defied classification by simultaneously embracing both a southern outlook *and* a pro-Federalist political stance. By the third year of Washington's first administration, leaders of the plantation South were already starting to detest Hamilton's centralizing programs, from which they gained little. Yet Charleston was a striking exception that would provide federalism with a strong southern base and two distinguished but now forgotten presidential candidates. What were the reasons for the paradox?

✳

FOR ONE, Charleston was the capital of South Carolina, a state already noteworthy for its prima-donna-like self-image of untouchable independence. And Charleston was particularly proud of its distinctive social patterns. It was a case study in how local customs and traditions confound broad political generalizations. All the local elites of America's young communities were somewhat intermarried, but this was most noticeably so in Charleston. Nothing said that more clearly than the makeup of the state's four-man delegaton to the Constitutional Convention. "General" (by virtue of Revolutionary service) Charles Cotesworth Pinckney was one of them, and his youthful second cousin Charles Pinckney—baby of the gathering at twenty-nine—was another. Serving with the cousins was John Rutledge, Charles Cotesworth's brother-in-law. Finally there was delegate number four, Pierce Butler, married to a cousin of Charles Cotesworth's wife. A fifth member never showed up. The following year he became young Charles Pinckney's father-in-law.

Absent from this virtual clan reunion was Charles Cotesworth's brother, Thomas. He was busy serving as governor. These two brothers would dominate and typify South Carolina federalism and be gratefully recognized as leaders by the party, which made Thomas its choice for vice president in 1796 and twice nominated Charles Cotesworth for president—in 1804 and 1808. Between them the two would hold almost all the state's important elective positions at one time or another, and both would receive crucial diplomatic appointments in Paris and Madrid, at a time when America's best, most loyal, and most cultivated minds were needed to negotiate successfully with experienced foreign envoys holding better cards.

Their unusual qualities came in part from an unusual mother. Eliza Lucas was brought to South Carolina in 1738 by her father, a British army officer who owned three plantations there. When duty called him back to Antigua, in the Leeward Islands, about a year later, he left Eliza—rather than her mother—in charge of one of them, despite the fact that she was then just seventeen years old. Wappoo was six miles from Charleston by water and seventeen by land, comprising six hundred acres worked by twenty slaves. The girl also supervised the running of the two others. "I have the business of three plantations to transact," she wrote to a friend, "which requires . . . more business and fatigue . . . than you can imagine."[1]

Perhaps Major Lucas was impressed by the adolescent daughter's seriousness (she referred to herself in a letter as possessing "gravity and love of solitude"),[2] but for whatever reason he also entrusted her with the job of trying to grow various West Indian plants on Wappoo, from seeds that he sent. One of them was the indigo bush, which yielded a blue dye indispensable to textile makers through a complicated and dicey process of soaking the leaves, agitating and aerating the liquid to extract the color, then drying it and pressing it into cakes. Eliza spent four discouraging years experimenting with planting techniques, losing crops to weather, and having batches of dye ruined by inexpert makers, but in 1744 she had produced seventeen pounds of "very good indigo," according to British experts who evaluated a batch. Her success inspired other planters to follow. By 1747, they shipped out a total of 135,000 pounds. Eventually annual exports totaled a million pounds. South Carolina had a booming cash crop to supplement the rice, forest products, and small quantities of cotton she had been selling abroad. The perseverance of a young woman with a passion for agriculture had helped to make the colony prosperous.

In 1744 Eliza married a widower, Charles Pinckney (the whole Pinckney clan had a confusing fondness for duplicating names), who was a distinguished lawyer much older than herself, and to whom she was devoted enough to subside happily into eighteenth-century wifehood. Charles Cotesworth was born in 1746, Thomas in 1750. In between there was another son who died in infancy and a daughter. Eliza noted in a book of personal resolutions her firm intention to be "a good Mother to my children, to pray for them, to set them good examples . . . to be careful both of their souls and bodys, to watch over their tender minds . . . and to instill piety, virtue and true religion into them."[3] In 1753 the family moved to London when Charles senior was named South Carolina's agent to the Crown. He returned home with Eliza five years later, leaving the two boys in English schools, and soon died of malaria. Widowed Eliza, never losing her pleasure in trying new crops in Carolina soil, managed the affairs of both his estate and her father's through succeeding years of war and revolution. When she died while visiting Philadelphia at the age of eighty, George Washington himself served as one of her pallbearers.

Her sons were reared as English gentlemen. "C.C." read law at Oxford, was admitted to the British bar, and finished off his formal education with a tour of Europe plus further study of natural sciences and a grounding in the arts of war at the French royal military academy in Caen. "Tommy" followed the same course. It was very much in the pattern followed by sons of wealthy West Indian planters—they were sent "home" for education. And Charleston was in fact West Indian in style. With its balconied townhouses open to languorous sea breezes, its scented gardens, its slaves still speaking in African-English dialects, its French-and-Spanish-accented customs and cuisine—and likewise with its perils from fevers and hurricanes—it was more like Guadeloupe or Jamaica than Boston or New York. Yet there was something different about the British colonists on North America's mainland—they steadfastly thought of "home" as on *their* side of the Atlantic. The nationalism that would be so severely tested in 1800 survived in part because its roots ran mysteriously back into the feelings of men like the Pinckney brothers.

Considering that they respectively spent sixteen and twenty years growing up in London society, it is surprising that they were not Tories. But Charles returned in 1769, promptly took a seat in the colonial legislature, and supported the boycotts and protests against Britain's tightening grip. Thomas got back in 1774 on the eve of the outbreak of fighting. Both were valuable to the state by virtue of their military training; both rose to become generals; both served actively. Portraits show them in uniform, full-faced and solemn (C.C. the more portly of the two), already looking like senior advisers to officialdom, though actually they were still in their thirties. Thomas had a leg shattered in one battle. Charles Cotesworth was taken prisoner when the British captured Charleston in 1780, and later exchanged. During his captivity he was offered a chance to switch sides. "No," was his answer. "I entered into this cause after much reflection, and through principle; my heart is altogether American."[4]

The brothers' American hearts led them both into support of the Constitution and then into federalism for two especially Charlestonian reasons. One was that the Charleston of the 1780s was a commercial town, needing a government with authority to protect and enlarge its trade. At any given time up to a hundred vessels, some built in Charleston yards, bobbed at anchor in the harbor waiting to be loaded with rice, cotton, indigo, and "naval stores," the tar, rope, and timbers that were the sinews of sailing fleets, bound for the Caribbean and the British Isles. Though land ownership still carried the highest social cachet, fortunes made in trade were respectable, and what helped trade, therefore, helped elite Charleston as much as it did any New Englanders or New Yorkers. Since a number of prominent Charlestonians had also lent money to the state and nation, they liked Hamilton's "assumption" plans, which would guarantee them repayment, as well as his banking policies to bolster American credit at home and abroad.

Even more attractive was federalism's defense of order and stability against the turbulence of too much democracy. South Carolina's growing "up-country" settlements were pushing the state in a Republican direction, but the wealth and social influence of Charleston's eight thousand whites (matched by an equal number of blacks) was able to slow the march. The capital was moved to Columbia in 1790, but duplicates of all state offices remained in Charleston. Religious and property qualifications for office were abandoned only gradually, and as late as 1860 South Carolina's presidential electors were still chosen by the legislature rather than voters at large. White, male, Protestant, and rich, the Pinckney brothers held the line for a leadership based on the presumed wisdom and virtue of the best-bred, which was a foundation stone of Federalist doctrine. Washington anchored the southern wing of federalism on them. Charles Cotesworth was successively offered—and declined—a seat on the Supreme Court, and then the offices of secretary of war and secretary of state, before finally taking the post of minister to France in 1796. Thomas was made the American minister to Great Britain in 1792 and to Spain in 1795. But neither was fated to rise higher. There would never be a president from South Carolina.

In light of South Carolina's later secessionist record, it still comes as a shock to think of the state's early federalism. It would not last long. Two events in the general vicinity of Charleston helped to start chain reactions that would wipe out Carolina's pre-1800 nationalism. In August 1791 a hundred thousand slaves in the French colony of St. Domingue—modern-day Haiti—burst into revolt against conditions so hellish that they made America's version of slavery seem almost benign by contrast. Cruelty bred cruelty, and within weeks hundreds of sugar, coffee, cotton, and indigo plantations had been torched, while in the lurid light of the flames, troops of blacks armed with machetes and crude pikes were butchering their former owners. Thousands of white refugees fled to nearby American ports, and Charleston was closest. The exiled French planter community filled the ears of Charlestonians with horror stories that confirmed their worst nightmares. Then a charismatic free black commander, François-Dominique Toussaint, who called himself Toussaint-L'Ouverture ("the beginning"), was recognized for a while as the de facto authority in the colony by the French revolutionary government. An island ruled by a black radical, only a few days' sail from Charleston—another nightmare realized! What would be the impact on the local "Negroes"? What ideas might it inspire in them? Charleston and all of South Carolina had long defended slavery on economic grounds, but now a racial paranoia gripped the state, which began increasingly to distrust the idea of sharing a union with opponents of slavery. Rebellious blacks anywhere made the South more nervously aware of its separateness—and black rebels in the Caribbean drew South Carolina closer to her sister slaveholding states.

Then in 1793 on a plantation near Savannah, just a hundred miles south of Charleston, Eli Whitney, a son of Massachusetts, changed the future of the city forever. Almost everyone knows that he invented the cotton gin. But fewer realize that Whitney was just the kind of "humbly" born, restless, gifted individualist who could rise to the top only in an open society not dominated by Federalist ideas. Whitney was a mechanically inclined farmer's son with a mind of his own. He turned down his father's offer to send him to college when he was twelve, puttered about his home manufacturing violins, nails, and hat pins, then decided at the advanced age of twenty-three to go to Yale, where he partially supported himself until his 1792 graduation by repairing the school's scientific and mechanical equipment. En route to a job as private tutor to the children of a Georgia planter—a stopgap until he could teach himself law—he met the widow of Connecticut's General Nathanael Greene, who had liberated South Carolina from British occupation in 1781–82 and planned before his early death to make a postwar living out of a southern plantation. She invited the footloose Whitney to be her guest and handyman, and it was at her dining table that he heard visitors discuss the cotton dilemma.

"Long-staple" or "sea island" cotton, grown in the hot and damp coastal lowlands of Georgia and South Carolina, was a useful export but could only be produced in limited quantities. "Short-staple" cotton flourished abundantly on higher ground, but its stubborn green seeds could only be plucked from the bolls by hard hand labor. A slave had to work all day to produce a marketable pound. In ten days Whitney contrived a wooden model of his cotton "gin" (short for "engine") that could clean and seed short-staple cotton fifty times as fast as black fingers. Within a year he and a partner were manufacturing gins; within seven more—by 1800—United States cotton exports had jumped from an annual 138,000 pounds to 35 million, about half of it exported, and the numbers were still rising. The boom was on. Pioneers would pour into the unsettled, still-unplowed acres of Georgia and the Carolinas, Mississippi and Alabama, Tennessee and Louisiana and Arkansas, and create the "cotton kingdom" of upstart newcomers who insisted that maintaining and expanding their slave labor force was indispensable to the future of the South.

Charleston would not share fully in the bonanza. The major ports of export for cotton would become New Orleans and, after railroads were invented, New York. As the country expanded, aristocracy was submerged in the tide of democracy (for white men only). Charleston began to look inward and backward instead of ahead. Her thinkers and writers produced intense and passionate defenses of slavery, states' rights, and eventually secession, and the town that had done so much to promote the Constitution in 1788 became the first to leave the Union in 1860.

So, acting as agents for history's blind forces, Toussaint-L'Ouverture and Eli Whitney, the black man and the Yankee, had helped to make the worldview of the Pinckney brothers an anachronism, and had done so virtually on the Pinckneys' own turf. But in 1800 slavery hadn't fully reentered the political stage, and South Carolina federalism stayed very much alive. It would have a decisive influence on the election's outcome.

✳

NEW ENGLAND'S sense of distinctiveness rested on several props, and especially on a harsh religious and political history. But nowhere was it paraded more vividly than in seagoing, trading Boston. The merchant first citizens of the town superficially resembled their Charleston counterparts who lived in fine houses and drove handsome carriages to busy countinghouses. But they were actually of a different breed. Circumstances forced them to be far more adventurous, more conscious of a new and widening business world. They were relentless in their search to find substitutes for the imperial markets closed off to them by British law after American independence was won. They had more practice at it, because even in colonial times the foodstuffs of New England, unlike the plantation crops of the South, were not admitted to Great Britain to compete with locally grown produce. So New Englanders had learned early to swap cheese and salted codfish for Barbados sugar and rum, sugar and rum for Spanish raisins and Portuguese wine, raisins and wine for Birmingham nails and Sheffield pottery, all in a sweeping orbit that took in the ports of the Caribbean, the Mediterranean, and the North Atlantic.

Following 1783 the orbit widened. In 1790 Boston celebrated the return to its harbor of the ship *Columbia*, Robert Gray, master, ending the first round-the-world voyage under the new American flag. Gray had gone all the way around South America, stopped on the Oregon coast to load furs, proceeded to Canton, China, with a stop in the Hawaiian Islands, and come back with a hold full of tea and silk. The *Columbia* was not the first American-flag ship in Canton; New York's *Empress of China* had been there in 1784, beating out Boston for the honor. But the Northwest fur trade, once established, made Boston, population sixteen thousand, a truly international port.

Equally remarkable was the maritime entrepreneurship of Boston's little neighbor Salem, only eight thousand strong. Salem sent locally built and manned ships around the Cape of Good Hope at Africa's southern extremity, to India for cotton fabrics and teak. From there they went on to Sumatra, Borneo, Java, and the Malay Peninsula for coffee and spices. Thence onward to the Philippines for hemp that made the indispensable ropes that rigged the vessel, and so home. New England's whale fisheries, too, expanded, and skippers out of New Bedford and Nantucket hunted their quarry in far Pacific waters, stopping to refit their storm-battered ships on little-known islands where their great-great-great-grandsons would fight battles in the 1940s.

The dangers were huge. Many of the little ships, not much bigger than modern pleasure craft, never returned with their crews and cargoes. They simply disappeared, wrecked on reefs in uncharted waters, capsized in typhoons, or captured by Barbary or Malay pirates. There was genuine risk for the investors, too—a skipper or supercargo with broad authority from the owners might load up on calicoes or sandalwood on a hint that they would fetch good prices, only to discover at the next port of call that the bottom had dropped out of the market. But the rewards for the winners were handsome. Boston shipowners could build themselves stately brick houses on the hills that overlooked the busy wharves crowded along the water's edge. They could decorate their parlors with scroll paintings and porcelain vases and carved teak chests and enjoy a life still full of hard work by later standards, yet far more comfortable than that of their austere, struggling Puritan ancestors. No wonder that a foreign visitor wrote: "Commerce occupies all their thoughts, turns all their heads, and absorbs all their speculations."[5]

Boston's mercantile outreach had national implications. It made an American presence in the world a reality to foreign nations. It planted the seeds of future commercial empire while the Constitution was still an experiment, and so supplied a tangible incentive to make it work. But it also made Yankees think of themselves as a separate people whose major contribution to the nation was disgracefully undervalued outside New England. And seafaring success colored Boston politics indelibly Federalist so long as federalism was dedicated to the nurture of trade. The social conservatism of Boston's Federalists owed something to the town's tough, seagoing traditions, too. The ship of state was meant to be run not by vote of the crew but by officers properly qualified and with unchallenged authority. So the voice of Fisher Ames, Harvard class of 1774, friend and supporter of Hamilton in the first Congress, dripped contempt for "mere democracy, which has never been tolerable nor long tolerated."[6] Equal skepticism about the people at large fell from the pen of Salem-born Timothy Pickering in the midst of the Revolution: "If we should fail at last, the Americans can only blame their own negligence, avarice, and want of almost every public virtue."[7]

The social and economic conservatism that made New England's Federalist leaders blindly and unwisely contemptuous of democracy also brought them to look more kindly on the former mother country and its solid institutions. It was a strange development less than a generation after boycotts and redcoat-baiting in Boston streets. But that was no stranger than the pro-British stance of Boston's mercantile elite in the 1790s in spite of the tight collar that London had clamped on their trade with Britain's homeland and possessions. One would have expected the opposite—yet there was an evident economic logic to courting British esteem. Britain was already the world's workshop and leading source of American imports. And Britain's far-flung and hungry dominions could benefit enormously from consuming American produce. Britain's potential value as a trading partner was incalculable. So it made far more sense to seek a deal with her than to fight with her, especially when she was so strong. To get such a deal, commercially minded New Englanders believed, should be a major object of United States diplomacy. So this became a major foreign-policy issue, debated more stridently with each succeeding election.

New England's inclination toward closer ties with Old England was merely an irritant to the South. But it made western politicians furious, because they were certain that both the older sections, the North and South, were always ready to sacrifice the special interests of the West. In 1794 this smoldering friction burst into flame in Pennsylvania over the seemingly simple matter of a national tax on distilled spirits. The fire's center was the raw town of Pittsburgh, and the panorama of words, whiskey, and warfare that unfolded there perfectly illustrated why the engine of constitutional government was sputtering and threatening to quit on takeoff.

✳

NO BROTHERLY LOVE was wasted in Pennsylvania between the coastal East, whose center was Philadelphia, and the mountain West, of which the informal capital was rough-hewn Pittsburgh, hardly a generaton away from its beginnings as a wilderness stockade. Westerners had a lengthy bill of particulars in a bitter indictment of both the state and national governments. They were outraged that too many eastern speculators held title to thousands of acres of good land. They wanted more help in fighting the Indians, more muscle for the puny and disorganized army of the United States, which in its first official battle under the Constitution was soundly beaten by Miami tribesmen under Chief Little Turtle. They wanted a tougher diplomatic stance against Great Britain, which they accused of stirring up the Indians and of hanging on to forts and fur-trading posts in the Northwest that were supposed to have been given up under the peace treaty of 1782.

They were also disgusted with the lack of pressure on Spain, the existing holder of the Louisiana Territory, to allow their exports to pass through New Orleans. That permission was crucial to them for still another reason that rankled, namely, the failure of Congress to appropriate money for decent roads connecting the backcountry with the coast. Lacking these, freight haulage was so slow and expensive that it ate up any profits from the sale of the grain, meat, furs, hides, and handmade articles that the new settlers needed to sell. It made better sense to float goods down the Ohio (which began at Pittsburgh) and then the Mississippi on flatboats and rafts and dispose of them to New Orleans merchants for reshipment, provided there was Spanish consent and no killing Spanish fees or taxes.

The whole crescent of settlement that clung to the flanks of the Appalachians shared these problems, and in fact the frontier from Maine to Georgia was still only tenuously bound to the distant and untested United States. More than once in those early years there would be talk of independence and possible separate deals for protection with London or Madrid. Ambitious individuals were rumored to be waiting in the wings to play the part of liberator. It seemed fanciful looking back later on, but it was not so in 1791 when secretary of the Treasury Hamilton got Congress to enact a seven-cent-a-gallon excise tax on distilled spirits. That tax was a fighting issue, especially in Pennsylvania.

There were good reasons. The tax struck a body blow at western Pennsylvania's economy by steeply boosting the cost of a major activity. Easily built stills, communally or individually owned, were scattered abundantly throughout the region. Grain was expensive to ship, but twenty-four bushels of rye could be reduced to a pair of eight-gallon kegs of whiskey salable at up to a dollar a gallon, and these could be carried to market easily on a mule's back. Where hard cash was lacking, the whiskey itself served as a strong backup currency in a system heavily dependent on barter. To farmers living on the margins of survival, those few extra pennies of tax, which could be paid only in cash, looked enormous.

And there was more. Whiskey was, in a literal sense, "the water of life" in frontier Pennsylvania. Drunkenness was deplored, but not drinking. Pioneers "drank good Monongahela rye to cure ague and snakebite, to season simple meals, to cheer at christenings and to console at wakes."[8] A whiskey tax had an irritating flavor of unspoken moral reprimand. An excise—by definition a tax on the manufacture, sale, or consumption of some commonly used article—was also intrusive. It allowed collectors to snoop in barns, closets, and cellars looking for hidden untaxed spirits. And anyone wishing to challenge an assessment had to leave home and farm untended in order to take his case to the federal court in distant Philadelphia. All in all, where Hamilton may simply have seen the tax as a simple revenue-raising device to pay the costs of government, the settlers felt that the clock was turning backward to pre-Revolutionary days. Hadn't the colonists been complaining about a faraway government in which they had no influence choking their economy with unjustifiable taxes and sneering at their local customs? Had the war been fought simply to replace London with Philadelphia as the seat of tyranny?

Frontiersmen in Kentucky, Tennessee (not yet a state), and western Virginia objected to the tax, too, and dragged their feet about paying it. But it was in Pennsylvania that resistance was strongest and centered in the counties surrounding and adjacent to Pittsburgh. At first it was simply a matter of ignoring the tax and summonses to court. But when, after more than two years of meager collections, the federal government began to make a real effort to collect, violence erupted. A few would-be collectors were physically attacked, had their heads shaven and their clothes torn off, were tarred and feathered and otherwise crudely humiliated until they agreed to resign their offices. It was not surprising. The frontiersmen were people whose lives were violent, painful, and often short. They died in infancy from untreated diseases, in adulthood from childbirth and accidents like falling trees, attacking animals, suddenly flooded valleys, blizzards that caught them in the open. When men fought they bit off noses and gouged out eyes. When men and women prayed at camp meetings they howled at full voice. Naturally, political protest also took strenuous forms.

On July 16, 1794, a crowd gathered outside the home of a wealthy local resident named John Neville who had accepted a commission as collector. Neville owned several stills himself but could afford the tax and did not regret that it might drive smaller competitors to the wall. There were shouts for him to resign the office. Neville, a veteran of the French and Indian War and the Revolution, was not easily frightened. He refused, and when shots were fired he shot back and mortally wounded one of the mob. They returned in force the next night. Neville had brought in about a dozen soldiers from Fort Pitt. There was another exchange of gunfire, more dead and wounded, and then Neville slipped out before his guards surrendered to the besiegers, who then burned the finely furnished aristocratic residence to the ground.

Blood had been shed. Leaders of the antitax forces called a mass meeting, and on August 1 seven thousand protesters carrying the weapons that were commonplace on the frontier gathered in a field outside Pittsburgh and threatened to destroy the town. It would not have been hard. There were only four hundred houses, all wooden, half a dozen taverns, a post office in a log hut, and a courthouse in front of which a stocks and pillory stood. A few inhabitants were rich, but most were small shopkeepers and craftsmen. A visitor a few years later warned that "a person coming [to Pittsburgh] . . . should do it under the conviction of making money & bettering his circumstances, but not of enjoying the pleasure either of a country or city life."[9] Usefulness, not refinement, was the purpose of Pittsburgh's existence.

But the future workshop did not go up in flames that August night. Moderate leaders who opposed the tax but also saw the futility and danger of a disorganized uprising managed to cool the crowd down. One of them was Hugh Henry Brackenridge, Freneau's old Princeton classmate. Another was Albert Gallatin, a Geneva-born immigrant and brilliant financier who would eventually play a major part in the Jefferson administrations. The two made sympathetic speeches to the roaring crowd. They promised political action to bring relief, and they also managed to arrange for the distribution of free food and liquor. The mollified rebels were persuaded simply to march through Pittsburgh and bivouac on the other side. After a short while, most of the prominent resisters agreed to sign a promise to obey the laws of the United States in the future, in return for a pardon for any past offenses.

The rebellion was really over in September 1794, but by then the situation had become deeply embittered. Hamilton, who rarely failed to show his worst side when thwarted even temporarily, insisted as usual that opposition to his will equaled subversion. In a cabinet meeting he urged Washington to make an example by punishing the ringleaders at whatever cost. Otherwise, he warned, "the spirit of disobedience . . . will naturally extend and the authority of the government will be prostrate."[10] The president did not basically disagree. He was upset that many of the dissidents had joined "democratic societies," social and political clubs that sprang up briefly to unite sympathizers with the French Revolution. He was "perfectly convinced" that if not "discountenanced . . . they will destroy the government of this country" and that further forbearance with the whiskey-tax resisters , in the hope of curing their "delirium and folly," would only "increase the disorder."[11] He agreed to muster a force some thirteen thousand strong of militia from three states rather than regulars, in deference to lingering anti-

Federalist fears of a "standing army" being employed to crush the people's liberties. Hamilton would not have been so scrupulous. He had "long since learned to hold popular opinion of no value."[12] Federalist newspapers were even more disdainful. "It is by force alone," one said, "that an ignorant herd can be governed." The malcontents were men of "vice, ignorance [and] idleness." Editors in Pennsylvania defending the westerners were not any more restrained. According to them, the real issue was "whether the powers of the government of the United States are held by an aristocratic junto or by the people." The punitive expedition showed the administration's hand, its conviction that "government can be carried on only by the pageantry of rank, the influence of money and emoluments and the terror of military force."[13]

So the "rebellion" came to a tragicomic end. The "army," a very large one for the time, gathered at Carlisle, to which Washington rode on October 4 to make the gesture of assuming personal (but temporary) command amid the boom of cannons and the ringing of bells. A local scribe was carried away with the scene. "THE MAN OF THE HOUR," he wrote, inspected the ranks "with a mien as intrepid as that of Hector, nor once turned his eagle eye from the dazzling effulgence of the steel clad band."[14] But this was no *Iliad*. Mountain cold, autumn downpours, washed-out roads, and a totally disorganized supply service made the march westward a horror. Many of the militiamen deserted. Others struggled on minus coats and blankets, sick and hungry, stealing food and firewood from local farms. When the forces of law and order finally reached Pittsburgh they dragged eighteen miscreants from their homes and kept them shivering outdoors for hours in snow and rain before locking them up. There were more arrests later, but many of these arrestees had already signed the pledge of obedience and some were wrongly identified.

Eventually twenty were dragged to Philadelphia on a winter return march. Arriving there exhausted on Christmas Day, they were paraded through the streets to edify jeering crowds who wanted to see the wild men from the West. When finally tried after nearly a year, only two were found guilty of treason and Washington, having made his point, pardoned both.

The Whiskey Rebellion passed into the history books as a glorious defining moment in establishing the authority of the new government. But there was something ugly lingering in the air at its conclusion. The actual bloodshed was small, but for a time men on opposite sides of a tax law had been enemies rather than adversaries; conspirators and anarchists, not fellow citizens. Torrents of anger were swirling, and disruption of the nation seemed thinkable.

Much of this passion reflected events abroad. The French Revolution and the wars it caused had started an earthquake in the entire Atlantic community of which the new American nation was very much a member. By 1794 it had shaken down many old structures, including the supposed walls of isolation between American and European affairs and the presumed harmony of feeling among all Americans that separated them from the troubled societies of the Old World. At the time that rebels were threatening to burn Pittsburgh, the situation could be completely understood only with reference to other violent events far away in Paris.

PART III

WAR ABROAD,

POLITICS AT HOME,

1793–1796

CHAPTER 7

Terror, Turmoil, and
Citizen Genet

ON JANUARY 21, 1793, before a cheering crowd in a Paris public square, the unbelievable happened. The drums rolled, the blade of the guillotine fell, and the severed head of Louis Capet, formerly His Majesty Louis XVI, toppled into the basket. The French had actually executed their king. The news took two months to reach Philadelphia. When it did, the shock wave rocked the newly begun second administration of George Washington. Where the first had been focused on domestic policy, this one would be dominated by foreign affairs. Again, Hamilton and Jefferson's clashing views would turn cabinet meetings into combat zones, as the new situation brutally intensified partisan feelings. Heavyset and lethargic Secretary of War Knox and the occasionally indecisive attorney general Randolph would sometimes intervene and sometimes evade, and as always the last word was the president's. But it was the tension between the secretaries of state and Treasury that drove the scenario.

The year 1793 was Jefferson's last in the cabinet and Hamilton's next-to-last. Their departure, however, did not calm the storms unleashed by their quarrels. The clashing ideas of these two men about the goals of an independent America went beyond the man-to-man rivalry of cabinet politicians. Their quarrels over the federal bank and the debts had become part of a developing party conflict on a larger national stage, because they touched basic and sensitive issues about the proper connections linking wealth, power, and republican government.

Now the stage broadened even more and took in the world. Put simply, the main business of 1793 for Jefferson was an effort to bring France and America, now sister republics, closer together while leaving Great Britain trumped and isolated. Hamilton wanted the exact opposite—to help Great Britain contain revolutionary France—and he more or less succeeded in winning over Washington, as he had done before. There were other forces, too, thwarting Jefferson's purpose—including robustly inept French diplomacy. But just as with the domestic issues, the fellow thinkers of Jefferson and Hamilton on the respective merits of France and England enlarged, multiplied, and further embittered the disagreements between the two men. Once again it was a matter of fundamentals. For the Franco-British struggle, too, went to the very core of social values—to opposed beliefs about the virtues of equality, tradition, stability, and progress. These feelings on both sides of the ocean could not be confined within George Washington's cherished framework of nonpartisan consensus on the public good. They were even strong enough to pierce his shell of immunity in his second administration.

As adversaries in domestic politics Jefferson and Hamilton were makers and mirrors of purely American divisions of opinion. But Jefferson and Hamilton as, respectively, defender and attacker of the French Revolution had prototypes the world over, who were causing bloodshed in European countries—and threatening to bring it to America.

The two men were not, of course, mere disembodied voices rallying support for their philosophies. They were also human beings, and while history is much more than a record of magnified personal encounters, it also remains rooted in individual personalities. The years of hottest battle between Jefferson and Hamilton coincided with personal crises for both. Jefferson began to feel a disgust with politics and a yearning for exit. And Hamilton was trapped in a private scandal that later would have extravagant political costs.

⁂

THE MISCARRIAGE of Jefferson's pro-French plans in 1793—the story to be told in the rest of this chapter—undoubtedly intensified what appears to have been a clear longing to wash his hands of public life at least for a while. In April Jefferson passed his fiftieth birthday, a time of stock taking for almost any man. He always had seen himself in spite of his high-living ways as a simple man of the soil, one of God's chosen "who labor in the bosom of the earth," in a familiar phrase that he penned in 1782. Though the manual labor was done by others, Jefferson's love of the landowning life was manifest. When he could get away to Monticello he spent happy, sixteen-hour days in the saddle, riding tall and easily, sometimes singing to himself, taking in every detail as he supervised his endless projects for improving his beautiful residence or boosting his crop yields. He faced real problems in making his eleven thousand acres, spread over several separate locations and worked by more than a hundred slaves, pay enough to reduce the thousands of dollars' worth of debt he had accumulated. He would try crop rotation, the replacement of tobacco with oats and rye, the establishment of a brickyard and a nail factory—anything to achieve the agricultural self-sufficiency that he believed was the only real foundation for independence. He always yearned to be as he described himself in 1795: "measuring fields, following my ploughs, helping the haymakers . . . and living like an antedeluvian patriarch among my children and grandchildren [of whom he then had two by his older daughter, with his younger on the verge of marriage] and tilling my soil."[1] There is an intriguing quality to his choice of the words "antedeluvian patriarch," considering the near certainty that he had a slave concubine, about whom rumors would soon begin to circulate.

In July 1793 Jefferson had been away from home on public business for almost half his life—twenty-four years—and felt genuinely weary. He had wanted to leave before the 1792 election, and now he told the president that he would quit at the end of September. Washington asked him to stay through the year and Jefferson had to agree, but when his friend Madison also urged him to think it over, he answered with irritation. He said he was "worn down with labors from morning to night, and day to day; knowing them as fruitless to others as they are vexatious to myself; committed singly and in desperate and eternal contest against a host who are systematically undermining the public liberty and prosperity. . . . cut off from my family and friends, my affairs abandoned to chaos and derangement, in short giving [up] everything I love, in exchange for everything I hate." No, he would hear of nothing but quitting and told Madison the subject was closed. "Never let there be more between you and me, on this subject."[2] The hardworking Madison may have disagreed about how "singly" his partner was contesting the enemies of liberty, but he argued no further. So Jefferson did reach Monticello at last in 1794 self-persuaded that "my bark will have put into port with a design not to venture out again; and I trust it will be the last [time]. My farm, my family and my books call me to them irresistibly."[3]

But with Jefferson it wasn't always possible to be sure. Did he really mean to abandon the fight against Hamilton and the "stockjobbers" to Madison and his allies? Only two years later, in 1796, he would reluctantly let his name be put forward for the presidency, aware that he was the strongest symbolic figure around whom almost all Republicans could rally. Only Jefferson would ever know for sure whether he jumped or was pushed into that decision. But many of his Federalist rivals never were convinced by his protestations of loving bucolic simplicity. Hamilton from the start said that Jefferson was aiming at the presidency. And John Adams, unlike Hamilton a longtime friend of the man, was blunt in assessment when the Virginian stepped down. "Jefferson thinks by this step to get a reputation as an humble, modest, meek man, wholly without ambition or vanity," he wrote. "He may even have deceived himself into this belief. But if the prospect opens the world will see and he will feel that he is as ambitious as Oliver Cromwell."[4]

For Hamilton, too, 1793 was not the best of years. It opened with a public attack on his integrity in the form of a set of resolutions introduced into the final session of the Second Congress, due to expire on March 4, by Virginia representative William B. Giles. Behind Giles were the hands of Madison and—in secrecy—Jefferson, who anonymously drafted one of several versions. Jefferson was thereby meddling in Treasury matters, but Hamilton on numerous occasions tried to undercut Jefferson's moves in foreign affairs. Each secretary was shameless in trying to thwart the other. The Giles resolutions in effect accused Hamilton of manipulating Treasury funds in disregard of congressional authority and for the benefit of speculators. Then as now, Congress would authorize specific appropriations for particular ends, such as paying off an installment of a loan. The charge was that Hamilton had switched specific funds around, applying them to different purposes as he saw fit. An explanation was demanded. To beat the mandatory adjournment date Hamilton needed to work at breakneck speed, but no one was better at it. He produced three lengthy documents that gave reasonable explanations of his management. The Virginians nonetheless introduced nine new resolutions of censure, all of which failed by wide margins. Jefferson privately grumbled to his son-in-law that the vindication came from an expiring House of Representatives "one-third . . . made up of bank directors & stock jobbers . . . and another third of persons blindly devoted to that party . . . [or] not comprehending the papers, or perhaps . . . too indulgent to pass a vote of censure."[5] He was saying, in short, that Hamilton's defenders could only be stupid, partisan, or venal.

The defeat of the Giles resolutions was a victory for Hamilton but also a signal that resistance to his plans for a sound national economy based on investor confidence would continue to plague him in the months ahead. And he was also aware of another gigantic vulnerability, which was, for the moment, still a secret but packed with devastating potential.

In November 1792 Hamilton's comptroller of the Treasury, a faithful Connecticut Federalist named Oliver Wolcott, jailed a pair of shady operators named James Reynolds and Jacob Clingman. The charge was that they were submitting claims against the Treasury that they had fraudulently obtained from legitimate government creditors. Clingman was well connected—he knew Senator Burr, former House speaker Frederick Mühlenberg, and ex-representative (from Connecticut) Jeremiah Wadsworth. Wadsworth interceded with Wolcott, who let the two go when they agreed to repay the government and reveal the source of the list of claimants whom they had bilked. But Wadsworth was stunned by a bombshell that Clingman and Reynolds dropped in order to win his support. They said that Reynolds had gotten money from Alexander Hamilton himself to use in "insider" speculation on Treasury notes.

Word was passed to Mühlenberg, who promptly took it to his friends Senator Monroe and Representative Abraham Venable, both Virginians and future Republicans, who decided to investigate further. Two of them called at Reynolds's home and spoke to his attractive young wife, Maria. They persuaded her to part with some letters from Hamilton to herself. Together with others furnished by Clingman, they showed that Hamilton had in fact been making payments to Reynolds.

On December 15 the trio—Mühlenberg, Monroe, and Venable—confronted Hamilton in his office and asked why they should not show the incriminating notes to the president. Hamilton, though badly flustered and angry, asked them to come to his own house that night and promised to explain everything to them and to Wolcott, whom he would also invite. When the group convened, thirty-six-year-old Hamilton, one of the shrewdest realists and keenest thinkers on public affairs in the world, made a confession of private stupidity and lechery. He had committed adultery, been caught, and let himself be blackmailed by Reynolds.

The story was classic, familiar, and ugly. One July day in 1791 Maria Reynolds, then a seductively good-looking twenty-three, was shown into Hamilton's office in Philadelphia. As the sister-in-law of a Livingston she was well credentialed socially, but she had a problem. Her scapegrace husband, James, had left her for another woman and she needed money to return to New York. Would Mr. Hamilton be neighborly and gallant enough to help a lady in distress? Mr. Hamilton did not have the money on him but promised to bring some to her address that night. She met him, showed him the way to her bedroom, and as he put it later, "it was quickly apparent that other than pecuniary consolation would be acceptable."[6]

The affair took the usual course, with secret trysts at her home, his home, and inns. Then a complication was introduced when, according to Maria, Reynolds returned penitent to her side. She remained Hamilton's mistress, however, while he cultivated her husband in order to avert suspicion. But finally the secretary began to wonder if he himself was not being used, and decided to break things off. At that point Maria tearfully insisted that she loved him and pleaded with him to stay. So, as he later put it, since "my vanity admitted the possibility of a real fondness," he decided on a "gradual discontinuance." But while that was in progress, the trap was sprung. In mid-December 1791 Maria came to Hamilton with terrible news—her husband had discovered all! However, Reynolds did not come raging to Hamilton with horsewhip or pistol in hand. Instead he wrote that his wounded honor would be satisfied with a payment of a thousand dollars, and once he got that he would decamp. Hamilton gave him the money in two installments and even took a receipt saying that it was payment "in full of all demands."

It was not, of course. Hamilton by now really wished to exit, but Reynolds urged him to go on seeing Maria, whose heart, he said, would be broken by her lover's abandonment. Warned of that impending calamity, in fact, Maria did pen some piteous, misspelled letters to the secretary: "I have kept my Bed these tow dayes and now rise from my pillow which your Neglect has filled with the sharpest thorns. . . . I only do it to Ease a heart which is ready Burst with Greef. I can neither Eat or sleep . . . for God's sake be not so voed [void] of all humanity . . . if my dear freend has the Least Esteeme for the unhappy Maria whose greatest fault is Loveing him he will come as soon as he will get this."[7] It is hard to know if Maria herself was a full participant in the scheme or the catspaw of Reynolds, but she must have been very winning in either role, because Hamilton went on seeing her and making further "loans" to Reynolds until the summer of 1792, not long before the blackmailer's arrest.

That was the story, supported by letters from the conniving couple, that Hamilton told Venable, Mühlenberg, and Monroe. Before he was finished the first two, at least, urged him to stop—they were convinced that his sins were private and wanted to hear no more. Monroe agreed, though somewhat more coolly according to Hamilton's later account. They would simply forget about the matter and not publicize the incriminating letters already gotten from Clingman and Maria the day before. Hamilton asked that they not return those to Reynolds in order to prevent their further use against him, and also requested copies. That was agreed to, and the originals stayed in the possession of Monroe. It appeared at the beginning of 1793 that the case was closed.

But Hamilton could hardly have been tranquil in mind. Nor could Jefferson, torn between his urge to block Hamilton and his unfulfilled longing to go home to Monticello. Among the leading figures of the administration John Adams appeared to be having the easiest time, thanks to finally accepting the insignificance of his job. While the Senate was in session he lived unstressfully in a Philadelphia boarding-house, reading, writing letters, and enjoying social dinners with friends like Benjamin Rush. He was troubled only by such unavoidable physical discomforts of an eighteenth-century man nearing sixty as teeth lost to pyorrhea and a slight tremor of the hands. He had, however, come to miss Abigail and his Peacefield retreat sorely—"I want my wife to hover over and about me. . . . I want my horse, my farm, my long walks and more than all the bosom of my friend," he wrote her.[8] So during the eight months of 1793 that Congress stood in adjournment he abandoned the capital and its debates for Massachusetts, a pattern that he would follow during the remainder of his vice presidency.

✳

SO MATTERS STOOD in April 1793, when a new development brought foreign affairs into the immediate foreground of Washington's recently renewed presidency. While Americans were still absorbing the significance of King Louis's beheading, a ship arriving late in March brought more explosive news. France had declared war on Spain, Great Britain, and Holland. The immediate, concrete, and dangerous issues facing the chief executive were enormous. The United States was still linked to France by the treaty of mutual defense concluded in 1778. And now France had two enemies who ringed young America on three sides. The British held Canada, and Spain owned the entire west bank of the Mississippi, the Gulf Coast, and all of Florida. Both of them had island possessions in the Caribbean a few days' sail from Charleston, Philadelphia, New York, and Boston.

What would be the result of honoring the French treaty? The British fleet could work its will in American coastal waters and on the United States merchant marine anywhere it chose. Spain was weak, but a young America with a token army and no navy did not need any additional enemies. On the other hand, France, too, had a major-league navy and West Indian bases. If she regarded American failure to support her as a hostile act, the results could be as damaging as any brought on by war with Britain. For the United States government, choosing sides between London and Paris was no longer a question of ideology but possibly of existence itself. The situation was serious enough to bring Washington, who had gone down to Mount Vernon after Congress adjourned, hurrying back to Philadelphia for an emergency meeting of his cabinet.

It was foreseeable that Hamilton and Jefferson would be at odds. Behind them and their cohorts were three years of disagreement as to whether to tilt U.S. foreign and commercial policy toward the British or French. One of Madison's first acts in the First Congress had been his failed battle to win discriminatory taxes on British shipping and increase the flow of imports from France. Both he and Jefferson were disturbed by the power London could exert thanks to America's dependence on British markets and manufacturers. Up to two thirds of the commerce of the United States was with Britain or with territories that flew her flag, a fact that seriously undercut American bargaining power in bitter disputes with the ex-mother country over how the peace settlement was being carried out. Hamilton, from his chair as the national finance manager, saw it differently. There was no realistic chance of a commercial French connection that would match the power of the thriving British trade to produce home prosperity, high tariff revenues, and cash for the national coffers. Picking commercial fights with King George would be self-defeating. (Ironically, the best long-term prospect of reducing the demand for British-made goods was Hamilton's own idea of encouraging American factories.) So when the Treasury and the State Departments repeatedly clashed over the course to take in a Franco-British war, there were basic questions of national interest at stake. The republican versus monarchical sympathies of the two secretaries, however, sharpened the dispute, and their personal antagonism poisoned it even more. Hamilton, using a curious adjective, saw Jeffer-

son as possessed by "a womanish attachment to France and a womanish resentment against Great Britain."[9] Jefferson fumed that "[Hamil-
ton] is panic-struck if we refuse our breech to every kick which Great
Britain may choose to give it."[10]

Behind the hard-edged questions of trade and war were the issues
that can best be understood only in the context of the French Revolutionary era as a whole. In the broadest framework, France's revolution
was an ongoing series of upheavals that hammered out the political
shape of the nineteenth and twentieth centuries and made them different from any that had gone before. The story is one from which the
United States cannot be isolated. The revolt against King Louis XVI
that began in May 1789 ran an erratic and violent course for some ten
years and culminated in the rise of Napoleon Bonaparte, who made
himself dictator and then, in 1804, emperor of France. His armies sub-
dued most of Europe in a string of wars that did not end until his own
overthrow in 1815. Napoleon was a new kind of monarch. At home he
was a despot but an upstart despot from a family of commoners. He
ruled in the name of the people, displaced the old aristocracy with a
new elite of his choosing, and kept many of the social changes of the republican regime he followed. In the countries he defeated and controlled, he imposed changes of the same kind on the rulers and clergy,
forcing them to redraw borders, write constitutions, empower new
classes, and forfeit old privileges. He force-fed Europe the principles of
nationalism, democracy, and revolution—that is, the theoretical sovereignty of the people composing a nation and the possibility of radically
breaking with the past. After him, the old bases of authority could never
be safely and totally restored. And this was taking place just when the
age of steam, iron, and electricity was beginning—when inventions
were introducing western Europeans to mass production, speedy transportation, and lightninglike communication, forces that completely
separated their life experiences from those of their ancestors. A modern
world was in birth, and the creation of the United States was part of the
process. Her breakaway from Great Britain belonged to a whole "age of
revolution" stretching forward to the late twentieth century.

The salient point is that the first decade of France's transformation, from 1789 to 1799 (when Napoleon took over), precisely coincided with the first ten years of American life under the Constitution. These were the ten years that were the keynote-setting precedent for the 1800 election. It took place precisely when, across the Atlantic, established certainties were falling apart and there was no sense of firm ground under society's feet. That was why feelings ran so high when the issues of democracy were on the table. Anything was possible, a condition that was potentially exhilarating or frightening. Was the unfolding story in France the sign of a new dawn in human affairs or a hint of approaching anarchy and chaos? Opinions on such a question could only be passionate.

Given Jefferson's intellectual radicalism, it is not suprising that he had warm feelings toward the French Revolution, at whose opening scenes he had a front-row seat as the United States minister in Paris. The process started when the king convened a body of notables called the Estates General to deal with a fiscal crisis. It gathered in May 1789 just weeks after Washington was inaugurated on the other side of the Atlantic, and for a brief moment it looked as if the American example was about to be followed in a French setting. In the first few months, almost without a fight, the feudal privileges of the clergy and nobility were abolished, a start was made on limiting the powers of the king, and a Declaration of the Rights of Man sounding similar to the opening lines of the Declaration of Independence was adopted. There were some ugly scenes of popular riot, but they could be understood as temporary results of a poverty deeper than anything well-fed Americans could imagine. So Jefferson thought. By the time he left for home in September 1789 (with more than three dozen boxes and trunks full of wine, delicacies, plants, artworks, instruments, and books), he was writing: "I have so much confidence in the good sense of man, and his qualifications for self-government . . . where reason is left free . . . [that] I will agree to be stoned as a false prophet if all does not end well in this country. . . . Here is but the first chapter in the history of European liberty."[11]

That seemed a safe prediction as two years rolled by in which France got a constitution and a legislative assembly. Americans in general applauded the march of their wartime ally toward freedom. France had a reservoir of goodwill on which to draw, filled with memories of Lafayette and other French officers and soldiers who had helped to defeat the British enemy, plus the general admiration of the educated classes for French thought and culture. But in 1791 and 1792 came new and destabilizing developments. The king tried unsuccessfully to flee the country, possibly to rally resistance to democratization from outside. He was forced back to Paris by his "loyal" subjects. After that, Austria and Prussia declared war on France, both to take advantage of her weakness and to stamp out the revolutionary virus before it infected the rest of Europe. Threatened and besieged, France hurtled leftward. During the autumn of 1792, after more street violence and murder, the king was actually imprisoned, a republic declared, and the war proclaimed a crusade for liberty everywhere.

When this news reached American shores after the usual delay of eight to twelve weeks, there was widespread rejoicing that the world had now seen a second people throw off the yoke of monarchy. In American cities "democratic societies" were formed, in which members wore tricolored cockades and other symbols of liberty and called one another "Citizen," parades flaunted the tricolored French flag alongside America's, and banquets celebrated the great event. The new French popular assembly, the National Convention, reciprocated with flattering gestures. It conferred honorary French citizenship on a number of foreigners, including Tom Paine, James Madison, Alexander Hamilton, and George Washington. Madison replied gratefully that as an American whose country had played a big part in "reclaiming the lost rights of mankind," he took "peculiar satisfaction" in "the public connection with France."[12]

But Hamilton and Washington neither wanted nor acknowledged the honor. By that point they, like other conservatives in the United States, had been repelled by the excesses of popular revolt. The events in Paris that culminated in the king's execution struck them as too rash, too swift, too ill-considered—too French. John Adams charged American Francophiles with being "blind, undistinguishing, and enthusiastic of everything that has been done by that light, airy, and transported people," and his friend Fisher Ames said more succinctly: "France is madder than Bedlam and will be ruined."[13] Events that followed the killing of King Louis deepened and seemed to justify the horror of Federalist commentators. Between the summers of 1793 and 1794, the ultraradicals known as "Jacobins" took total control of the National Convention, introduced conscription and price fixing, changed the Christian calendar itself, tried to launch a "religion of reason," and guillotined thousands of opponents in the so-called Reign of Terror. Though it lasted only a year, it confirmed in Federalist minds the identification of revolutionary France with murderous atheism and amorality.

But the more that Federalist spokesmen insisted on that identification, the more Republicans were convinced that whipping up anti-French sentiment was a covering device for Federalist plans to overturn American freedom. France had to succeed if monarchy and aristocracy were to be checked at home. "We have every motive in America," Madison wrote to a friend, "to pray for [France's] success, not only from a general attachment to the liberties of mankind but from a peculiar regard for her [i.e., America's] own." Should the Revolution fail, "it would threaten us with the most serious dangers to the present forms and principles of our government."[14] Every fresh mailbag of foreign dispatches drove the wedge deeper. "The war," Jefferson noted—meaning that on the continent of Europe—"has kindled and brought forward the two parties with an ardour which our own interests merely, could never excite."[15]

Such was the situation on the morning of April 19—by coincidence the eighteenth anniversary of the first shots of the Revolution—when Hamilton and Jefferson, in icy politeness, joined Washington, Knox, and Randolph in a meeting to respond to the hard question that the aging president had thrown before his quarrelsome advisers the day before. To what extent, if at all, should the United States honor the 1778 treaty that had made American independence possible? Its terms called on the United States, should France be at war, to guarantee her possessions in America (in effect the French West Indies) against any attack and to allow France, but not her enemies, to recruit, supply, and outfit privateers in American ports, to which those privateers (but not those of France's enemies) could bring their captured prizes. French warships would have the same exclusive right. France promised reciprocal privileges if America was fighting a third power. Full compliance with these provisions, however, would be a virtual declaration of war on Great Britain.

The privateering clauses were especially sensitive because they were the likeliest to be soon invoked. Privateering was a form of sea war by private contract—or in less polite terms, by licensed piracy—in the age of sail, not abolished in international law until 1856. A belligerent nation could issue "letters of marque" to a shipowner to raid the commerce of her enemy. A skipper with a light, fast vessel carrying a small number of cannon could easily overtake and compel the surrender of a clumsy merchantman. If he could eventually bring the "prize" before an admiralty court somewhere, both ship and cargo would be sold and part of the proceeds divided among himself and his crew. For the privateer the incentive was booty. For the licensing nation it was a cheap way to enlarge its regular naval forces and to harass and effectually blockade a foe. Plenty of American sailors stood ready on short notice to become maritime mercenaries and join the hunt for prize money under French authorization.

No one in the cabinet, Jefferson included, wanted Anglo-American hostilities. What he hoped for was to reaffirm friendship with France and hold off a strong, formal statement of neutrality while waiting to see if the British might offer some diplomatic concessions to keep the United States from joining the fight against them. Jefferson also argued that constitutionally it was up to Congress, not the president, to decide a question such as the one before them, which could lead to war, since Congress alone had war-making power. Hamilton, by contrast, thought it a dangerous idea to keep Great Britain guessing. She might preemptively take hostile action against America, a real calamity that needed to be staved off by an immediate announcement of neutrality. The official excuse for backing away from the 1778 alliance would be that it had been made with the king of France and was no longer binding. And, Hamilton added, there was no need to consult Congress—the president had full power to to handle the matter by simple executive order. So once again the fight was joined over the meaning of the Constitution, with one side represented by those who, in Madison's words, "would stretch it to death" and the other by those who "would squeeze it to death."[16] This round went to Hamilton. The president issued an official Proclamation of Neutrality on April 19, and Hamilton, who freely leaked the substance of cabinet meetings to British minister George Hammond, assured him that Washington intended to observe it strictly.

That led to a second matter, on which Hamilton did not do as well. Dispatches from the government of the recently created French Republic reported that a new chief envoy, Citizen Edmond Charles Genet, was on his way to Philadelphia. He had, in fact, already landed in Charleston. The question was whether or not to receive him, which implied official recognition of the end of the monarchy. Hamilton believed and no doubt hoped that the king's heirs might be restored to the throne by war. His idea was to reject Genet's credentials while waiting to see who would finally rule legitimately in Paris. Jefferson countered by proposing what would eventually become official recognition policy. The United States should do business with whatever government the people of a nation established or changed by their own will. In this case he was the one who prevailed with Washington. The final outcome of the deliberations was a split verdict—the republic would be recognized but the treaty not implemented. Then everyone waited for the arrival of Genet.

Jefferson had high hopes for the Genet mission, almost a personal stake in its success. If he and the ambassador could work out some kind of friendly cooperation between their respective nations, carriers of the torch of liberty as he believed them to be, the United States could help advance the republican cause everywhere without being dragged into war. Rarely have hopes been so cruelly disappointed so quickly. Genet turned out to be like an assistant on a household job who, in helpful zeal, breaks tools, spills paint on the furniture, and sets fire to the curtains.

✳

EDMOND GENET was very bright, very young, and very spoiled. His father was a royal official, his sister became one of the queen's ladies-in-waiting, and he grew up amid the splendors of Versailles, tutored privately in ancient and modern languages, fencing, horsemanship, and all the gentlemanly arts. He was only twenty-four in 1787 when he got a foreign service posting to the court of Catherine, empress of Russia. But as a diplomat he was not discreet. During the early stages of the Revolution he apparently spoke too warmly for Czarist taste in favor of limited monarchy and was sent home in July 1792. The same liberal views, however, recommended him to the French republicans who soon were in charge. They gave him the assignment to America. Gouverneur Morris, the American minister in Paris, shrewdly described Genet in letters to President Washington. He had an "ardent temper" and an opinion of himself "a little too high," which probably explained his troubles in Russia. After having him to dinner, Morris further concluded: "He has, I think, more of genius than ability and . . . at the first blush the manner and look of an upstart."[17]

Genet's ardent temper led him to a generous interpretation of his American mission. His plans called for outfitting up to three hundred privateers—he was carrying that many blank letters of marque with him—plus organizing, arming, and financing expeditions of American volunteers from the West against Louisiana and Canada. His early reception at Charleston gave him the impression that the American people were burning for war on France's side. The banquets and salutes of Charleston's Republicans were so exhilarating that after lingering there to put two privateers in commission, he began a slow northward tour through more American cities and more receptions. "The people received me in their arms," he wrote back home, "and under their modest roofs . . . I was clasped in the arms of a multitude."[18] He did not get to Philadelphia to present his credentials until mid-May, but there he met with a cold shower of reality. His reception by the president was decidedly cooler than he had anticipated, consisting (he later told Paris) of a formal restatement of American neutrality with no expression of sympathy for the Revolution. Moreover, although the secretary of state was personally hospitable, it soon became clear that he neither could nor would support Genet's proposals for advance payments on the U.S. debt to France, or an immediate mutual free-trade pact between their two countries, or any other steps likely to spark a clash of arms with the British. Genet simply could not fathom that Jefferson, however anti-British and pro-republican, would put the best interests of the United

States first. Later on he would angrily denounce "this man of half-hearted convictions" whose aim was to "maintain himself in a position which would keep him in office, whatever the turn of events."[19]

What turned the young envoy's head was the increasing heat of republican rhetoric. The Democratic Society of Pennsylvania was on record in defense of "the spirit of freedom and equality" that was in danger of being "eclipsed by the pride of wealth and the arrogance of power." Its counterpart in Boston resolved that "the present struggles of the French people are directed to the subversion of Aristocracy and Despotism, and to the lasting improvement and happiness of the human race." And that in Charleston proclaimed that those who supported "the combined despots of Europe, particularly, Great Britain," were "treacherous and hostile to the interests of the United States."[20] Even George Washington himself at last came under fire from Freneau's *National Gazette* in June for signing the Proclamation of Neutrality. He had been misled, the paper suggested, by an "opiate of sycophancy" into intruding on powers that were properly those of Congress. Perhaps he was simply too isolated from genuine popular sentiment. Had he forgotten that his tenure was only at the pleasure of the electorate? Was he "so buoyed up by official importance [as] to think it beneath his dignity to mix occasionally with the people?"[21]

Listening only to voices like that and ignoring his own unfamiliarity with the tub-thumping vigor of American political style, Genet came to believe that gigantic majorities were on his side and that he could successfully fight the government to which he was accredited. He continued his activities in the very shadow of the capital city. In May a French warship brought a captured English merchantman called the *Little Sarah* into the port of Philadelphia. Genet had her outfitted with fourteen cannon, renamed the *Petite Democrate*, and prepared to take to sea as a privateer in flat violation of the Proclamation of Neutrality. The news got to Jefferson on July 7, while Washington was out of town. To let the ship sail could start the dreaded war with England. Pennsylvania militiamen could prevent that by boarding and seizing the ship, which was what the other members of the cabinet wished. But that could bring on a serious crisis with France. Jefferson went to Genet and bought some time by getting him to delay the departure of the *Petite Democrate* until Washington could return. When the president did so, he was furious but decided against grabbing the privateer by force. At the same time he wanted Genet told in no uncertain terms that it must not sail. "Is the Minister of the French Republic to set the acts of this government at defiance *with impunity?*" raged Washington to Jefferson.

In Genet's mind the answer was yes. Ignoring the order, he sent the *Petite Democrate* on her destructive way.[22] Luckily the British chose at that particular moment not to make it a fighting issue. Genet's success thereupon sent him into headlong abandonment of common sense. He got an appointment with Washington and apparently—no other witness was present—lectured him on his treaty obligations and even announced that he would go over the First Citizen's head and appeal directly to the public to reject neutrality. The story of that threat soon exploded in public, the source being Pennsylvania's governor and secretary of Pennsylvania State. They claimed to have gotten it from chief justice Jay and New York senator Rufus King. King and Jay had received it, on the quiet, from a resourceful Hamilton, who correctly judged that a storm of outrage would break over Genet. Losing ground, Genet denied it but then had the brass to ask attorney general Randolph to bring libel prosecutions against Jay and King. When refused, the French firebrand grumbled that "America is no longer free."

By early July, Jefferson decided that "never in my opinion was so calamitous an appointment made, as that of the present Minister of France here. Hot headed, all imagination, no judgment, passionate, disrespectful and even indecent towards [the president], urging the most unreasonable and groundless propositions in the most dictatorial style."[23] The next month a formal request for Genet's recall, endorsed by the whole cabinet, was started on its slow ocean trip to Paris. When he heard about it, Genet blustered on, demanding a chance to put his case to the incoming Congress. But he was finished. Even the French government was urging him to keep cool, warning: "Do not delude yourself any longer concerning the brilliance of a false popularity."[24] In January 1794 a replacement minister arrived carrying not only the revocation of Genet's own powers but an unpleasant surprise—instructions to return home at once to stand trial. The triumphant Jacobins had put Genet on their enemies' list and he would face certain execution. If he did not go of his own will, the United States was asked to extradite him.

The story has a positively romantic ending. Genet appealed for asylum to the president he had been busily attacking, and Washington granted it. Whatever his failings, the ex-envoy must have kept a certain residue of charm as well as some private money. With it, he bought a small farm on Long Island and in November 1794 married twenty-year-old Cornelia Tappen Clinton, daughter of New York's wily veteran governor, whom he had been wooing for the past year. In time he became an American citizen and sired American children; he is buried at the site of his final home just outside Albany. He died there in 1834, at seventy-one, after long and busy years of amateur agricultural and scientific experiments and futile efforts to collect nine thousand francs still due him from France.

But his brief career through the china shop had left a mark on United States politics. He had not only destroyed Jefferson's hopes for Franco-American amity but also pushed Washington further into the arms of Hamilton and frank partisanship. The president, after all his efforts to avert faction, had been severely stung by the verbal brickbats that opponents of neutrality flung at him, especially the accusation of acting like a king. At the meeting that authorized Genet's recall, he lost his temper and fumed that he would rather be in his grave than subjected to more slander from the likes of "that rascal Freneau."[25] His anger at the "self-created" democratic societies would boil over again during the Whiskey Rebellion. From mid-1793 onward on he leaned more heavily than ever on the advice of Hamilton and conducted what was clearly a Federalist rather than a national administration.

Jefferson's exit from the cabinet confirmed that reality. It did not merely end the open skirmishing between himself and Hamilton, but it likewise signaled more or less the final waning of Washington's ideal of a government of all the country's best combined talents. In 1794 there would be new turmoil, as the opening year found a nation buffeted between two great warring powers, a people more divided than ever, and a still-evolving constitutional system under severe strain. Soon a controversial treaty with London would further compound those problems.

CHAPTER 8

John Jay's Divisive Treaty,
1794–1795

ON FEBRUARY 22, 1794, the boom and clang of salutes and bells and the stamp of parading feet marked Washington's birthday. The president was sixty-two, and nearing the end of his fifth year in office. The morning was spent in business as usual and included the formal reception of Joseph Fauchet, Genet's successor as minister from France. In the afternoon the members of Congress called and were served cake and punch. The evening featured a ball in the First Citizen's honor. Geniality reigned.

Sixty days later the country was in a full-dress war crisis with Great Britain and convulsed with internal debate on how to handle it.

It was the second hard year in succession for Washington's second administration. His first had been warmed by the sunshine of expectation. This successor term, however, was shadowed by the realization of some of his worst fears. The country was splitting into violently partisan camps—and what was worse, each of the parties had allied itself with a foreign power. Two centuries later Americans would take it for granted that "politics stopped at the water's edge" and that bipartisanship was the bedrock of foreign relations. Not so in the 1790s. The Genet affair had already exposed the raw divide separating friends of

France from those of England. The 1794 clash with Britain drove the knife deeper into the prospects for national unity. It was resolved by a treaty which was not entirely a bad treaty but caused such bitterness that it tainted the election of 1796—the first without the harmonizing presence of Washington—and cursed unlucky winner John Adams with four years of near-disintegration of the still young and experimental Constitution.

Jay's Treaty, named for its negotiator, was the dominating foreign-and-domestic policy event of 1794. The Whiskey Rebellion opened new partisan wounds and demonstrated federal muscle, but it was essentially a local story. On close scrutiny, there was less to it than met the eye. But Jay's Treaty nearly tore the whole country apart. To make sense of the tempest it awakened requires a small excursion into the complicated feelings in the hearts of voting Americans toward England.

The French connection so warmly evoked but then so rudely shaken by Citizen Genet's tour of duty was easier to explain. To America's educated elite, France was the home of culture and the Enlightenment. Below their intellectual plateau was another level of pro-French thought after 1792, shared by "plain" Americans resentful of the influence of local aristocracies. They identified with the people of France who had toppled their own snobs and wealthy overlords. And then there were thousands of "Gallomen," as the enemies of the Francophiles called them, who were automatically anti-British and therefore partisans of France by default.

But England, unlike France, was the mother country, and in Americans she evoked all the complicated feelings of dependence, resentment, fear, love, admiration, and anger that parenthood carried. On the one hand Americans high and low had good reason for attachment to the island nation to which, according to the 1790 census, the majority of them traced their roots. Up until the very moment of declaring independence the colonists had appealed to their rights as Englishmen. Even in rebellion most colonists thought they were imitating Great Britain's Glorious Revolution of 1688–89, when Parliament threw out one king, picked another, and established itself as the true ruler of the realm. After America's own revolution was won, conservatives like the

Federalists felt free once more to openly admire the "unwritten" British constitution that seemed to keep the king, the aristocrats, and the middle class pulling so smoothly in harness. Even haters of Britannia could not escape the fact that they shared a language and a set of religious, legal, and business customs cast in English molds. It was one of the things that made it possible to create the United States.

But there was a reverse side to the coin. England was still the ex-oppressor, the parent whose yoke was cast off and from whom the respect due an adult was now demanded. And it was not forthcoming! High-handed British policies that treated the United States with a hard-boiled disdain for her obvious lack of power were infuriating. They seemed to send a message that American freedom was not yet real. To that resentment "agrarian" thinkers like Jefferson added another grievance. Too much taste for British imports (though he himself shared it) could breed imitation of British social divisions. Then what would happen to the Republican ideal of a nation of simple-living independent farmers?

Britain's war against revolutionary France alternately stoked and cooled American Anglophobia in rhythm with the ups and downs of war. On one hand, the empire in mortal combat used its sea power more aggressively than ever against neutral traffic with her enemy. But by the same token there were moments when things went badly for British armies and fleets—and then London was inclined to offer sweeter deals. France, too, played friend or bully according to how the tides of battle turned, so a weak America lurched from crisis to crisis with both fighting giants, each fresh standoff having a strong impact on party politics. For all the sound and fury, however—and it was something that foreign diplomats had to learn—both parties put American interests first at the bargaining table. Neither "Anglomen" nor "Gallomen" seriously looked for status as a satellite of London or Paris—but neither trusted the other not to do so.

There were curious complications. One was that the group that seemed to suffer most harm from Britain's noose on neutral shipping—that is, the mainly Federalist merchant class of the Northeast—was also the most reluctant to provoke war. The reason was not their pro-British sentiment but the news from their countinghouses. American commerce and shipbuilding were doing well, thanks to the wartime boom in foreign demand. Troublesome losses were incurred when English high-seas cruisers seized or delayed shipments intended eventually to reach French hands. But full-dress hostilities would bring a destructive total blockade, and a generous half loaf was much better than none. So Federalist policy toward the British asked much and settled for little. Republicans were more consistently warlike in their Anglophobia, but the wiser among them knew that peace alone kept prosperity shining on their farmer supporters who were providing the foodstuffs for foreign tables.

Another complication too easy for modern readers to forget was the time lag in communications in the age of sail that made trans-Atlantic diplomacy like a game of blind man's buff. Each party reacted many weeks later to a "new" situation—which might already have changed. The wonder is that long-term policy could be made at all. It was still another thread woven into the controversies that rocked Congress and the country in the stormy two years—from early 1794 to the election springtime of 1796—that it took to negotiate, ratify, and guarantee funding for the implementation of Jay's Treaty.

✳

THE WINDING COURSE began with the unfinished business that Jefferson left on the desk for successor John Randolph when he left the State Department at 1793's end. He and British minister George Hammond had been in a long wrestling match over the unresolved issues between their two countries, each of which blamed the other for not fully carrying out the terms of the 1783 treaty ending the Revolutionary War. For Hammond it had been especially discouraging. He was only twenty-eight and eager to succeed when he arrived in October 1791 as the first minister sent by George III to the land of his revolted subjects. Oxford-educated and rosy-faced, Hammond won the heart of an American girl (just as Citizen Genet was to do—there was something attractive about educated foreigners!) and married her early in his mission.

But his charm made no impression on the American secretary of state. Jefferson required that all communication between them be in writing and mandated a long, recriminatory exchange of notes debating which side was not acting in good faith. This lasted until May 1792, and when poor Hammond sent the whole correspondence back to London with a request for instructions, he was left to dangle for weary months without an answer. Neither the government behind him nor the government to which he was accredited seemed to care much for him, and he was a happy young husband when at last relieved in 1795. On the homeward-bound ship Mrs. Hammond wrote to her father that George's "cold, formal manner . . . has been thrown off and everybody, observes how agreeable he is in company."[1]

The issues between the two nations were differently weighted. There were disagreements, partly based on simple geographical ignorance, about the actual boundary between the United States and Canada. Then there were dollars-and-cents matters. The treaty bound each side not to interfere with the efforts of the other's creditors to collect prewar debts. Almost all of them were owed by the Americans to British suppliers, but American state courts had widely ignored the bargain and instead supported American debtors who contested payment. Another article engaged the United States government to use its best efforts to get fair recompense for Loyalists (Americans would have said Tories) whose properties had been confiscated during the war. That too, the British insisted, had been ignored. A monetary demand by the Americans was based on a violation of Article 7. It stipulated that British forces should evacuate all American soil "without causing any Destruction or carrying away any Negroes or other Property of the American Inhabitants."[2] Some British-occupation commanders, however, had offered freedom to slaves who came into their lines to fight or work for them. They took these volunteers along when they sailed away, on the humane ground that otherwise they would be reenslaved. The owners wanted them back or at the very least to be paid for them—a point that Jefferson, the apostle of freedom, was perfectly agreeable to pushing hard with Hammond.

Beyond these bread-and-butter questions were two on which neither government could give ground without serious political damage at home. The British had not left all soil as promised but were holding on to some half-dozen garrisons on the American side of the Great Lakes. Their purpose was to protect and facilitate the profitable operations of Canadian fur traders working those areas. Violent objection to this cheating came not so much from American fur dealers as from American pioneer farmers. No other British action stung them into such fury. They knew that the traders were providing firearms as well as the usual axes, kettles, blankets, and knives to the Indians, and it was an article of faith among them that British officials incited attacks on American settlements.

The Indians, the unacknowledged third party in the conflict, needed no "stirring up" and were not the unprovoked aggressors shown in the stereotypical (though truthful) woodcuts of burning cabins and tomahawked women. They were trying to hold on to lands that had been promised to them by treaty with Great Britain before the Revolution but then were given—without consulting them—to the United States, with whom they then had to renegotiate on very hard terms. The five nations of the Iroquois Confederation had been pushed out of their holdings in upper New York, and the United States was demanding big new cessions of land from Indian peoples to the west, in the area north of the Ohio River. When these were refused, a five-year campaign of subjugation began with the despatch of a U.S. expedition of some fifteen hundred men, mostly local militia, in 1790. They burned crops and villages—for some of Ohio's Indian peoples were not the nomadic hunters of myth but settled cultivators—and these acts of an ongoing war were the counterparts of Indian "raids" on white properties. In 1791 Washington sent out a larger force of regulars and militia, six thousand strong, and the Indians thrashed it near present-day Fort Wayne, Indiana, leaving nine hundred Americans dead.

So the "savages," who knew something of diplomacy as well as war, looked to the British in Canada for help. They were aware that Englishmen did not love them any more than Americans did, but British interest in collecting pelts was not inconsistent with leaving large areas of land in Indian control. The relatively few inhabitants of Canada did not need more acres to till. American policy, on the other hand, had behind it the explosive pressure of a multiplying agricultural population whose land hunger, it appeared, could be fed by nothing less than the total expulsion of the "redskins." For their part, the royal governors in Quebec were glad to have Indian friends to help them hold off a tide of expansion-minded Yankees who had eyes on Canada. They did encourage Indian resistance to the Americans. All was fair in imminent war.

So the question of the fur posts was really one of getting the British to abandon their Indian clients engaged in a war against the United States. Americans were absolutely determined to win, because victory was the key to their future—to occupying the huge, resource-rich Northwest Territory that would in time become Ohio, Indiana, Illinois, Michigan, and Wisconsin. There was some domestic opposition to westward expansion from a minority of Federalists. But for a clear majority in America evacuation of the posts was a nonnegotiable demand.

On their side the British were equally locked in place on a commercial issue created when the Americans left the empire. That was their long-standing "mercantilist" policy of importing as little as possible, exporting as much as possible, and doing both in British ships only. With independence won, American ships—now "foreign"—could only bring homegrown products into British ports. That meant little because most of those products were foodstuffs, which were barred from sale in Britain to protect local growers. Americans were also forbidden to carry to British markets any goods they bought elsewhere, including the lucrative plantation crops of the nearby British West Indies. That door was firmly shut, and American shippers were desperate to get it reopened. But London's policymakers rigidly believed that to do so would overturn 140 years' worth of "navigation acts" under which the kingdom had gotten rich. Changing them was not to be thought of.

All the same, there were businessmen and politicians in Parliament and the cabinet who recognized that American customers couldn't pay for British purchases unless they earned credits by selling to Britons, a good argument for some easing of the rules. So Hammond was authorized to explore a possible commercial treaty with the United States, but he never got that far. Resolutely anti-British, Jefferson preferred trade war in the form of retaliation. His choice was to kick rather than to talk the door open.

Hammond got some unofficial comfort from private conversations with Hamilton, whom he found to have a "just and liberal way of thinking." Hamilton regretted the "intemperate violence of his colleague"[3] in Jefferson's notes denouncing British perfidy. He was sure it did not completely represent the opinion of either the president or his other advisers. He advised his young friend that new federal courts would eventually do justice to British creditors, and if Britain got out of the Northwest posts, fair arrangements could be made to protect Canadian interests. He especially hoped that the question of trade restrictions could be compromised, which would be easier if Hammond's government showed a little flexibility on trade with the West Indies, his own boyhood home. In this back-door effort to soften Jefferson's hard line, Hamilton was not simply getting at his detested enemy. Anticipating free trade arguments of the next two centuries, he wanted to lay the groundwork for increased Anglo-American commerce that would help everyone in both countries to make money.

The war of 1793 brutally intruded a whole new question—the neutral rights of the weak United States against the claims of Britain, ruler of the waves. The first impact of war seemed helpful to American shippers. The French government invited them to sail freely into its ports, including those in the previously closed French West Indies. That brought an immediate protest from London, because it broke a rule of international law, such as it was, which said that a belligerent could not, in wartime, open a trade closed during peace. The idea was to prevent a weak naval power from "cheating" a blockade by having neutrals carry its traffic. This "rule of 1756" carried the stamp of the expiring eighteenth century, when conflict between sovereigns was supposedly regulated as formally as a chess match. Other such rules of engagement, especially cherished by neutrals, were designed to protect private property on wartime oceans. One provided that neutral ships might freely carry cargoes of a belligerent power except for "contraband," narrowly defined as military hardware. The shorthand phrase was "free ships make free goods." Another would protect neutral noncontraband property even if bound for a belligerent port on a belligerent's merchant-man. If captured, it had to be allowed through, or at least paid for.

Using definitions like those, Americans expected neutrality to pay them handsomely as suppliers to the warriors.

But strong nations bent or broke these "laws" at will. And for Great Britain, the war on the Jacobins had gotten beyond a chess game. As Minister Hammond expressed it to Hamilton, "All the dearest interests of society were involved . . . [in] a contest between government and disorder, virtue and vice, and religion and impiety."[4] This was the language of total war, and in fact and fairness the French had already raised the curtain to it in the *levee en masse,* an emergency conscription decree crying that the entire nation-in-arms must resist foreign invaders and that everyone from children to graybeards would have a part to play. In that case, every citizen of the French Republic could be considered an enemy "soldier," and so to starve a populace was a lawful act of combat. The British, anticipating modern times, were determined to expand "contraband" to include food and other civilian necessities. American forces in Ohio were following exactly the same principle in setting fire to Indian crops. But that did not keep Americans from believing that the battle for sweeping neutral rights was a struggle for their own commercial lives. The difference of opinion put the two nations on a direct collision course, and the British pressed on at full sail with a June 1793 "Order in Council"—that is, a king's cabinet decision—that made it "lawful to stop and detain all vessels loaded wholly or in part with corn, flour or meal, bound to any port in France, or . . . occupied by the armies of France."[5]

The news reached American ears not long before the Third Congress convened in December, the members trickling nervously by twos and threes into a Philadelphia still mourning the dead of the summer's yellow fever plague. Though party organizations had not yet crystallized or taken official names, more and more senators and representatives were by then consistently recognizable as Republicans or Federalists. (These were the names that came into common use, though in a few places enthusiasts for the French Revolution called themselves "Democratic-Republican" when running for office. Some historians attached that label to the whole Jefferson establishment, which allows the modern Democratic and Republican Parties each to claim him as an ancestor.)

The first order of business was to receive the president's annual message. Jefferson, preparing to leave the government, had persuaded him to include a passage strongly criticizing Great Britain for the impasse over the 1783 treaty obligations. There were citations from Jefferson's correspondence with Hammond, emphasizing his own arguments, suppressing Hammond's, and generally putting the British case in the worst possible light. To expose ongoing foreign-policy exchanges to the public eye in that way was a break with custom bitterly resented by Hammond. And not Hammond alone. John Adams saw it as dirty politics and poor statesmanship. Writing to Abigail, he defended secret diplomacy. "How a government can go on publishing all their negotiations with foreign nations, I know not. To me it appears as dangerous and pernicious as it is novel."[6] But Washington was himself irritated with British policy, and this time he overrode the judgment of the rest of the cabinet to insert Jefferson's charges in his text.

Jefferson followed up this victory with another parting shot. It was an open report to Congress on the state of commercial relations with France and Britain. It admitted but soft-pedaled any problems with the French but was strenuous in slamming British restrictions, which he implied were deliberately planned not so much to help England as to hurt America. In Hamilton's angry words, Jefferson "threw this FIRE-BRAND of discord into the midst of the representatives . . . and instantly *decamped* to Monticello."[7]

After Jefferson left, Madison reopened the fight in the House for retaliatory taxes and duties to force the British to soften their "aggravated violations of our rights."[8] But American businessmen were not asking for his strong medicine. American flour, fish, and lumber were in fact reaching the British West Indies, sometimes in foreign bottoms and often in American, through a loophole that let royal governors of individual islands make "emergency" exceptions to the navigation laws. A rising tide of imports was getting financed somehow. Shipyards were busy. "Trade flourishes on our wharves, though it droops in speeches,"⁹ said Federalist representative Fisher Ames in debating Madison. He and William Loughton Smith, voicing the views of Boston and Charleston, blamed Jefferson's stiff-necked attitude for the failure to reach agreement with the British. Swayed by the fear of war, House members stalled Madison's proposals on the floor.

But then came fiery news from the Caribbean and Canada that made debates on economic pressure look pale and obsolete. In March 1794 Philadelphia learned that the previous November a new Order in Council had authorized the seizure of anything bound to or from the French West Indies, and that British captains were zealous in executing the blockade. Two hundred fifty American ships, some of them merely suspected of heading for French ports, had been stopped and forced at cannonpoint to trail their captors into British harbors. Of these, 150 had been condemned and confiscated. American owners were robbed of their investments. American officers and crews, left with nothing but the clothes on their backs, were stranded and hungry. At almost the same time, New York's Governor Clinton relayed leaked information from the North. Governor Lord Dorchester had made a speech to a deputation of Indians in Quebec saying that he expected war with the United States within a year. If they helped him push Canada's borders southward, Americans would be thrown out and the king would look kindly on Indian claims.

As it happened, the British had already limited the blockade and were considering some reparations in January. But boiling-mad Americans did not know that. Nor did they know or care that Dorchester's speech was possibly unauthorized, and that Dorchester himself was worried about the intentions of a new and strengthened American force under General Anthony Wayne moving into the Northwest Territory. War fever raged throughout March and April. In secret session the House debated a total embargo on supplies to the British West Indies. That would be a piece of belligerency as valuable to the French as a Caribbean naval victory. Eventually it failed by just two votes. House members also considered "sequestration," meaning the suspension of all debts owed by American citizens to British subjects until damages were paid for the seized property. Hamilton was horrified. If it passed, foreign bankers would think long and hard before lending another cent. Another bill gave the king a six-month ultimatum to surrender the fur posts and pay maritime damages or face a total suspension of commerce with the United States that would cost his own exporters millions. That one passed the House and was killed in the Senate only when Vice President Adams cast a tiebreaking "nay."

The Republican press was raging, pouring out its vials of wrath in hyperbole strange to modern ears. "Our blood is in a flame. . . . The avenging arm of America once uplifted, should chastise and pursue a corrupt and base tyrant till his worthless life is terminated upon a scaffold."[10] Street crowds shouted insults at Hammond and his embassy clerks as they walked to their residence. Hammond found to his amazement that even Hamilton, in private conversation, spoke of American grievances "with some degree of heat." Elevating his gentlemanly chin, Hammond answered that he was astonished to hear from his friend such ideas, only "entertained by the demagogues of the house of representatives, and by the uninformed mass of the American community," but left in peace.[11] He didn't realize that the Federalists, too, had been pushed too far. Their spokesmen in Congress were asking an immediate increase of fifteen thousand in the size of the army, authorization to the states to raise eighty thousand militia, a start on a navy, and new supportive taxes. That caught the Republicans, who seemed hottest for war, in a bind, because all such politically irresistible measures violated their ideal of keeping government small, weak, and inexpensive.

However, the Federalists were also in a squeeze. A second Anglo-American war in eleven years, besides the other disasters it threatened, would help revolutionary France. That was the very last thing they wanted. In this crunch, Federalist leaders approached Washington with a modern proposal—a last-chance, edge-of-the-cliff negotiation through a special envoy, to emphasize how seriously the United States took the situation. They must have realized that it would bypass the regular American minister in London, former South Carolina governor Thomas Pinckney, but as a loyal Federalist he would understand and might receive later rewards. Washington thought the idea over for a while and eventually agreed, though he disliked the weak appearance of first shaking a fist at the British and then asking to talk things over. Who would the envoy be? Washington liked the idea of Jefferson, but he—or any other Republican—would hardly be acceptable to the British. Hamilton would be a good choice, but was too controversial to be sure of Senate confirmation. So the mantle fell on Chief Justice Jay. He was experienced—one of the draftsmen of the 1783 treaty, in fact—available from a Supreme Court with little to do, eager for some action after having been swindled out of the governorship of New York by Aaron Burr, and able to win approval in the Senate, where the Federalists had a majority. He got it, 20–8, on April 19.

It took political bravery or innocence for Jay to accept the mission. Much of the country disliked the whole idea, and if the chief justice came back with anything less than a triumph, he would suffer multiple slings and arrows. But a triumph was unlikely. Whatever the prowar tub thumpers might say, the United States was the weaker party, and so at a diplomatic disadvantage. Though his mission statement formally came from secretary of state Randolph, it was mainly drafted by Hamilton. In essence he was to do his best to get indemnification for seized cargoes, limitations on the definition of "contraband," some concessions on the West India trade, and some sort of compromise on the unsettled issues of debts, recompenses, fur-trading rights, and boundaries. He boarded ship on May 12. Luckily, it was not until May 20 that another news item from Canada arrived in the capital. Still worrying about a U.S. invasion, Lord Dorchester had sent a force to occupy another fort well inside American territory, near today's Toledo. Had word gotten to Congress ten days earlier, Jay's mission might have been scuttled.

✳

JAY WAS politely received on his arrival at the royal court, where his blue-ribbon lawyerlike style and Federalist politics made him highly acceptable. He spent four months in the peacemaker's familiar rituals and sleepless drudgery of composing and exchanging drafts and memorandums. His case was helped by the progress of war in North America and Europe. On August 20, 1794, General Wayne's army of pacification attacked and defeated a major Indian force on an Ohio field strewn with trees downed by a recent storm. News of the Battle of Fallen Timbers may have strongly suggested to foreign minister Lord Grenville that the Americans could not be held indefinitely at bay in the West. And during the autumn, French troops scored victories in Belgium and Holland, more bad news that inclined Grenville to put a slightly higher value on keeping America neutral. He worried about that, especially when he learned that the new United States minister to France, James Monroe, had received a "fraternal kiss" in mid-August from the president of the French Convention and returned the favor with lyrical remarks about sister republics. Unable to fathom why America's president should send a Federalist envoy to London and a Francophile Republican minister to Paris, Grenville saw signs of a French tilt in United States policy that he may have tried to counteract by yielding slightly in negotiations with Jay.

But any "give" was very slight. The final draft, signed on November 19, was heavily loaded in England's favor. The major concession to the Americans was on the fur posts. The British would pull out of them within a year and a half. But Canadian fur traders could still freely cross the border. However, neither party was supposed to supply Indians warring against the other. In an unusual breakthrough, Jay and Grenville agreed to "mixed commissions" of British and American representatives, to arbitrate disagreements about the exact location of the Canadian-American border, about how much Great Britain owed in damages for her recent "spoliations" at sea, and how much the United States would pay to compensate British creditors. What Jay gave up for these points, however, was considerable. British goods would be received in the United States on a most-favored-nation basis, meaning no charges could be imposed on them higher than those in the best deal offered to any other country. That killed off the cherished Republican idea of discriminatory retaliation. The British rules of sea war would not be challenged—cargoes belonging to belligerents could be taken from neutral ships, "contraband" was broadly defined, and a trade closed in peacetime could not be opened in war. These concessions worked heavily against France, and as an additional stick poked in her eye, Jay agreed that warships, privateers, and prizes of Britain's enemies would be excluded from U.S. ports.

There was an almost insulting token prize for United States exporters. They could send American-produced items to the British West Indies in ships of no more than seventy tons "burthen," a term for a vessel's cargo-carrying capacity. For goods like foodstuffs, heavy in proportion to their size and value, this was trifling. And there was a price for this, too. The same Article 12 said that Americans could not carry any molasses, sugar, coffee, cocoa, or cotton anywhere in the world except home—shutting them out of the richest carrying trade they knew. Jay lamely defended that article as "breaking the ice" of the navigation acts, but it was a narrow crack in a huge floe.

The treaty said nothing about compensation to Americans for lost slaves (which could hardly have troubled Jay, who was an early abolitionist) and made no promises to restrict "impressment," the practice by which shorthanded British naval commanders stopped American ships and plucked out English-speaking sailors who could not prove U.S. citizenship. In all, it seemed a sorry bargain. Yet it got much of what Hamilton's instructions had asked for, and it made strategic and economic sense. The British opened the door to American expansion on the continent, and the Americans recognized Britain's manufacturing, commercial, and maritime supremacy as at least temporary facts of life. The long run would favor a growing United States. What point was there in a 1795 challenge leading to war? "If there be a foreign power which sees with envy or ill-will our growing prosperity," Hamilton wrote in a newspaper essay defending the treaty, "that power must discern that our infancy is the time for clipping our wings. We ought to be wise enough to see that this is not a time for trying our strength."[12]

But thousands of Americans did not like reminders that they lived in an infant nation. When Jay brought the treaty home in March 1795 he was carrying dynamite. It would be safe for a few months, because the terms would remain secret until the treaty went before a special session of Congress called for June. In the interim, Jay was able to get himself elected governor of New York. That allowed him to quit the chief justice's office before angry opponents could try to get even by impeaching him.

After months of rumor, the closed Senate debates were stormy.

Even Federalists choked on Article 12, the one that would have, among other things, banned the sale of cotton abroad just as Whitney's gin had switched on a sixty-five year boom in the crop. The treaty finally squeaked through on June 24 with the exact minimum two thirds needed, 20–10, on a straight party-line vote. But Article 12 was rejected. The president was authorized to ratify the whole treaty only if it were suspended or changed.

This made a new, precedent-setting dilemma for Washington. Here was another one of those situations not precisely covered by the Constitution, which said nothing about the Senate consenting to some but not all of a treaty. It was like sending a partially eaten dish back to the kitchen. Should he renegotiate a substitute version of Article 12? And if so, should he submit that to the Senate before putting it to the British? And if he did that, would it mean that all future treaties would need to be wrangled out clause by clause with the senators?

Washington mulled this over with the cabinet, missing the presence of Hamilton, who had quit in January to go back to private law practice and a decent income in New York, though he still freely gave advice by post. Oliver Wolcott took over at the Treasury, and there were two other new faces. Timothy Pickering of Massachusetts had replaced Knox as secretary of war, and a Pennsylvania judge, William Bradford, had become attorney general. Randolph, at State, was the last holdover from the first cabinet, the last link to the sunny, early days of promised unity. Now he kept stalling indecisively in giving Washington his opinion on ratification. The president was annoyed, and more so when two new developments shook his celebrated composure. The Royal Navy, under a new so-called "provision order," had recently seized several American grain ships bound for France. It turned out to be a temporary policy and the cargoes were eventually paid for, but it looked like fresh evidence of British contempt. Then, although Jay's Treaty was not yet supposed to be published, the inevitable happened. A senator leaked a copy to a Republican editor. Within two weeks, as fast as the mails could function, it had appeared in print throughout the United States and set off a firestorm.

Republican sympathizers raged that Jay had betrayed France, truckled to King George, and brought his own country into contempt. "To what state of degradation are we reduced," ran a typical comment, "that we *court* a nation more perfidious than Savages."[13] Governor Jay himself later said that he could travel from one end of the country to the other by the light of his burning effigies. Private citizen Thomas Jefferson privately denounced the treaty as an "infamous act, which is nothing more than a treaty of alliance between England and Anglomen of this country against the legislature and people of the United States."[14]

Neither British nor Republican behavior was making Washington's decision any easier. He left the capital on July 15 to think matters over in the quiet of Mount Vernon. But within days the mailbag brought more bad news of a hot and angry summer. Protests were pouring in from every major city. In New York on July 18 Republicans called an open meeting of citizens to discuss the treaty. The crowd, gathered in Wall Street, yelled for a chairman and accepted William S. Smith, Vice President Adams's son-in-law. But Smith could not keep control. Alexander Hamilton tried to speak and was shouted down. Then a shower of stones drove him, bleeding from a cut in the head, off the platform. Opponents of the treaty, some waving French flags, marched off to burn copies in front of Governor Jay's residence on the Battery. Five days later there was a demonstration in Philadelphia itself, attended by respectable citizens like Stephen Girard, Chief Justice Alexander Dallas of the Pennsylvania Supreme Court, and ex-Speaker of the House Mühlenberg. There a prominent local Irish businessman waved a copy and bellowed: "What a damned treaty! I make a motion that every good citizen in this assembly kick this damned treaty to hell!" On that signal, a group stuck it on a pole, marched to Minister Hammond's residence, set the paper ablaze, and shattered his windows.[15] The experience undoubtedly increased Hammond's gratitude at being recalled to London shortly thereafter. In these scenes Republicans saw democracy at work, while Federalists shuddered at the Jacobin frenzy and wondered if, the next time, heads instead of treaties would be carried on poles.

To ratify or not to ratify? Washington was eager to do what was in the national interest but unwilling to yield to pressure from the Senate, the

British, or the "demagogues." Delay might only bring more agitation. Then a disturbing letter arrived from secretary of war Pickering. "I feel extreme solicitude," said the secretary, "and for *a special reason* which can be communicated to you only in person."[16] It was the final push that led Washington to cut his vacation short and start back to Philadelphia. When he got there on August 11 he was thrown into eight days of anguished private and political drama that finally produced his decision.

Fifty-year-old Timothy Pickering's solicitude wasn't easy to evaluate because his rigid convictions made his normal stance one of disapproval. Thin-faced and long-nosed, he looked like a caricature of a Puritan forced to live among sinners. Son of a Salem merchant who put him through Harvard, he had tried practicing law and dropped it, then had a fling at business and failed. But intelligence and industry won him public office. During the Revolution he served in the Quartermaster's Department but somewhat to Washington's displeasure showed more zeal in unearthing graft than in keeping the supply wagons full. He undertook farming in Pennsylvania afterward—unsuccessfully—and then got back into government, first as a negotiator with the Seneca Indians, then as postmaster general, and finally as head of the War Department, although he was not the first choice.

Washington got into town and sent word to Pickering to call on him at home. When Pickering arrived, the president was in amiable conference with Randolph, whose latest advice was that the president should hold up ratification until the British canceled the latest "provision order," which meant starting a slow new round of diplomatic correspondence. Washington excused himself momentarily and stepped into an adjoining room with Pickering to find out what was on his mind. Pickering pointed a theatrical finger at the door behind which Randolph sat and announced: "That man is a *traitor.*"[17] He gave Washington a packet of material for later study, and they politely returned to the unsuspecting secretary of state's company.

What Washington read alone that night was an incomplete set of intercepted despatches, about a year old, from the French minister Fauchet to Paris. They had been taken from a ship captured by the British, delivered to the Foreign Office, sent from there to Hammond in Philadelphia, and through him finally reached Pickering. What they seemed to show at their worst interpretation was that Randolph had been in frequent intimate conversation with Fauchet, talked freely about secret matters, and suggested bribing some of the leaders of the Whiskey Rebellion to keep it going. Randolph himself, his friends, his biographers, and some later historians of the period argued vigorously that the Fauchet letters were possibly inauthentic or at least misread and twisted by his enemies to frame him.[18]

Whatever the elusive final truth, the material convinced Washington that his fellow Virginian was, if not an actual traitor, a dangerous and foolish pro-French saboteur in the heart of his official family. Now he understood why Randolph had been so insistent on further delay that would give opposition time to build. And so his mind was made up. At next morning's scheduled cabinet meeting, he pronounced five simple words: "I will ratify the treaty."[19] He meant with Article 12 dropped altogether, which turned out to be no problem. For another week he continued to behave toward Randolph as if nothing had happened, while the official papers for Hammond to take to London were drawn up. Then he called Randolph to a morning conference with Pickering and Wolcott, who looked on frostily while Washington handed over one of the incriminating despatches and asked for an explanation. Randolph struggled for a while, then asked for and got leave to withdraw and compose a more considered written answer. Before the day was over he had resigned. Later on he published a long *Vindication* that bitterly attacked Washington as a tool of the British faction in America.

It was a sign of fast-changing times that Randolph had gone in just eight years from being the bright young star of nationalism at the Constitutional Convention to a disgraced casualty of partisan warfare. Pickering replaced him at the State Department, and between his influence and Wolcott's the atmosphere of the cabinet was finally and unmistakably Federalist. Washington himself never officially admitted losing the hope he expressed in a letter to Hamilton, which referred to the Jay Treaty but might have been about any issue, "to learn from dispassionate men, who have knowledge of the subject . . . the genuine opinion they entertain . . . that I may see . . . ultimately, on which side the balance is to be found."[20] But some time after Randolph was gone, Washington said that he could no longer appoint anyone to a major office "whose political tenets are adverse to the measures . . . [of] the general government . . . for this, in my opinion, would be a sort of political suicide."[21] He would not follow the ideal of impartiality over the edge of a cliff.

With the ratification decision made, the tempest surrounding the treaty did die down in the fall. But there was a last act still to play. In mid-March 1796, the trumpet call for a final Republican charge was sounded by the need for money to cover the costs of carrying out the treaty, such as the expenses and salaries of the mixed commissions. The first recognizable congressional party caucus ever was held when Republican members of the fourth House of Representatives, elected in 1794, gathered to plan a challenge. Appropriations had to originate in the House. If it was the job of the House to pay for a treaty, they decided, then the House as much as the Senate had to approve the entire agreement. A resolution was introduced and passed, calling on Washington to submit the executive documents relating to Jay's mission. Wearily facing another hard excursion into the unknown territory of his exact powers, Washington refused. The Constitution made it clear, he answered, that treaties should be made by him and consented to by the Senate. That was done, the word of the United States was given, and the House had no right to meddle.

Politically, however, the president was boxed in. The healthy 62–37 margin by which the call for papers had passed showed that the votes were there to kill the treaty by fiscal starvation. Controlled as always, Washington held his tongue in public but fumed in a letter that the sponsors "resolved to . . . render the treaty-making power a nullity without their consent; . . . worse, to render it an absolute absurdity." They had "not only brought the Constitution to the brink of a precipice but the peace, happiness and prosperity of the country into imminent danger."[22]

During April (which happened to be the month during which Washington sat for the famous, serene-looking Gilbert Stuart portrait) the battle surged back and forth in the House Chamber. Madison, who was the obvious expert on the Constitutional Convention, defended the claim of the House to a share in treatymaking but had to resort to a "broad con-struction" like that of his ex-friend, Hamilton, to make his case. He had help from a new member whose career as a Republican mainstay was just taking off. Geneva-born and French-educated Albert Gallatin came from frontier Pennsylvania, whose legislature had earlier named him to the Senate. That election was thrown out because he lacked the seven years' residence requirement, but his admiring neighbors reacted by electing him a representative. Gallatin and Madison seemed to have marshaled enough votes to win, but powerful counterattacks were made by Federalist spokesmen. One came from an ill Fisher Ames. He tot-tered from his seat and begged the House to indulge his weak voice for a few moments, then spent a rousing hour and a half (at a time when a good speaker could still persuade a small legislature) vividly picturing the commercial and military disasters—especially on the Indian fron-tier—that would follow the rejection of the treaty.

Ames had the facts on his side. Republican treaty haters from the West were wavering. They were happy to see the British packing up to leave the fur posts in another few weeks. Besides that, two other agree-ments enormously pleasing to them were up for ratification. One was the Treaty of Greenville, made with the Indians whom Wayne had beaten. They had to give up most of Ohio. The other, the Treaty of San Lorenzo, was the work of Thomas Pinckney. After he was bypassed as chief negotiator with Great Britain, Pinckney caught a lucky break in an appointment as special envoy to Madrid to work out problems with Spain. The Spanish were far easier to handle in 1795. They were about to make peace with France, they were afraid that it would get them into a war with the British, and they were ready for any deal to keep the Americans from grabbing the chance to attack Spanish Louisiana. Pinck-ney got the westerners their cherished dream, a water outlet to markets. They could flatboat their corn, meat, lumber, and whiskey down the Mississippi through New Orleans or warehouse it there for up to three years, all without encumbrances or strangling fees. There was also an agreement favorable to the Americans on the location of the boundary with Spanish Florida. Pinckney's treaty and the Treaty of Greenville between them opened the Northwest and the Southwest to floods of migration. They easily offset the supposed humiliation of Jay's Treaty.

As for the maritime issues, prosperity cotinued to survive the British lion's roar. Even the infamous ban on West Indian trade was lifted again and again by emergency exceptions. Other trades were opening to Yankee enterprise, and altogether the *Columbian Centinel* [*sic*] had it right: "The affairs of Europe rain riches upon us; and it is as much as we can do to find dishes to catch the golden shower."[23] The golden shower put out the fire of resistance among enough House Republicans to change the balance. On April 29, a 49–49 tie on a procedural vote to send to the floor an appropriation bill for the treaty was broken by Republican Mühlenberg's vote in favor. The next day there was another defection and the money was voted 51–48. The precedent was set—thereafter the House of Representatives would not demand an equal share in approving pending treaties. President Washington had won a big but a very close victory. Only a two-vote swing could have given a different result and interpretation. And while hindsight makes the precedent look decisive, there was no guarantee in 1796 that it would be followed another time.

The major losers by Jay's Treaty were the Indians abandoned by their British backers, and the French, whose 1778 alliance with the United States was now a dead letter. Among the people of the United States, the two-year crisis had produced practically nothing but winners. But the price was exorbitant. The savage debates had dug both parties into fortified positions from which they would hammer each other with hotter and hotter fire. Even Washington had lost his armor against criticism, and one Republican editor at least had accused him of "the supercilious distance of a tyrant" and "the insolence of an Emperor of Rome."[24] He was happier than ever with his firm decision to leave office at his term's end, though he was under no constitutional obligation whatever to quit. On the day that the House gave up its challenge he had been on the job for precisely seven years. And seven months were left until electors would gather in their state capitals to cast their votes for his successor. What would the first presidential election without him be like?

CHAPTER 9

Jefferson and Adams's First Round, 1796

IN THE STORY of presidential campaigns, the departure of Washington was a dividing line between the overture and the curtain raiser. In 1788 and 1792, when his name appeared on the ballot of every single elector as one of the two allowed, the Constitution's original system had caused no problems. But that unanimity would never recur. The year 1796 would see the first genuinely contested election for the chief executive's post. As such, it would at a minimum be more complicated than the earlier two. The point of distinction was the clear emergence by 1796, admittedly or not, of two political parties. But that was the only recognizable resemblance to the elections of later centuries.

Each party wanted to provide its electors with a clear Presidential choice as well as a number two candidate for vice president, who must get fewer votes to avoid a tie. But there was no nominating structure, only understandings among small numbers of scattered unofficial leaders dependent on a poor network of communication. Even the faithful did not always get—or follow—the word. Besides that, some electors still ran as independents. Further, in different states electors were chosen by different methods and on different dates, leading to a long wait for complete results. A cloud of uncertainty and rumor overhung the whole process, right through the official deposit of the electors' ballots in their state capitals in December and the official count before the Senate in February. Until the the last minute the candidates themselves did not know which job, if either, they would win.

The number one choices for both Federalists and Republicans were clear. No one on the proadministration side had anything like the credentials of John Adams—not merely his services, sacrifices, and risks during the Revolution but his seven years of loyal support in the mausoleum of the vice presidency. He understood as much. "I am heir apparent, you know," he wrote to Abigail. The idea was pleasing, though it had negatives. Being "the butt of party malevolence" would be "bitter, nauseous and unwholesome."[1] Besides, he had gotten to enjoy the long, quiet months at Peacefield when the Senate was not sitting and the gentle intimacy with Abigail of an aging couple whose love had survived hard times. One bitter winter morning she wrote him that it was cold enough to freeze the blood in her veins, but "not the warmth of my affection for him for whom my heart beats with unabated ardor through all the changes and vicissitudes of life." And when, in another letter, she said that a man of sixty ought not to spend much time away from his family, his reply was: "How dare you hint or lisp a word about 'sixty years of age.' If I were near I would soon convince you that I am not above forty."[2] Both of them enjoyed having leisure to visit daughter Nabby and lawyer son Charley and their grandchildren in New York and to write long letters to their eldest, John Quincy, who had started a diplomatic career as minister to the Netherlands in 1794, taking brother Tommy with him as his secretary. And neither liked the social prospect of becoming president and first lady and the discretion that it would demand from their frank natures. She said that if it happened, "I must impose a silence upon myself when I long to talk." And he wrote back: "I hate speeches, messages, addresses and answers, proclamations, and such affected, studied . . . things. I hate levees and drawing rooms. I hate to speak to a thousand people to whom I have nothing to say."

In spite of all that they both believed that he should not, could not, and would not say no when asked. "I have a pious and a philosophical resignation to the voice of the people," he told her, and her answer was that "the Hand of Providence ought to be . . . cheerfully submitted to." His only worry was about coming in second once more, in which case he would resign, unwilling to play accompanist to anyone but Washington.[3]

Jefferson appears to have fought harder than Adams against the "Hand of Providence" that made his "nomination" automatic. In February Madison wrote to Monroe: "The Republicans, knowing that Jefferson alone can be started with hope of success, mean to push him. I fear much that he will mar the project . . . by a peremptory and public refusal."[4] Madison, as a good political manager, dodged that risk for months by simply never asking Jefferson. Jefferson persisted in telling friends, "I have no ambition to govern men; no passion which would lead me to delight to ride in a storm."[5] He was happy at Monticello with his bricks, nails, and building projects, his crop experiments, and the nearness of his two daughters and their families. Opponents were skeptical of these disclaimers, and with Jefferson there was always a slight cloud of ambiguity about his exact political intentions. He did let his name be submitted finally, but when it appeared clear that he had not become president his reaction was: "On principles of public interest I should not have refused; but I protest before my God that I shall . . . rejoice at escaping."[6] He was certain that no man left the office with the good reputation that brought him into it.

It is hard to believe that either he or John Adams could resist the call, given the intensity of their alarm about the future of the country they had made and loved. During the final Jay Treaty battle, Adams, looking on, believed that if House Republicans killed the pact, it would "be then evident that this constitution could not stand." The mere fact of debating an already concluded agreement—of "whether national faith is binding on a nation"—showed "no national pride—no national sense of honor." The Francophiles would "throw this country into the arms of a foreign power, into a certain war and as certain anarchy."[7] Jefferson was just as passionate in his way. He wished for an "ocean of fire" to separate America from England, whose corruption threatened to infect the pure republican morals of America's people. He lamented that "an Anglican, monarchical, & aristocratical party" had sprung up, composed of "timid men who prefer[red] the calm of despotism to the boisterous sea of liberty . . . [and] speculators & holders in the public funds." Even good men [like Washington, by implication] had "gone over to these heresies," men who were "Samsons in the field . . . but who have had their heads shorn by the harlot England."[8] Granted that these outbursts were in private letters and that both Adams and Jefferson could be colorfully excessive in their correspondence with intimates, they were not the sentiments of political veterans ready to quit the fight and become onlookers.

The two men were still on good terms despite their differences. The Adamses simply believed that their old friend was misguided. "Though wrong in politics . . . my friendship for him has ever been unshaken," John informed Abigail, who answered that her own fondness for "that gentleman" had "lived through his faults and errors—to which I have not been blind."[9] Jefferson was equally open in his liking for the blunt Yankee he had known since they were working together for separation from Britain in 1776. The two had much more in common with each other than with many of their own political allies. They were farmers at heart, swapping long paragraphs of information about frosts, fences, manures, and yields. Neither really cared much for cities or their throngs of unpropertied workers. Both of them were omnivorous and wide-ranging readers with solid grounding in the classics. Adams may have lacked some of Jefferson's intense love of architecture, music, and natural science, but his own constant study of history, biography, and political philosophy in search of the essence of human nature matched the Virginian's. If he came up with a more hard-boiled assessment of humankind's frailty than Jefferson did, the disagreement was respectful. Jefferson's revolutionary anarchism and Adams's distrust of too much freedom were theoretical positions that each man knew could not be strictly applied to the realities of American life. Finally, while Adams did not share Jefferson's loathing for "stockjobbers," neither did he care much for fellow Federalist Hamilton's cultivation of the banking elite. He had, in fact, a lingering Puritanical distrust of usurers and sharpers. In the same way, Jefferson's speculative flights sometimes put a slight distance between him and his friend Madison, who tended to focus his own fierce intelligence strictly on political issues.

The Adams-Jefferson friendship was unusual, for partisanship was dividing both friends and families. John's cousin Sam Adams, the old Boston radical democrat, ran for Republican elector in Massachusetts. (He lost there, but fifteen Republican electors from Virginia made him their second choice for president.) In South Carolina, cousin Charles Pinckney broke with Charles Cotesworth and Thomas to become a Republican. Nothing quite matched what happened to Pennsylvania's Frederick Mühlenberg. Two days after he crossed the party line to vote with the House Federalists in favor of Jay's Treaty, his Republican cousin stabbed him, though not fatally. In Philadelphia, according to Jefferson, men who had known each other for years crossed the street and looked the other way to avoid greetings.

In spite of that the election was relatively quiet. The "campaign" did not begin until Washington formally announced his retirement in September. The four understood candidates did not say anything on their own behalf in public. It was considered unseemly and, in the case of the Federalists' choice for vice president, Thomas Pinckney, impossible. He was en route home from his diplomatic stint, literally "at sea" until mid-December. Burr, the Republicans' number two man, always preferred to work offstage. So such debates as there were took place in newspapers, pamphlets, and public meetings to promote individual electors in the four states where they were chosen by district, or to push statewide electoral slates in the two states where that was the law. In ten states the only way to register one's preference for president was to vote for a state legislator who promised in turn to vote for an elector supporting that candidate. So much indirection did not encourage a large turnout, nor did the tendency of local editors to touch only lightly on the presidential contest. The only state in which the election had a somewhat modern cast was Pennsylvania. Its fifteen electors were chosen on a statewide basis, meaning that the winning party got them all (as nowadays), and the Republicans mounted a tremendous organizational and public relations effort, ably coordinated by John Beckley, to get a slate of well-known names, have the names written out on thousands of prepared tickets, and have the tickets put in voters' hands. And since Philadelphia was the capital of the United States, the papers there gave plenty of room to diatribes on national issues.

The rhetoric was harsh enough. Jefferson was charged with atheism and cowardice, among other things. His supporters scattered handbills like the one that declared: "*Thomas Jefferson* first framed the sacred political sentence that all men are born equal. *John Adams* says this is all farce and falsehood; that some men should be born Kings, and some should be born Nobles. Which of these, freemen of Pennsylvania, will you have for your President?" Even so, the Pennsylvania turnout of some twenty-five thousand voters was only a quarter of those eligible—and the Republicans won by a margin of no more than one or two hundred votes.[10]

The real spice in the election was provided by two out-of-the-ordinary attempts to influence the result, one through bullying and the other by backstairs intrigue. The first involved the latest French ambassador, Pierre Adet. Both he and his home government reasonably believed that a Republican administration would be more friendly to France and made the mistake of trying to help produce one. Just around the time of the voting in Pennsylvania he informed secretary of state Pickering of a new French policy to counteract the Jay Treaty. Hereafter they would treat American shipping as roughly as the British did. Adet sent a copy of his official notification to the violently antiadministration Philadelphia newspaper, the *Aurora*, from which it would be later picked up by other sheets around the country. Then—again with copies to the press—he announced the suspension of diplomatic relations in a message bitterly criticizing the Federalists' betrayal of the 1778 alliance. The implicit message to the electorate was that voting Republican would prevent being sucked into war with France. Unluckily for him, Adet sounded more as if he intended to frighten than to persuade Americans by referring to his nation as one "terrible to its enemies, but generous to its allies." The results were probably counterproductive overall. Adet's meddling let Federalist pamphleteers paint Jefferson as the disloyal tool of a foreign power. The envoy himself knew better. What he warned Paris in December was that "Jefferson likes us because he detests England . . . but he might change his

opinion of us tomorrow, if tomorrow Great Britain should cease to inspire his fears." And he added: "Jefferson, I say, is American and as
such, he cannot be sincerely our friend. An American is the born enemy
of all the European peoples."[11]

Besides Adet's open, undiplomatic attempt to help the Republicans, there was an underhanded effort by Hamilton to make Thomas
Pinckney president instead of John Adams. The plot sprang from the
rich soil of Hamilton's personal distaste for Adams. Pinckney, thanks to
the popularity of his treaty, and because as a southerner he could pull
electoral votes in what was heavily Republican territory, was a good
Federalist choice for second place, but clearly no more than second
place. Now, however, Hamilton secretly tried to arrange that every Federalist elector should cast one vote for Pinckney, knowing that a few in
the South would give their alternate choice to someone other than
Adams. That would bring Pinckney in ahead of Adams, the exact opposite of what was supposed to happen. Hamilton's official excuse was
that Adams was lagging in the anticipated count, Jefferson was a threat,
and it was all-important to have Pinckney and Adams get the two highest vote totals in no matter what order. But word of his strategy leaked
out and enraged New England Federalists, who gathered perfectly well
that Hamilton was trying to reverse the party's preferences. Thereupon
some of them scratched Pinckney, which resulted in dropping his total
below Jefferson's. Hamilton's maneuver simply backfired.

When news of the bungled intrigue reached the ears of John and
Abigail Adams, their own rage at Hamilton bubbled like lava in their letters. She called him "as ambitious as Julius Caesar, a subtle intriguer. . . .
His thirst for fame is insatiable." John's view was that Hamilton was "a
proud-spirited, conceited, aspiring mortal . . . As great a hypocrite as any
in the U.S." Both of them apparently suspected him of sexual miscon-
duct, an unforgivable affront. He had "as debauched morals as old
Franklin," John reported, and she readily agreed. "I have read his heart
in his wicked eyes many a time. The very devil is in them. They are las-
civiousness itself."[12] This mutual Adams-Hamilton hatred—not always
understandable but as violent as that between Hamilton and Burr—
would soon have explosive results.

When the ballots were finally counted, John Adams had 71 of the total 138 votes, just one more than the 70 he needed, and just 3 more than Thomas Jefferson, with 68. Pinckney had 59, and Burr a miserable 30. Pinckney owed his third-place finish partly to Hamilton's interference and partly to local politics in his own South Carolina, where the legislature gave him 4 electoral votes and 4 to Jefferson. Burr was hurt most by getting only 1 vote from Virginia's 20 Jefferson supporters and only 9 from Republican electors in the rest of the South. He would not forget that four years later.

The sectional dividing line was bright and clear. All of New England—plus New York, New Jersey, and Delaware—went for Adams. South of Maryland he picked up only 2 electoral votes. Jefferson swept the South and the two new western states of Kentucky, admitted in 1792, and Tennessee, which had just joined the Union. Only Pennsylvania in the North joined the Republican column, thanks to a strong western element. Her 14 electoral votes pushed Jefferson ahead of Pinckney.[13]

In mid-December, when there was still a chance that Jefferson and Adams might be tied and the choice thrown into the House of Representatives, Jefferson sent instructions to Madison. Republicans were to be clearly told that he, Jefferson, wanted Adams to have the presidency. "He has always been my senior,"[14] the letter graciously explained. With authorization, Madison made it public, much pleasing Adams. A possibly more cynical explanation might be Jefferson's awareness that it was not a good time, in his phrase, to take the helm. Sectional ties were stretched to the screaming point, and war with France was on the horizon. Referring in another letter to the outgoing Washington, Jefferson noted: "The President is fortunate to get off just as the bubble is bursting, leaving others to hold the bag."[15]

On December 28 he sent Adams generous congratulations on his election, for by then he was sure of the outcome. He said he had always preferred that Adams should win. He was sorry that Adams had been forced to endure efforts of a scheming supposed "friend" (meaning Hamilton, whom he did not name outright) to defeat him. The new president would deserve all the glory if he could keep the peace. And finally, in spite of a few "little incidents" here and there, there was no break in the "solid esteem" of the old days together. It was a warm, lovely, nonpolitical note. All the same, Jefferson showed it first to Madison for his opinion. Madison, knowing that it might in the future make a fine campaign document for the Federalists, advised against sending it. And it was never sent.

With or without that letter, however, the new president and vice president were not formal adversaries when they took their inaugural oaths on March 4. Chubby Adams in his pearl-gray suit and sword and tall Jefferson buttoned into a long blue frock coat made an amusing contrast, but there was something heartening about their presence together in those roles, twenty years and eight months to the day after they had pledged their lives, fortunes, and sacred honor to American liberty. For a magic moment it looked as if the electoral system of the Constitution was a good one after all. The two nationally known figures best qualified to follow George Washington had been chosen. If they were not personal enemies, there might be a fleeting chance of their rising above party to share their knowledge and talent.

It was not to be. They did, however, make a try. When Jefferson arrived in Philadelphia, Adams called on him to say that he was planning to send a three-man deputation, representing both North and South, to Paris to talk peace. What would Jefferson think about being a member? They talked it over and agreed that it would not be a fit assignment for the vice president, and in any case Jefferson said he was not interested. Adams then wondered out loud if James Madison, who was retiring from the House, would go. Jefferson promised at least to ask him. A couple of days later they met again at a dinner given by Washington and exchanged news. Jefferson relayed Madison's refusal. And a slightly embarrassed Adams explained that it was just as well. He had already held a cabinet meeting (dominated by three very ardent Federalists), and they had objected to the nomination. Jefferson recorded that he was never afterward asked about "any measures of the government," and Adams's recollection was: "We parted as good friends as we had always lived, but we consulted very little together afterwards." There was simply too much "party violence," which, in old age, Adams laid at Hamilton's door.[16]

Shortly after that farewell dinner, Washington set off for Mount Vernon, happy to be out of office, especially under such lowering skies. On inauguration day Washington, suited in unobtrusive black, seemed to be enjoying himself more than Adams, the presumed star of the moment. Adams noticed, too, and confided his opinion to Abigail: "Methought I heard him say, 'Ay! I am fairly out and you fairly in! See which of us will be the happiest.' "[17] Relief rather than happiness was probably the dominant emotion in the First Citizen's mind. His hopes of a nation as orderly as Mount Vernon, a people as self-restrained as he had always tried to be, had not come to pass. In his farewell address of the preceding September he had warned "in the most solemn manner against the baneful effects of the spirit of party." In governments based on the people's will, it was "seen in its greatest rankness and is truly their worst enemy." And he had gone on especially to counsel against "passionate attachments" to foreign nations or automatic animosity toward them, which could fuel a self-defeating foreign policy. It was "folly in one nation to look for disinterested favors from another." There would always be a price.[18] But as the horses' hooves carried him southward he knew that the advice was having as little effect as most good advice. The remaining year and nine months of his life would be troubled by the turbulence his own extraordinary example had not been able to control. He was not superhuman, not the man of marble that idolizers would make him, but he was quite unlike any American who followed him in his capacity to unite Americans and set a model for them. Now his day was passing. Behind him he left a fire burning in an ammunition dump, on which John Adams sat.

PART IV

TOWARD

DISUNION,

1797–1800

X, Y, Z, and the
French Connection, 1798

BACK in the spring of 1796, while he was working through the pros and cons of choosing between the "great cares" of the presidency or the "small cares" of retirement to Quincy, John Adams fell into his lifelong habit of scrutinizing his own soul. "I have looked into myself," he wrote to Abigail, "and see no meanness or dishonesty there. I see weakness enough but no timidity."[1] It was rare for him to be so generous to himself, and in this instance, he was completely correct. The political cost of his lack of "timidity" was huge.

At the very best, Adams would have had a hard time filling the empty shoes of Washington, and the conditions of his presidency were far from the best. He inherited the excruciating foreign-policy dilemma that had dogged the still-experimental nation since 1792, the preservation of its freedom and prosperity in a world at war. Realism seemed to shout from the rooftops that Washington's choice—neutrality—was still the best answer. The United States lacked the muscle to make war independently. But alliance with either France or England only promised grim alternatives as the contending powers grew more desperate. If America picked the losing side, she would suffer at the peace table. And if she were yoked to a far more powerful winner, she could become a satellite.

Staying neutral, however, was not simple. The rights and dignity of American citizens traveling or trading abroad had to be upheld somehow; the flag could not be contemptuously ignored without some form of reaction. Peace at any price was not an option. A defense buildup of some kind would therefore be necessary—but it would meet stiff resistance from congressional Republicans devoted to small budgets and a weak central government. And the growing virulence of party spirit added to the problem. From ardently pro-British Federalists and pro-French Republicans came a constant clamor for shows of belligerency toward the "enemy" power. A policy that seemed to favor one side or the other would be violently divisive. Yet a stance that looked weak would outrage everyone who shared the budding spirit of nationalism that the Constitution needed in order to be successful. Any step taken to keep peace abroad could lead in the direction of civil war at home.

Adams was independent enough to make his own choice. Though undeniably a Federalist and enemy to "Jacobin" France, he was not ready to take Britain's side or yield to her further than Jay's Treaty already stipulated. But if the French were provocative, what would he do? And what would be the impact in 1800?

*

PEACEKEEPING WAS HARDER for the second president of the United States because he was not in control of events. He could not predict what foreign secretaries and war offices in Paris or London would do in their unending efforts to starve each other. He could only react. And, hard as it is to realize in a more organized age, he could also never be sure of restraining American citizens from private war-making initiatives. One proof of that was an incident that took place just four months after his inauguration, when the Senate expelled a member for the first time. His name was William Blount, and he came from the new state of Tennessee. His offense was the possible incitement of war with Spain.

Foreign policy was driven in the 1790s by two perspectives. The Atlantic-facing states were preoccupied with building a commercial future. For them, diplomacy's chief goals were to break down trade barriers and keep the high seas safe for American cargoes. But frontier communities facing westward had a different, though not necessarily conflicting, incentive. What they wanted was to plant the American flag over more of the virgin West (even though the territory within United States boundaries was still mostly empty). The strength of Great Britain put realistic limits on any hopes of moving against Canada. But once-mighty Spain was now a feeble shadow of an empire, hardly capable of making a vigorous defense of any of her North American holdings—Mexico, Florida, or the huge Louisiana Territory between the Mississippi and the Rockies, which she had gotten from France by treaty in 1763 as a winner's share in a European war. Her weakness put before the eyes of ambitious American schemers a steady temptation. A leader who could raise a few hundred men to overwhelm the Spanish garrisons and possibly negotiate a little foreign help could carve off a huge chunk of territory and then— who knew what? Keep it as a personal empire? Join it to dissatisfied parts of the American West in a new confederation? Offer it as a base to the highest-bidding European protector? Who could say what opportunities were open in that faraway land that still lacked settlement and law?

Blount apparently was one such dreamer, though his "plot" was driven more by pocketbook considerations than by soaring ambition. Son of a North Carolina settler of modest means, he was both handsome and persuasive and so was able to make a career of public office from 1780 onward. He was elected to the state legislature, then the Confederation Congress, then the Constitutional Convention, at which he said nothing recorded. His standing with the Federalists was good enough to get him appointed governor of Tennessee while it was still a territory. When it became a state in 1796, by which time he had become a Republican, he was elected as one of its first two senators. Like so many of his peers, he made land investments that turned out badly, and while feeling the pinch of need he concocted the idea of raising a combined force of frontiersmen and Indians that would capture at least parts of Florida and Louisiana and turn them over to Great Britain, which would provide naval cooperation by seizing New Orleans and, presumably, some kind of reward for Blount as well.

Unluckily for him, a letter intended to woo the Cherokees into participation fell into the wrong hands and wound up in Adams's possession. The president indignantly turned it over to the Senate on July 3, 1797. The "conspiracy" sounded somewhat mad and in fact, when proposed to the new British ambassador, Robert Liston, was rejected by his superiors.[2] But the evidence of it must have been powerfully damning to Blount, for the senators took only five days to expel him by a vote of 25–1. The middle-aged would-be warrior (whose Revolutionary War experience had been as a paymaster for North Carolina troops) left for home while Federalists in the House prepared to make some political use of the event. They voted articles of impeachment against him for treason, even though that word hardly described his offense, since he had neither levied war against the United States nor "adhered" to its enemies. But was a senator an impeachable "civil official" like a judge? Senators of both parties were reluctant to think so for fear of opening themselves to floods of partisan-inspired impeachments based on similar stretches of logic. Blount refused to leave the shelter of Tennessee and return to Philadelphia to appear in his defense. When the case finally got an official presentation a full year and a half later, the Senate voted closely (14–11) to refuse to try it, leaving open the question of whether they did so to declare senators unimpeachable or because the case was moot since Blount had already been kicked out.

The burlesque did Blount no political harm. He was elected to the Tennessee state senate and chosen Speaker by its members. His further rehabilitation was cut short by death in 1800. But the nation easily forgave sins like Blount's where expansion was concerned. George Rogers Clark, an outstanding hero of the Revolution who had captured the entire Northwest for America, accepted (from Citizen Genet) a general's commission in the French army to carry out the conquest of Spanish Louisiana. It never happened, but Clark survived a brief exile and returned to Kentucky to die in peace and alcoholism. James Wilkinson, at one point the highest-ranking officer in the United States regular army, received a pension from the king of Spain while on duty under the American flag, then contemplated double-crossing him, and in either case lost no official standing in the eyes of the U.S. War Department until 1806. Then he got into trouble for some mysterious dealings with Aaron Burr, part of a long sequel to Burr's role in 1800.

All such plots had the air of a bad spy novel about them, but they were serious matters for any president until the West was solidly under American jurisdiction. Underhanded dealings with France, Spain, and England could at any time start a war or split the Union. And politicians who even indirectly supported such dealings could be and were charged with selling out their country, which added to the poisonous atmosphere surrounding politics and peacemaking as 1800 approached.

✳

THE MOST URGENT PROBLEM facing Adams his first spring in office concerned France, with whom relations were steadily deteriorating. The French were still incensed by the pro-British tilt that American government had been taking since the Jay Treaty was ratified. Part of their response was the set of decrees published in fall 1796 that suspended diplomatic relations and ordered France's naval commanders to treat American ships exactly as the United States allowed the British to treat them, to wit, forcing them into some French-controlled port to be plundered of alleged contraband. Meanwhile, Secretary of State Pickering had recalled pro-French James Monroe as ambassador to Paris and replaced him with Charles Cotesworth Pinckney, an orthodox Federalist. In March 1797 President Adams learned of the French countermove. They refused to recognize or receive Pinckney, in effect saying that they would not even discuss the situation unless the United States changed its tune.

France's hard line reflected her growing sense of international power. Since 1795 the pendulum of revolution had been swinging back toward the center. There was a new constitution and a new government, with a two-house legislature and a curious five-member executive committee known as the Directory. The Directors were little-known men committed to no firm principles, who were trying to steer a middle course between radicals and reactionaries while saving the country and their own necks. Whatever their domestic record, the war against the monarchist European coalition was going very well for them at the start of 1797. Spain and Prussia had given up the battle, Holland was conquered, and the Austrian Empire that sprawled across the middle of Europe was on the ropes. Belgium, which was then an

Austrian province, was French-occupied, and twenty-six-year-old General Bonaparte, in a lightning campaign that left enemy generals gasping, swept into Austria's possessions in northern Italy. By October 1797 he forced the Vienna government to sign a treaty of surrender and was well on his own way to glory. France seemed invincible on land and still had a significant naval force to threaten Americans on the seas.

Such successes accounted for the Directory's arrogance toward America. Adams's cabinet, when consulted, inclined toward a fighting answer. Its members were, by his choice, holdovers from the Washington administration: Pickering at State, Wolcott in the Treasury post, and James McHenry of Maryland as secretary of war. The president was initially unaware of the extent to which those three were loyal followers of Hamilton, with whom they were in steady contact. Only Charles Lee, the attorney general, was the outvoted exception. Adams listened to their advice, then took the presidential privilege of the deciding vote in favor of a halfway step. First, he pleased the Francophobe elements among the Federalists by calling for a special session of Congress to meet on May 15, 1797, and greeting it with a statement of defiance of French threats. He promised that they would be "repelled with a decision which shall convince . . . the world that we are not a degraded people, humiliated under a colonial spirit of fear and a sense of inferiority."[3] He also called for an enlarged army and navy. But then, two weeks later, responding to Republican outcries against such militarism, he announced his intention to try again to open the door by creating a special, new mission to France to "dissipate umbrage" and "adjust all differences by a treaty between the two powers."[4] Pinckney would not be replaced—the French would not have that satisfaction. Yet he would be supplemented by two other negotiators. One would be a Virginia Federalist, John Marshall, possibly named to remind southern supporters of Adams that they were not forgotten. The other was, like Adams himself and like Pickering, a Massachusetts Yankee—but to the consternation of conservatives, he was Elbridge Gerry, an occasional Republican sympathizer, who had been Adams's friend (and Jefferson's) since the days when they all served together as young, pro-independence "radicals" in the Continental Congress.

They were interesting choices, men of temperaments as determined as Adams's own. Gerry was one of the three delegates to the Constitutional Convention who had refused to sign the final version. There his cranky objections to anything promoting either "tyranny" or an "excess of democracy"—to standing armies, to infrequent elections, and to a host of other ideas—had led to a feeling among the other delegates that he automatically resisted anything he did not propose himself. His troublemaking exterior, however, masked a talent for friendship with men from different political and sectional camps. Gerry simply could not be typecast. Though a Harvard graduate (in 1762, at age eighteen), he preferred his family's codfish-exporting business in Marblehead to a professional career. He did not marry until he was in his forties. He opposed ratification of the Constitution but supported (and, as a holder of government securities, personally profited by) Hamilton's centralizing economic policies. He distrusted party dogmas and could be equally critical of the British or the French. In time he would become vice president of the United States under James Madison and die in office in 1814.

Marshall, the future chief justice who would almost single-handedly make the Supreme Court the final authority on the Constitution, was then a forty-one-year-old rising star among Virginia's few Federalists. He came from the western part of the state, still a frontier when he was born, and even while he battled for the rights of large property holders he was a homespun democrat in person. Tall and athletic, always casually dressed, he was a fond husband and good neighbor. He enjoyed pitching horseshoes, cheering his favorites at horse races, and sitting in on a friendly card game. His education consisted of a little private tutoring, mostly from his much admired farmer father, also a popular local official. Young John Marshall had no academic training in law except for two months of attendance at lectures given at William and Mary in 1780. At that time he was still in the army awaiting reassignment after four years as a junior infantry officer in the continental line. War was the shaping force of his nationalism. He faced death in four major engagements under Washington, whom he revered, survived the miseries of Valley Forge, and as he later wrote, became "confirmed in the habit of considering America as my country and Congress as my government."[5]

By 1787 Marshall was building a successful law practice. He won over judges and juries by a gift for shrewd and concise arguments based more on logic than on precedent. Disgusted with what he saw as the shortsighted self-interest of pro-states'-rights Virginian politicians (including Thomas Jefferson), he stood out as a strong supporter of the Constitution and then of Washington and Hamilton. Washington was duly appreciative and had offered him the attorney generalship in 1795, but Marshall then preferred to stay close to his land investments and court work in Virginia. Two years later, however, he felt ready to accept Adams's invitation to make a debut on the national stage.

Gerry's appointment predictably irritated the three dedicated Federalists in the cabinet. Secretary McHenry warned that the chances were "ten to one against his [Gerry's] agreeing with his colleagues."[6] But Adams persisted, and after some maneuvering, Gerry's name went to the Senate and was confirmed. By August he and Marshall were en route to France. Adams himself retreated to Quincy for the summer and fall to restore his spirits and escape Philadelphia's fevers.

What happened to the three commissioners in France was a mixture of diplomacy, intrigue, and, if the results had not been so dangerous, possibly near comedy as the Americans argued with one another and with representatives of the Directory's cynical foreign minister, Charles Maurice de Talleyrand-Perigord.

Talleyrand is the rare historical figure who lived through the executions and banishments of the French Revolution, held high office in one republic, one empire, and two monarchies, outlasted them all, and died peacefully in his own bed. In 1797, after a four-year exile, he was back in France through the grace of friends who had come to power with the Directory. Born to an aristocratic family in 1754, Talleyrand entered the church and was a bishop by his midthirties but was defrocked when he took the side of the Revolutionists in renouncing clerical privileges. He was posted to London as a diplomat, escaped the Reign of Terror there, and then took refuge in the United States until 1796, observing American politics and little realizing how much his future actions would shake them up.

A European who took the world as he found it, Talleyrand enjoyed backstairs dealings for which Marshall, Gerry, and Pinckney were hardly prepared. When they got to Paris early in October, he refused to receive them officially for a full five months. Instead, he worked through three cultivated go-betweens, referred to later in the public version of the Americans' letters to the State Department as "X," "Y," and "Z." X and Y were Swiss-born bankers Jean Hottenguer (who knew Pinckney) and Pierre Bellamy, who had American business connections. Z was Lucien Hauteval, a refugee from the Santo Domingo rebellion. He had made Gerry's acquaintance in the United States. So had Talleyrand. Later on came still another banking agent, "W." Talleyrand's views were also urged by a charming Parisienne, Madame de Villette, who owned a house in which Gerry and Marshall roomed. Both men appeared somewhat smitten. She was "one of the finest women in Paris," according to Gerry, known for "her excellent morals & the richness of her mind." Marshall described her as "very accomplished . . . very sensible and I believe a very amiable lady," leading Republican gossipmongers to charge that he had been more than a mere tenant.[7] In time, Talleyrand also made use of Pierre Beaumarchais, author of *The Marriage of Figaro*, who might have scripted the whole affair, and who had a lawsuit pending in a Virginia court, with Marshall as his attorney.

Hottenguer first called on the three at Pinckney's lodgings. He said that M. Talleyrand couldn't begin formal negotiations because his superiors, the directors, were furious over President Adams's anti-French remarks before Congress. There would have to be an apology first, plus an agreement for the American government to pick up any debts owed by France to American citizens, plus a loan, and finally, "there must be something for the pocket . . . for the private use of the Directory and Minister."[8] Two nights later, on October 20, Hottenguer came back with Bellamy, who played the hard-liner. *"You must pay money,"* he told the trio. *"You must pay a great deal of money,"* and he indicated that the bribe (concealed of course by some bookkeeping ruse) would cost about a quarter of a million dollars. Marshall was for breaking off the private talks then and there but agreed to more meetings. Once more the question of a private payoff was raised, to which the shouted answer of Pinckney (the only one of the commissioners who spoke French) was, "No! No! Not a sixpence."[9] All the same, the Americans were "un-officially" willing to consider money for the pockets of the directors in exchange for a halt in the attacks on U.S. shipping. A secret bribe was preferable to an open loan, which the British could regard as an act of war, and which the commissioners were not sure they had the authority to promise (and could not find out without a three-month delay). But the Directory, puffed up by the triumph over Austria, was conceding nothing. Talleyrand himself had a "social" meeting with his American friend Monsieur Gerry, there were other visits from his messengers, and arms were twisted. France was irresistible; she was going to conquer England soon; neutral countries would be wise to keep her friendship; other nations were not too proud to pay for peace. And finally, if Marshall, Gerry, and Pinckney did not cooperate, the "French party in America" would make sure that "the British party"—that is, the Federalists—got the blame for the disasters to follow.[10]

This political threat was the last straw, and the Americans promptly announced that they would talk no more until officially received. What made all the bullying and insulting so important was that it was fully described in despatches home that were certain to rouse fury if and when made public. Meanwhile the mission itself was at a standstill. The Americans waited on through the winter of 1797–98 in a frustration that wasn't entirely unpleasant. "Paris presents one incessant round of amusement and dissipation," Marshall wrote to his wife, Polly. "Every day you may see something new, magnificent and beautiful, every night . . . a spectacle which astonishes and enchants the imagination."[11] But he and Pinckney were getting increasingly angry with Gerry, and that, too, had its political results. Gerry was more conciliatory than they were, and Talleyrand began in February to woo him away from the other two with private, confidential conferences and hints that the two of them could work something out if left alone. Bitter quarrels within the split delegation followed, leaving lasting antagonism. "I have never met a man with less candor and so much duplicity as Mr. Gerry," Pinckney wrote to a fellow Federalist.[12] Marshall felt much the same. Eventually, after complicated and slow exchanges of messages, Pinckney and Marshall left for home in April 1798. Gerry, too, was recalled but hung on through August. By then, faced with some changes in the European picture, Talleyrand had done a turnabout and was looking for peace with the United States. Gerry, unfortunately, no longer had the authority to negotiate. But when he got back to America, his report of the French change of heart would open the door to a fateful decision by Adams.

What kept Gerry lingering in Paris? Was it pro-French bias? An implicit Talleyrand threat that his presence was now the only thing preventing war? Or was he thinking politically, trying to cheat the Federalists out of a fight with France that would play well with patriotic voters at home? If that last was the case, his effort failed.

⁂

POLITICS WERE BECOMING harsher throughout 1797. While Adams summered in Quincy, Hamilton—the other giant of federalism—suffered the unexpected exposure of the affair with Maria Reynolds that he thought was buried. In June a gossipmongering newspaperman named James Callender—who, like many of his journalistic colleagues of the era, would be deeply and unapologetically enmeshed in partisan campaigns—published a set of pamphlets carrying the self-inflating title *A History of the United States in the Year 1796*. One of them revealed the whole story, including Hamilton's 1792 confession to Senator Monroe and Representatives Venable and Mühlenberg, with all the damning corroborative correspondence. Worse, Callender insisted that the original charges were true—that the sums handed over to Reynolds were not mere hush money but were meant for disguised speculation on Hamilton's account.

Hamilton went into an agonized rage. He was making money at the bar again; a sixth child was on the way; and he had three disciples in the cabinet helping to set administraton policy, with which he had no quarrel at that point. Now this disaster! Who had broken the gentlemen's agreement to keep those letters secret? Hamilton fired off notes to Monroe, Venable, and Mühlenberg, insisting that they now say publicly what they had assured him then—there was no evidence whatever of any *official* wrongdoing. Monroe, who was visiting New York, stalled in replying. Hamilton, along with his brother-in-law and a friend, called on him on July 11 and, "very much agitated," accused him of being the source of the story. Monroe denied it. Hamilton said the denial was "totally false." If you say that, Monroe answered, "you are a scoundrel." "I will meet you like a gentleman," Hamilton shouted back, and Monroe snapped in return: "I am ready, get your pistols."[13] The two other men present calmed them down, but it was not quite over. In the next few days Hamilton found out that Monroe had never been totally convinced of his story, and letters passed with more demands for clarification and more refusals and mutual accusations, until it looked as if pistols at dawn were the only possible outcome. But things were diplomatically smoothed over by the friend whom Monroe chose as his possible second. That was Aaron Burr, who himself, seven years later, would have the most celebrated duel in American history, with Hamilton. What would have been the result if a fatal exchange of shots had taken place between Hamilton and Monroe instead?

Hamilton believed that only partisanship kept Monroe and the other two from doing the right thing and clearing him—that by now the Republicans were simply determined to color him corrupt, no matter what the facts. He was correct in that, but he had the wrong culprit. The most likely "leaker" was the Republican man-of-all-work John Beckley, to whom Monroe had given copies of the incriminating letters for safekeeping. The Federalist-controlled House of Representatives of the Fifth Congress had, in May 1797, thrown Beckley out of his eight-year-old post as clerk. The job was supposedly nonpartisan, but Beckley clearly was anything but that and was the kingpin of the effort the preceding fall that had swung Pennsylvania's electoral vote to Jefferson. His firing was clearly payback, and he probably gave Callender the Hamilton story as his own (and the party's) revenge. It was effective.

To counteract the political impact, Hamilton was forced to go public in a pamphlet that appeared in New York on August 25, entitled *Observations on Certain Documents . . . in which the Charge of Speculation against Alexander Hamilton . . . Is Fully Refuted, Written by Himself*. He was in no way, he said, linked to Reynolds by any financial scheme. "My real crime," he added, "is an amorous connection with his wife, for a considerable time with his . . . connivance . . . with the design to extort money from me. This confession is not made without a blush."[14] Not for another 201 years would a notable public man have details of his sex life so mercilessly exposed to a public that professed to be scandalized but bought the pamphlet by the thousands. But in the rancorous political climate of that summer the embittered Hamilton (whose wife, at least, forgave him) saw no other choice.

Monroe kept the rancor alive through December with a long, printed attack on the Federalists who had forced his recall as ambassador to France. Then at the end of January came a less solemn moment of party fury. During a congressional debate a Vermont Republican representative, Matthew Lyon, spat in the face of Connecticut Federalist Roger Griswold. Two weeks later, in mid-February, Griswold walked over to Lyon's desk and began to beat him with a hickory cane. Lyon snatched up a pair of tongs from one of the fireplaces heating the House Chamber and returned the blows. The yelling gladiators rolled on the floor for a time before being separated. But the comic relief was short. Suddenly a new war crisis erupted and divisive passions flared higher than ever.

On March 4, 1798, Adams was advised that the State Department had received late January dispatches from the team in Paris. As usual, they were in cipher, for no nation could be trusted to maintain the inviolability of the diplomatic pouch. The very first confirmed what he had already heard as a rumor from abroad—the mission was hopeless. For many nights thereafter Adams would sit late at his desk drafting and redrafting sulfurous messages denouncing France—but stopping short of trumpet calls to battle. He was always struggling to control his private irascibility in order to fulfil his public duty. Now he needed to get the country to follow that hard middle road, for he seemed to be persuaded that the right course was to build up America's military capabilities but to avoid war. So his communication to Congress the very next morning only passed on the undetailed news that the mission was a failure. But as further decipherments unfolded the full record of French hostility and contempt—potential dynamite—Adams had to consider his follow-up steps with care. He sounded out the cabinet. Attorney General Lee was ready for a war declaration, and so was Picker-

ing, who wanted to join Great Britain formally in the worldwide ideological struggle "against the universal dominion of France."[15] But Wolcott and McHenry argued for a limited response, confined purely to the
defense of American interests. That happened to be Alexander Hamilton's opinion of the moment, and it was also Adams's. He reported
again to Congress on March 19. "Mature consideration" of the
despatches, he said—still not releasing the full text—left no reason to
assume that France would make any agreement "compatible with the
safety, the honor, or the essential interests of the nation," and he
wanted legislation allowing for the arming of merchant vessels to defend themselves.[16]

The Republicans thought even that too bellicose. Vice President Jefferson privately called Adams's message "insane." He was anticipating
that the French would invade England, end the war, and remove the issues of neutrality and military readiness from America's political life. He
wondered if the president was whipping up anti-French feelings by exaggeration. What did those dispatches actually say? Perhaps "their information if made public would check the disposition to arm."[17] Others had
similar ideas. On the last day of March Virginia representative William
Giles introduced a resolution calling on Adams to turn over all the materials relating to the mission. Inside of three days it was passed, and
Adams, without resistance, delivered the documents. In another three
days Congress agreed to open them to the public. Within weeks they had
created a furor against the French and their Republican friends in America, plus a call to arms, that could not have worked better for the Federalists if John Adams had planned it. Perhaps he had. Both he and
Jefferson, heading for their confrontation at the polls, constantly disclaimed political motives while taking inexorably political actions. In any
case, by forcing disclosure, the Republicans sprung a trap on themselves.

"Stand-behind-the-leader" resolutions poured in from everywhere.
"Since man was created and government formed," wrote one amazed
Federalist, "no public officer has stood higher in the confidence and affection of his countrymen than our present President now does."[18] Abigail Adams wrote to her sister, "The Jacobins [her favored term for the
opposition] in Senate & House were struck dumb, and opened not their

mouths." Congressional Republicans were indeed silent, and some ran for cover by going home to their districts, leaving the Federalists even larger working majorities. Speech makers outdid one another in bombast. Pinckney's "No! No! Not a sixpence" was elaborated into a Federalist toast: "Millions for defense, but not one cent for tribute." The wife of British minister Liston attended the theater in Philadelphia one night when Adams came in. "Nothing could equal the noise and uproar," she reported; "the President's March was played, & called for over & over again." The crowd threatened to pitch a man who began singing a French Revolutionary song over the balcony rail. Mrs. Liston happily noted that "at this moment the British are extolled for having so long resisted the Tyrants of France." A few weeks later she observed: "This country is preparing for war . . . The insolence of the French has done its work."[19] Students at Princeton sent a message "applauding your administration and energy of government."[20] Over a thousand young men of Philadelphia, wearing black cockades in their hats (the Federalist answer to the tricolor cockades of French supporters) paraded to the presidential residence to testify their support. Adams received them in a dress suit with a sword at his side.

Anything less than rampant patriotism was unacceptable. "To be lukewarm . . . is to be criminal," one New York newspaper proclaimed, "and the man who does not warmly reprobate the conduct of the French must have a soul black enough to be *fit for treasons, stratagems and spoils.*"[21] Federalists were boiling for combat. Fisher Ames wrote to Pickering in June: "The members [of Congress] still talk too much of *peace* as if we had our choice. . . . We have war & the man who now wished for peace holds his country's honor & safety too cheap."[22] And two weeks later Pickering had written to his own son, "The Rubicon is passed. War is inevitable."

The anti-French fever had a double political result. In June the Federalist-controlled Congress passed—and John Adams signed—laws designed to punish dissenters in general, and in particular foreign-born "agitators" for republicanism like Albert Gallatin. These Alien and Sedition Acts were massive exercises in overreaching, so grave in their results that they must be dealt with in a separate chapter.

The other spurt of legislation was military. In the heat of 1798's spring and summer, the United States got the Navy Department and the Marine Corps. An undeclared sea war was authorized, and plans were laid for a greatly enlarged army, which Alexander Hamilton, reverting to his youthful dreams of military glory, hoped to lead into battle. When John Adams frustrated that fantasy, he and Hamilton finally became open enemies, ripping their apparently triumphant party apart on the eve of the next election—in which one of the key issues would be whether a republic could coexist with a large "defense" establishment.

✯

THE FEDERALISTS ENJOY the credit and responsibility for creating the United States Navy. Naval expansion was far less of a problem than building an army because the foundation had been laid under the ever-popular Washington in 1794, when the crisis with Great Britain gave congressmen the political courage to authorize the building of six frigates—ships of thirty-two to forty-four guns each. The expense, which provoked considerable opposition, was justified as a step to protect commerce against Algiers, one of the Barbary States of North Africa—autonomous provinces of the Ottoman Empire, whose small and lightly armed but highly maneuverable pirate vessels easily captured slow-moving merchantmen in Mediterranean coastal waters. The rulers then sold the cargoes and enslaved or held the crews for ransom. The young United States, like other nations, had found it cheaper to buy protection by paying "tribute" to the Dey of Algiers than to keep expensive warships stationed in the region, and soon after 1794 Congress went back to that practice, approved a renewal of "tribute" to Algiers, and cut the order for frigates in half. One of the three that finally came out of American shipyards was the USS *Constitution*, "Old Ironsides."

✯

THE NEW WAR SCARE of 1798 rekindled the pronavy sentiment and made it temporarily irresistible. April saw the passage of a bill allotting nearly a million dollars—one sixth of the preceding year's total federal budget—to buy, build, or lease twelve fighting ships of up to twenty-two guns each. Creating the fleet became the job of a new Department of the Navy. The man whom Adams chose as secretary was no sailor but a knowledgeable middle-aged Marylander in the shipping business, Benjamin Stoddert. He turned out to be a fine administrator. Confronted with the job of letting contracts, buying and moving materials, finding officers and crewmen—all with a small staff working by hand—he got ships afloat in time to keep pace with galloping demands. Congress voted in July to tear up the 1778 treaty with France and ordered the infant navy to capture any French ships interfering with American commerce. So began what the official documents still call the "Quasi-War Between the United States and France." The marine corps, created as part of the expansion, was allotted 33 commissioned officers, 96 noncoms, 720 privates, and 32 "drums and fifes."[23] By December 1798 the navy already had four squadrons on duty in the West Indies where the heaviest French depredations were driving marine insurance rates through the roof. Stoddert's first annual report to Congress boldly asked for money for a major fleet, including a dozen more frigates and a dozen 74-gun ships of the line, the eighteenth-century equivalent of heavy battleships. He argued that the millions to be spent would be only a fraction of the commercial losses already inflicted on an unprotected merchant marine. Though his requests were pared down, he got more fighting ships and marines, plus appropriations for dockyards, timber, and supporting services. "Public opinion is getting more and more in favor of the Navy," he reported to one of his commanders.[24] It stayed that way throughout 1799 as the quasi war went well. Americans won most of the sea fights, which were usually with privateers who surrendered quickly, rather than the brutal duels between wooden men-of-war, which pounded each other at close range until one or both were sinking or dismasted and the decks were slippery with the blood of sailors crushed by falling spars, torn open and dismembered by flying splinters, or shot by marksmen in platforms high up on the masts. Two such murderous matches ended in victory for the USS *Constellation.*

It all sounds rather modern: a businessman secretary of the navy skillfully building a big-fleet constituency, with victories in an undeclared war to back him. But then as now, "defense" could not be separated from sectional politics. Southern and western Republicans, though outnumbered, battled against growing navalism. Why, they clamored, should they pay to protect a commerce that only enriched the busy ports and shipyards of the northeastern (often referred to then as merely the "eastern") states? They were especially stung when the Federalists, in order to defray war expenses, authorized a heavy "direct tax" on houses and lands, the major source of southern and western wealth—a step that extended the resentment against the commercial "oligarchy" spurred by Hamilton's fiscal measures of 1790.

But while a big naval establishment was controversial mainly on the grounds of expense, plans for a European-sized land force struck a far deeper vein of resistance in the American mind, where standing armies and tyranny were often linked.

✴

AVID READERS of history, the Republican elite of the 1790s remembered that winning generals like Julius Caesar and Oliver Cromwell had easily made themselves dictators. In 1800 Napoleon would prove that the feat could still be accomplished in a modern age. (The Federalists read their own lessons from the past and saw all critics of their government as plotters like those who had from time to time threatened the Roman republic.) What was more, eighteenth-century regular troops were not the citizen-armies of the future. The officers were aristocrats whose loyalty was mainly to their own class, while the common soldiers were the sweepings of the underclass, brutalized first by the poverty from which they escaped by enlisting and then by floggings and other savage punishments to enforce discipline. Such rootless professional killers were mercenaries at the disposition of kings who wanted to snuff out opposition. "A Standing Army," wrote Sam Adams, John's rebellious cousin, "is always dangerous to the Liberties of the People."[25] The classic example, in his eyes, was the 1775 Boston "Massacre," a minor affair that his prose and Paul Revere's engraving worked into an indelible and exaggerated image of soldiers stiffly firing into an innocent crowd of freemen. Years later good Republicans were still outraged at the very idea of being "plundered and bullied by the very dregs and refuse of mankind, who are too lazy to apply themselves for an honest livelihood."[26]

For the Republicans, the Federalist effort to create an army in the spring of 1798 was one more sign of a desire to crush the liberties of the people, and therefore one more embittering partisan issue. But even for moderate Federalists who were calculating businessmen, the cost factor of a large military establishment was a serious drawback. A combination of votes from these two camps kept the preparedness bills of spring 1798 from enjoying the success of the naval buildup. What was first asked was a fifty-thousand-man "provisional army," a kind of inactive reserve, with officers and men given a few days' annual training but not mobilized and paid until actual wartime. Republicans saw even this as a trick to give central government more power and patronage in the form of commissions to award. Their solution was to authorize and help the states to train more militia. The myth of the minuteman springing to arms from the plow furrow remained strong in spite of the Revolutionary War's proof that in the long run professional leadership and training were necessary. The whole up-and-down history of United States military readiness is the result of political compromises trying to balance the need for a competent and ready army against the potential threat it poses to democracy. And in 1798 the debate sizzled. Federalists could only see Republican resistance as part of a plan to keep America disarmed before the "Jacobin" menace, and Republicans were certain that Federalists really wanted a large force in order, in the words of one of them, to confront not only "invaders of our country . . . [but] the turbulent and seditious insurgents . . . [the] daring infractors of the laws."[27] Finally, after three months of arguing and slashing, came passage of a bill for a "New Army" of twelve regiments of infantry of approximately a thousand each to be added to the four existing regiments, plus four of mounted "dragoons."

The new army of twelve thousand was still a long way from what Federalists believed would be necessary to take on a French force of thirty thousand. But that idea was preposterous to John Adams. Where would the French land them? How would they transport them from the

nearest French possessions, the West Indies? And, in Adams's formula-
tion, "What would thirty thousand men do here," far from any base, and
in a country bigger and stronger than the one France had helped from
1778 to 1781?[28] In autumn he told the secretary of war that "at present
there is no more prospect of seeing a French army here, than there is in
Heaven."[29]

Adams's antimilitarism pitted him against so-called High Federalists or Arch Federalists raging to declare war on France. It lined him up
instead with the midroaders for whom a firm diplomatic stance plus
"unofficial" naval battles with French ships were enough for the moment. Certainly one motive for his fear of a big army was his awareness
that the man whom his cabinet was pushing on him for the command
of it was Alexander Hamilton, in his eyes "the most restless, impatient,
artful, indefatigable and unprincipled intriguer in the United States if
not in the world."[30] Picking successful generals would be a hard problem at best—Adams remembered the days of the Revolution when
quarreling prima donnas in uniform scrambled for pay and rank, in his
words, "like apes for nuts." And Hamilton? When the name was put before him by Secretary McHenry, his immediate answer was, "Oh, no! It
is not his turn by a great deal."[31] But the last word was not his.

To forestall more pressure in favor of choosing Hamilton as commander in chief, Adams acted swiftly and surprisingly by sending to
Congress the name of George Washington for the post, even before he
had consulted him. It seemed a bold stroke, a nomination that no one
could possibly challenge. But now it was Adams who walked into a trap.
Washington was still greatly influenced by Hamilton and, what was
more, had in retirement become more of a Federalist. Hearing that
some Republicans were applying for commissions, he expressed doubt
about their sincerity, saying, "you could as soon scrub the blackamoor
white as to change the principles of a professed Democrat . . . [who] will
leave nothing unattempted to overturn the Government of this country."[32] So when Adams sent Secretary of War McHenry down to Mount
Vernon with a politically balanced list of potential new generals that included such Republican war veterans as Peter Mühlenberg and Aaron
Burr, Washington turned them down and made his own wishes explicit.

At sixty-six, he would not take the field except in case of actual invasion. But he would exercise overall command from Mount Vernon through his chosen subordinates, three new major generals—Alexander Hamilton, Charles Cotesworth Pinckney, and Henry Knox. Hamilton would be in the top spot with the additional title of inspector general and, as Washington's right-hand man, would be the de facto head of the great new army.

It was an arrangement that Washington and his onetime aide had discussed by letter, and it appalled Adams as well as Knox and Pinckney, both of whom, as generals in the Revolution, had far outranked Colonel Hamilton. The sitting president tried hard to get the former president to revise the order of his recommendations, and the former president, while politely and constitutionally conceding that the final authority was with his successor, refused to change his mind and hinted that he might resign if his wishes were ignored. Adams knew what a public-relations disaster that would be for his administration. He could not win a popularity contest with the nation's hero, much as he may have longed to escape from his shadow. He had unwisely kept Washington's cabinet by choice, and now he had to swallow Washington's protégé. He made the appointments as proposed, a political decision that would have long-range political results. Pinckney accepted his new commission, but Knox refused his, rather than serve under General Hamilton.

Hamilton put Pinckney in charge of the forces in the South and gave himself a double job as field commander of all the rest as well as inspector general, where his administrative talents were badly needed to help a floundering War Department. Secretary McHenry—Irish-born, genial, and totally loyal to Hamilton and Washington—fitted the description given him by a fellow delegate at the Constitutional Convention—"a man of specious talents with nothing of genius to improve them."[33] He was overwhelmed by the job of speedy mobilization, and as papers piled up on his desk during 1799 it was plain that the new army was not coming together. Camps were not ready, equipment was missing, clothing and provisions were not showing up at the right times and places. Working day and night, Hamilton improved the situation. But he had not given up his revived lucrative law practice and put his

old uniform back on merely in order to sit at a desk. He had more ambitious ideas.

Hamilton had caught the "throw-out-the-Spanish" fever. Like
Blount or Wilkinson (with whom he was in friendly contact), he was
thinking of an expedition to conquer Florida and Louisiana, possibly
with British help. There was actually a practical side to this fancy.
France might persuade or coerce Spain, who was now her ally, to turn
the two provinces over to her. Then there would be a place to land one
of those French armies that were terrifying Europe and launch it
against the United States. A preemptive seizure would check that
threat. Beyond that there was a possible goal consistent with Hamilton's expansive view of the American future. With Florida and New Orleans in hand, the United States would become a major power in the
Caribbean and perhaps be able to push southward and batter down the
trade barriers surrounding Spanish-owned Latin America. Hamilton
had even discussed such plans with an unsubstantial Venezuelan adventurer named Francisco Miranda, who was seeking support for a
scheme to liberate Spanish New World possessions.

And still beyond that prospect of a pan-American commercial empire there was possibly a personal hope of winning the military glory
that a poor, dependent West Indian orphan boy toiling as a clerk had
once craved. America might even be as grateful to General Hamilton
for his conquests as the French were to General Bonaparte, also born in
obscurity. There is no evidence that Hamilton had dictatorial expectations, but his enemies—especially John Adams—were always ready to
suspect him of the worst. Adams told Elbridge Gerry early in 1799 of
his belief that "Hamilton and a Party were endeavoring to get an army
on foot to give Hamilton the command of it & then to proclaim a Regal
Government, place Hamilton at the head of it & prepare the way for a
Province of Great Britain."[34] Years later he claimed that his reaction on
learning of Hamilton's proposed march against Louisiana was: "The
man is stark mad or I am."

Mad or sane, Hamilton was not in complete control. As a military officer, he needed a declaration of war to use the army for any part of his
plans. While a civilian in the spring 1798, he had bitterly hated revolu-

tionary France, but nonetheless he had not favored going beyond recommending (through McHenry) essentially defensive measures like
building up coastal fortifications. A year later, figuratively in the saddle
with sword drawn, he was eager for formal hostilities to start. But that
decision still belonged with the Congress and the president, who remained decidedly not in favor.

Politically, Adams sensed that the war fever was dying down. En-
listments were lagging, officerships were going vacant for lack of applicants. The Federalists had run into trouble in the 1798 congressional
elections thanks in part to antitax resentment. In southeastern Pennsylvania, in March 1799, an active tax-resistance movement led by John
Fries broke out among the usually orderly German inhabitants of Bucks
and Montgomery Counties. Fries led an armed group that compelled
federal officials to release some protesters they had arrested. He was in
turn pursued, captured, and tried for treason in a case not concluded
until 1800, which became part of that year's story.

For Adams these signals that peace was desirable were reinforced
by mounting evidence that it was possible. In the autumn of 1798 Gerry
finally returned from France and in a private conference explained his
late departure and described Talleyrand's change of heart toward the
United States. There was also a personal interview with Dr. George
Logan, a well-meaning Quaker conscientious objector, who traveled
from Philadelphia to Paris on his own to persuade the French government that Americans were a peace-loving folk who would react favorably to a softening of the war on their merchant marine. (That did, in
fact, take place. But an outraged Congress, in its next session, passed
the Logan Act, still in force, forbidding such private diplomatic efforts.)
Then there was information from a "back channel" of communication
that Talleyrand established through the United States embassy to the
Netherlands. The American representative there was a faithful Federalist, a soft-featured, thirty-eight-year-old Marylander named William
Vans Murray, son of a rich doctor who had sent him in 1784 to study law
in London, where he first met and admired his young country's ambassador, John Adams. Talleyrand ordered a French legation official to tell
Murray "unofficially" that if a new United States negotiator were sent

over, he would this time be greeted with "the respect due to a proud and free people." As expected, Murray passed the word to President Adams, who gave it the close attention that a letter from a friend of fourteen years' standing deserved.

Adams also had significant reports from his brilliant oldest son, John Quincy, whom he had appointed minister to Prussia over the Republicans' bitter protest of what they considered nepotism. John Quincy, already a veteran diplomat at thirty-one, described the shakeups inside the French government and the 1798 military setbacks that explained the peace feelers. Napoleon had taken an army to Egypt to attack the British lifeline to India, but it was cut off and stranded there when Admiral Horatio Nelson, in a major sea battle near Alexandria, destroyed all of the expedition's shipping. The best thing about the news from John Quincy and William Murray was the courier who brought it. This was the president's second son, Thomas Boylston. After five years of serving as official secretary to his older brother, Thomas came home on a January day in 1799, announcing his intention to stand on his own, stay in America, and practice law. Like any aging couple, John and Abigail were overjoyed to reclaim their handsome "boy" (of twenty-seven) after so long a separation, especially since Abigail had been deathly ill during the summer and never expected to see him again.

Finally there came a really important piece of "peace intelligence" in the form of a letter from General Washington, enclosing another written to him by Joel Barlow, a Connecticut Yankee living in Paris. Barlow, a part-time poet, part-time businessman, and full-time radical in an age where it was not impossible to be all three, was friendly to the French Revolution—actually had been awarded French citizenship, like Tom Paine—and had contacts in high places. He asked Washington to throw his weight behind one more effort to negotiate "before you draw your sword." It wasn't Barlow's word that impressed Adams—he had no respect for the "worthless" freethinker—but Washington's covering letter, in which he volunteered to answer Barlow if it would help in "restoring peace and tranquillity to the United States upon just, honorable and dignified terms," which was the "ardent desire" of all her friends.[35] Adams knew then that Washington, at least, would not oppose a new bid for peace, which would have created an impassable road-block.

On one hand, then, the network of Adams's personal and trans-Atlantic contacts was buzzing with signals in favor of another try at diplomacy. On the other hand was the certainty that it would produce an explosion among High Federalists, and that another failed mission would be a disaster. John Adams made his decision alone. On February 18, 1799, without consulting anyone in his cabinet, his party, or his family, he sent to the Senate a terse message: "I nominate William Vans Murray, our minister at the Hague, to be minister plenipotentiary of the United States to the French Republic." The president, at whatever risk, had come down on the side of a final try for peace.

Congress and the country were "thunderstruck." Never did the flinty, shadowy personality of blunt and brilliant John Adams display it-self so fully. Endless competing explanations would thereafter roll through the annals of biography. It was an impulsive decision to resolve Adams's own inner uncertainty, or a calculated step that followed Adams's consistent, balanced policy of firmness without rashness. It was a move that rose nobly above party expediency—or a gamble that the party would benefit from a shift toward peace in popular opinion. It was a sturdy expression of willingness to do what conscience dictated—or was merely the revenge of a bruised ego against Alexander Hamilton. All may be partly or entirely true, and none subtract from its unique example in the record of the presidency. Adams knew that. Years later he would express a wish to have his tombstone read: "Here lies John Adams who took upon himself the responsibility of peace with France in 1800."[36]

It was a move that spawned the expected tempest, which was probably enjoyed by Vice President Jefferson, presiding silently over the Senate. High Federalist reactions were frenzied. "Surprise, indignation, grief and disgust" were expressed, according to one of them. Another was convinced that it was an "embarrassing and ruinous measure," the product of "a vain, jealous and half frantic mind."[37] Adams was forced to enlarge the mission by the addition of two other Federalists, Governor William Davie of North Carolina and Connecticut's Oliver

Ellsworth, who had taken over as chief justice of the Supreme Court. But he stuck to his pacific intentions in spite of attempts by McHenry and Pickering at sabotage by delay. The two of them, plus Wolcott, continued to leak every inside move to Hamilton and to support his views rather than those of the chief executive who had appointed them. One example was Pickering's insurbordinate letter to Murray, the president's chosen peacemaker, which in effect told him not to follow through. Part of it read: "[N]egotiation for a treaty with a government so totally unprincipled, so shamelessly perfidious as that of France, would give us no security. . . . There will not be any safe treaty . . . until its government (not the tyrants who successively administer it) shall be changed."[38] Weeks dragged on without Pickering's drafting the instructions for the envoys.

Adams could play a waiting game himself, and as soon as Congress adjourned in March he took off for Peacefield, where he stayed for a full seven months, single-handedly conducting the official business of the presidency by mail each morning. Whether this was because of a sudden rush of uncertainty about the peace mission or because he was expecting even more cooling of the war fever was unclear. In any case his absence aggravated the two members of the cabinet—the attorney general and the secretary of the navy—who stood behind him and were left to fight alone, as well as other supporters needing decisions that only he could make. One of them wrote sharply: "The people elected you to administer the government. They did not elect your officers."[39] Finally, in October, Adams felt ready to come down to the capital, which was temporarily in Trenton, New Jersey, since Philadelphia was having still another outbreak of yellow jack. Whatever passed there between him and his official family, the orders were written and Ellsworth and Davie were told to sail by the month's end. The fight was over and Adams had won.

His satisfaction was greatly increased by a meeting with General Hamilton, who either had some business to transact with the secretary of war in Trenton or made some in order to get to the president. Only Adams's description survives. He claimed that he sat quietly smoking a cigar while Hamilton, seeing his hopes of conquering glory slipping away, pleaded with increasing agitation for at least a temporary suspen-

sion of the mission. Frantically (according to Adams) he predicted that
the French government would soon be replaced by a restored monarchy, which was sure to take offense at American dealings with the as-
sasins of the Revolution. It was only common sense to wait and see.
"Never did I hear a man talk more like a fool,"[40] was Adams's retrospective judgment on his emotionally battered adversary. The tables
were turned. A year earlier General Washington had forced Hamilton
on Adams. Now Hamilton had to beg Adams, whom he had tried in
1796 to do out of the presidency, to save his hopes from wreckage. But
Adams's satisfaction carried a price tag. When Hamilton walked out of
the conference, defeated but still a mighty power in federalism, his
mind was almost surely made up that at all costs he would keep Adams
from winning reelection the following year.

Two men who had together helped create a free United States now
faced each other across a deep gulf of hate. The Revolutionary War era
was passing. On December 14, 1799, it lost its most cherished figure. Two
days earlier General Washington returned from a horseback ride in a
snowstorm and developed a severe sore throat. Not yet sixty-eight, he was
still a vigorous outdoorsman, but it took his ignorant eighteenth-century
doctors less than forty-eight hours to bleed and dose him to death. For a
brief moment politics stood in suspension as the nation mourned its unifying "Father." Then John Adams's stormy presidency headed into a new
year and century. Already Federalist Rufus King, of the prowar faction,
had predicted that if Adams should "temporize," then "the next Election
will convulse the Country, and may . . . deliver it to the same ruin that con-
tinues to desolate Europe."[41] Now the "next Election" was at hand.

The domestic impact of the three-year war crisis had been excruciating, too. It had produced America's first "Red scare," then a blatant
trampling over a First Amendment on which the ink was hardly dry, and
then a counterblast from the South that held the first, dark anticipations
of secession. There was good reason to worry about a prospect of "the
same ruin" that had overtaken France.

CHAPTER 11

Gagging the Press,
1798

AMONG THE MANY THINGS that made the election of 1800 a crucial moment of national definition, there was one towering circumstance that set it apart from the three that preceded it and the fifty that followed in the next two centuries. It was the only election conducted while there was a law on the books that could and did put men in jail for criticizing the sitting president, who was one of the candidates. And it was a law that some of the men who had made the Constitution thought was overdue.

The Sedition Act of June 1798 (and its companion statute making it easy for the president to deport aliens he found undesirable) has drawn the fire of historians ever since as a gigantic stroke of partisan overkill by Federalists trying, in the heat of a war scare, to muzzle the opposition. But even allowing for a healthy measure of truth in the charge, critical hindsight fails the test of perspective—of seeing how things might have looked in 1798 to Federalist voters and lawmakers. For them the First Amendment, only ten years old, had not yet taken on its semisacred character. They saw a world ablaze with "destructive" democratic ideas, which few people had any notion would become commonplace in another couple of generations. And the Republican press was not entirely an innocent victim of legislative mugging. Readers and viewers of the year 2000 outraged by the slither of political debate into a cesspool of "negative" and "attack" ads may find it almost reassuring news that two hundred years ago campaign tactics were not a bit purer.

The main vehicle of political discourse ten years after the relatively decorous—and secret—debates in the Constitutional Convention had become the printing press. Conditions were still not ripe for large-scale political rallies, so what candidates and their advocates had to say was said in pamphlets and, increasingly, in newspapers. Those papers were the private and exclusive property of colorful egotists who called themselves not editors or publishers but printers, as they were. They wrote their own copy and for the most part helped to set and print it with their own inky hands. They operated from shops attached to their homes; their presses and workrooms were visible from the street; and their windows were cluttered with specimens of job printing, books, and stationery for sale. Journalism was a small-scale and personal business.

It was also a growing and risky one. The number of newspapers had jumped from the ninety or so of 1789 to around two hundred in 1800. But of those, only twenty-eight were survivors of the 1789 ranks. It took very little money to acquire a press and put out a few hundred weekly copies—dailies were a scarce big-town novelty—but the earnings were proportionally tiny and uncertain. The papers were sold only by subscription and usually on credit. The advertisers whose label-sized "notices" marched in rows up and down the front and back pages also were allowed credit. In far too many cases, payment never came and the journal expired. The city papers that did succeed, however, had considerable influence, thanks to those who read the copies supplied by public eating and drinking places, and also to cheap postage. They were carried throughout the states, and their contents copied as "exchanges" by country journals.

Perhaps the very fact that a newspaper was so much of a gamble attracted especially adventurous owners given to loud and passionate opinions. Or perhaps intemperate language was a simple fact of life in young America. In the early nineteenth century one British traveler would write a familiar-sounding complaint that "[d]efamation exists all over the world, but it is incredible to what extent this vice is carried in America." Another would add that the "war of politics seems not the contest of opinion supported by . . . enlightened argument . . . but the squabble of greedy and abusive partisans, appealing to the vilest passions . . . and utterly unscrupulous as to their means of attack."[1] Those might simply be passed off as stuffy upper-class judgments on a robust democratic society and a wide-open and therefore self-correcting marketplace of ideas. Back in 1798, however, when the makers and the readers of newspapers were in live daily contact, printed insults were nothing to be taken for granted. They could and did bring on fistfights, beatings, duels, and riots. And with party feelings at the boiling point, uncivil discourse might even possibly stoke the fires of civil war. The journalism of the capital city was a good example, as the careers of several of Philadelphia's most notorious press warriors showed. Three would run afoul of sedition laws, one would be driven from business by a libel suit, and all of them would help to create an atmosphere that produced the bitterly contested attempt to shackle the press that colored the approaching 1800 campaign.

There was, first, Benjamin Franklin Bache (pronounced "Beech"), named for his illustrious grandfather. Bache inherited the unofficial post of principal Republican printer after Philip Freneau abandoned the *National Gazette* and fled from the yellow fever epidemic of 1793. From a personal viewpoint Freneau's decision was a smart one. He lived on to be eighty, whereas the returning yellow jack would kill his old rival John Fenno, of the *United States Gazette,* in 1798. From a political point of view, however, the folding of Freneau's paper left a vacuum that Bache filled with a journal he had begun when he received a small legacy in 1790, the Philadelphia *General Advertiser.* In 1794 he added the name *Aurora,* by which it soon became notorious.

Born in 1769 to Franklin's only daughter, Sarah, and her businessman husband, eight-year-old "Benny" was taken along on Franklin's dangerous 1777 trip to Paris to win support for the American revolutionaries. His parents seem to have been merely spectators of his education, which Franklin supervised as carefully as if the youngster had been his son. There was boarding school in France; then more board-

ing school in Geneva for a contrasting taste of life in a Protestant republic; then private training as a printer and typecaster; finally, return
home at age fourteen for "finishing" at the University of Pennsylvania,
which focused on modern languages, geography, science, and economics rather than the traditional classical curriculum. As chief architect of
this model practical upbringing, Franklin provided Bache with plenty
of good advice, primarily by letters. The young man's hunger for personal affection was warmly satisfied by his happy marriage for love, at
age twenty-one, to Margaret Markoe. Peggy, as she was known, was the
daughter of a deceased sugar planter in the Danish West Indies and
stepdaughter of a well-known Philadelphia physician, so the young
couple fitted well into Philadelphia's cosmopolitan elite of established
families.

Bache's passionate nature and French education quickly enrolled
him among the Republican radicals supporting the whiskey rebels, Citizen Genet, and France's embattled regimes in general. He opened the
Aurora's pages to fellow Republican sympathizers like Jefferson, Madison, Gallatin, and John Beckley as well as to émigrés like the English
radicals Thomas Cooper and Joseph Priestley, run out of their homeland
during a clampdown on dissent inspired by Britain's war against Jacobins. It was that very attempt of reactionary Europe to crush the
French Revolution and France's answering crusade to spread her gospel
everywhere that really radicalized Bache. It brought out a messianic and
pugnacious streak, which grandfather Franklin, a rebel but a prudent
one, would hardly have recognized. "Consider what the prospect por-
tends!" Bache wrote in the summer of '93. "The associating of the
champions of Liberty against the conspiring supporters of despotism . . .
in various quarters of the globe . . . now strike the mind as approaching
CONVULSIONS OF THE WORLD."[2] Outbreaks of unrest in Rus-
sian-occupied Poland, British-controlled India, in Ireland and Canada all
showed that freedom was on the march everywhere, falling in line behind America and France. The future would be theirs.

But to Bache the most powerful oligarchy blocking the path to that
better world was Great Britain, and to his horror the Federalists in the
United States had become her minions. For that reason, the Jay Treaty,

devised by "the wicked arts of Britain to entrap us into an . . . alliance, . . . [and] the tame surrender of Republican freedom at the feet of Aristocracy & Kingly pageantry," drove him nearly mad,[3] at least in his editorial role.

His writing became more strident, more embittered, and more personally aimed—even at the untouchable General Washington, who had signed the infamous pact, showing his "most pointed contempt" for the will of the people. "Louis XVI, in the meridian of his power," Bache cried out in print, "never treated his subjects with as much insult." The performance better fitted "the omnipotent director of a seraglio" than "the first magistrate of a free people." The president had revealed a "new character," which should "shake off the fetters that his name has hitherto imposed." The years of Washington's stewardship had been "a series of errors or of crimes,"[4] which the *Aurora* went on month after month to particularize, not omitting retrospective glances at the general's entire career that produced withering accusations. Washington had callously killed a French officer under a flag of truce in the French and Indian War. He had been slow to renounce loyalty to King George. He was inept as a battlefield commander, and it was really thanks to France's help that independence had been won.[5]

Washington, whose residence was only a block and a half away from the *Aurora* office, was denounced as a hypocrite who spoke of liberty and held slaves (a criticism that Bache did not apply to southern Republicans like Jefferson). His ceremonious presidential style had been merely the "apish mockery of Kingship."[6] A series of columns by "a Calm Observer," who was most probably the inexhaustible Beckley, charged that the president had overdrawn his salary from the Treasury by a considerable sum. "Will not the world be led to conclude," asked Calm Observer, "that the mask of political hypocrisy has been alike worn by a CAESAR, a CROMWELL and a WASHINGTON?"[7] And when the Father of His Country, stung by the loss of his previous immunity from criticism, passed up a third term and delivered his final address to Congress, Bache, unrelenting, described the outgoing administration as tainted with "dishonor, injustice, treachery, meanness and perfidy" and issued an oft quoted valedictory: "If ever a nation was debauched by a man, the American nation has been debauched by WASHINGTON. If ever a nation was deceived by a man, the American nation has been deceived by WASHINGTON. Let his conduct be an example to future ages . . . a warning that no man may be an idol."[8]

Washington made no public answer that would bring him to the level of a malicious scribbler who, as he told a private correspondent, "has . . . celebrity in a certain way, for his Calumnies are to be exceeded only by his Impudence, and both stand unrivalled."[9] But among his inner circle he reacted explosively to being flayed in terms that "could scarcely be applied to a Nero, to a notorious defaulter, or even to a common pickpocket." Jefferson (who was a friend of Bache) once saw the poker-faced president glance at a copy of the *Aurora* and then slam it to the floor with a fervent "Damn!"[10]

John Adams got off more easily at first, but as his military buildup proceeded during 1797, Bache turned his guns on "old, bald, blind, querulous, toothless crippled John Adams" as well.[11] Adams never shook off the conviction that Bache was simply carrying on a feud between grandfather Franklin and himself that had started when both were in Paris twenty years earlier. Bache ranted that Adams, in naming thirty-year-old John Quincy minister to Prussia, was trying "to provide handsomely for his son, especially . . . at public expense . . . an appointment repugnant to every idea of propriety."[12] What could be expected of "JOHN ADAMS . . . [who] would deprive you of a voice in choosing your president and senate, and make both hereditary?"[13]

And Adams's naval-enlargement program? What was it but a scheme to enrich contractors and buy the votes of their employees? That particular line of attack earned Bache a drubbing. In April he went down to the Delaware riverside shipyard owned by the builder and naval architect Joshua Humphreys for a look at the unfinished frigate the *United States*. Humphreys's son Clement saw him standing on the deck and ran over and delivered a set of sharp raps on the head with a cane or a piece of wood. Bache managed to win a court judgment of fifty dollars for the assault nine months later, and he kept on his prickly course.

More than once in 1798 stone-throwing crowds shattered his shop windows. In August, while walking on the street with John Beckley,

Bache was attacked again, this time by the son of John Fenno, whom the *Aurora* had called "the dirty tool of a dirty faction" and a man who cheated his creditors and took cash payments for attacks on Vice President Jefferson.[14] Fists flew, Fenno bit Bache's finger, and Bache whacked him with a cane. After bystanders separated them, both young men retired to their respective offices and wrote their versions of the battle, each accusing the other of cowardly retreat.

By the summer of 1798 Bache, sometimes referred to as "Lightning-Rod Junior," was already a public enemy from the Federalist point of view. So was one of his *Aurora* collaborators, William Duane. Nearing middle age and recently bereft of his wife by cholera, Duane was a radical Irishman, only recently landed in the United States. He had, for two years, been scraping together a living by assisting various Philadelphia editors, Bache included. His pieces for them flashed a vivid style that owed more to the lively chatter of ordinary people than to classical sources. Duane was actually born near Lake Champlain on New York's colonial frontier but was taken home to Ireland as a child after his father was killed fighting Indians. He was a natural rebel. On reaching manhood he married a Protestant woman, flouting the expectations of his mother, who promptly disinherited him. Learning the printer's trade, he headed next to Calcutta and began a newspaper, the *Indian World*. It was free in its criticism of the East India Company, the de facto corporate ruler of India at the time, and in short order Duane was arrested, his press and other property were confiscated, and he was deported back to England. There he became a reporter of parliamentary debates. But the political climate was not hospitable for an outspoken troublemaker suspected of pro-French sympathies and Irish nationalism. So in 1796 he took a ship to America, already the haven of all restless challengers to order. He would soon add the Federalists to a list of enemies that already included the Catholic church, the East India Company, and the British government.

Bache and Duane both sincerely hated monarchy on principle. There was no discernible principle in James Callender, whose work also appeared from time to time in the *Aurora* but whom both Bache and Duane later disowned. Duane would claim in fact that they briefly hired Callender in 1798 only to keep him from being bought as a propagandist by the British minister Robert Liston—though at the time Callender was counted among Republican propagandists for having forced Hamilton's adultery scandal into the open. Callender was a Scot from Edinburgh, born in 1758, who had acquired enough education to become a vigorous writer. In 1793 he showed his skill in an antigovernment pamphlet that landed him in a king's court, charged with sedition. He fled to America and began to cover congressional debates. Like any refugee from royal tyranny, he was automatically befriended by Madison and Jefferson. Feeding a wife, four children, and a heavy drinking habit kept Callender chronically broke. From time to time he was given small sums of money by Jefferson. Jefferson described these as charitable handouts, but Callender believed them, possibly with some reason, to be payments for personal mudslinging at Hamilton and other Federalists. Callender would probably have remained unnoticed by history except for two things. First, he became a target of the Sedition Act, and second, he ungratefully turned on Jefferson and was the first to put in print the rumor that Jefferson kept one of his slaves, Sally Hemings, as a mistress and by her had fathered "several children," including a son who greatly resembled him.[15] This came to pass after 1800 and was a part of the surprising aftermath of the election.

If calling Washington a thief, Hamilton a seducer, and Adams a senile warmonger and monarchist was acceptable Republican journalism of the 1790s, Federalist standards were not any higher. Bache's best-known rival, for example, was not the veteran Federalist insider Fenno but still another immigrant newcomer, William Cobbett. Shrill and merciless, he further illustrated the rowdy aspect of a free press in times of wrath and revolution. A red-faced six-footer, Cobbett was a self-tutored English farm boy who had fled rural poverty to become a clerk in London, then joined the army. He served eight years, some of them overseas in Canada, and in that harsh environment he won his way up to the rank of sergeant major, which carried heavy responsibilities while the credit went to titled junior officers. Back in England Cobbett quit the service and brought court-martial charges against some of those officers whom he had caught swindling. He lost but then made his case in a mutinous

pamphlet, *The Soldier's Friend,* so intemperate in its attacks on the military hierarchy that in 1792 he had to run first to France and then to the
United States. He was still only thirty. He settled in Wilmington,
Delaware, and initially earned his scanty bread as a teacher and French
translator but was soon sucked into pamphleteering again—surprisingly, for the Federalists.

Cobbett's antiestablishment and populist rage should normally have
lined him up with the Jeffersonians. He had "imbibed principles of republicanism" in his reading, but in real-life contact bumptious Americans rubbed him the wrong way and pushed him toward the high
conservatism of England's Tory party. As he explained it, when given
an actual "opportunity of *seeing* what republican government was," he
found himself "under a set of petty, mean despots ruling by a perver-
sion of the laws of England."[16] His political tracts turned into Tory
broadsides over the well-chosen signature of "Peter Porcupine," whose
quills were decidedly sharp, since Cobbett's gift for invective was
matchless. In March 1797 he started his Philadelphia daily, *Porcupine's
Gazette,* with a booming declaration of war in an open letter to Bache. "I
assert that you are a liar and an infamous scoundrel," it began. "Do you
dread the effects of my paper? . . . You will get nothing by me in a war
of words, and . . . may as well abandon the contest while you can do it
with good grace. . . . I am getting up in the world, and you are going
down. [F]or this reason it is that you hate me and that I despise you."
The feud would go on, Cobbett warned, "till death snatches one or the
other of us from the scene."[17]

Porcupine's Gazette quickly became popular, and hardly a day passed
by in which the two Federalist papers in town did not launch new
salvos at Bache. Fenno had the advantage of official subsidy through
printing contracts, but page for page, Cobbett was more colorful and
stinging. One typical attack described his rival as "the notorious Jacobin
BACHE, editor of the *Aurora,* Printer to the French Directory, General
of the Principles of Insurrection, Anarchy and confusion; the greatest
fool and most stubborn sans culotte [i.e., lower-class Frenchman] in the
United States." Another declared that "all the world knows and says he
is a liar; a fallen wretch; a vessel formed for reprobation; and therefore

we should always treat him as we would a TURK, a JEW, a JACOBIN or a DOG," all four being equal in Cobbett's view. Still another commented that any reasonable defense of the government was certain to awaken Bache's disapproval and "excite the corrosion that is destroying his malignant heart, where envy, baseness, and every passion which render a mortal detestable . . . have fixed their abode."[18] So it went, on and on, without truce or abatement either for Bache or for any of the administration's other enemies. The Republicans in general were "a hardened and impious faction whose destructive principles . . . [might] one day render the annals of America as disgraceful as those of the French revolution." The Whiskey Rebellion was "paid for with French gold." Defenders of democracy were "a sort of flesh flies that naturally settle on the excremental and corrupted parts of the body politic."[19]

Other Federalist papers, like the *Commercial Advertiser* in New York (run by Noah Webster of dictionary fame) or the *Columbian Centinel* of Boston, reprinted these blasts and originated plenty of their own. Republican printers in other major cities answered in kind. Combat was not confined to the nation's capital, where, then as now, politics was the local industry and preoccupation. In every population center, editorial practices between 1798 and 1800 were setting passions on fire. It was in that glare, rather than in political science or philosophy classrooms, that the issue of press freedom would be fought out in the election to come. Both sides had their provocative incendiaries. But in June and July of 1798 it was the Federalists who had the presidency and the congressional majority, and they struck first and hard. The opening salvo, however, was aimed not at printers but at immigrants.

✷

"I DO NOT WISH to invite hordes of wild Irishmen, nor the turbulent and disorderly of all parts of the world, to come here with a view to disturb our tranquillity, after having succeeded in the overthrow of their own governments."[20] So spoke Harrison Gray Otis, who was first in his Harvard graduating class of 1783 and had evolved by the summer of 1798 into a rich Boston barrister, investor, social role model, and member of the House of Representatives. Federalists like him were intrin-

sically suspicious of the thousands of foreigners—"hordes of ruffians . . .
[and] revolutionary vermin"[21] in a newspaper's less elegant phrasing—
whom war and political turmoil had washed ashore on American soil.
Many of these were French and indiscriminately labeled "Jacobins,"
though the majority of them were expropriated refugees from the Paris
guillotine or the black revolts in Santo Domingo. But it was the "wild
Irishmen" driven here by poverty and hatred of England whom American conservatives most feared.

In May and June of 1798 there was an actual (though quickly defeated) uprising on Irish soil aided by a French landing force. It was the
conservatives' nightmare scenario for America—and two of the leaders,
Theobald Wolfe Tone and James Napper Tandy, had spent brief peri-
ods in the United States. But there was a more imminent threat from
the Federalist point of view, namely, that American Irishmen might
take power nonviolently through the ballot box by voting the "pro-
French" Republican ticket. So the first thing Federalists chose to do to
capitalize on their sudden surge of post–XYZ affair popularity was to reduce the pool of Republican voters by making it harder for new arrivals
to become eligible.

That was the force behind a Naturalization Act passed on June 18.
It revised a three-year-old statute that let an immigrant become a naturalized citizen after just five years' residence, with a three-year wait between the declaration of intent and final papers. Now the residence
period was boosted to fourteen years, with a five-year waiting period.
The act was a very limited victory, however. It sent thousands of resident aliens rushing to register under the old system before it expired,
and besides that, the states could, in 1798, make their own, more liberal
rules for naturalizing state citizens, who at that time automatically then
became United States citizens as well. (The practice stood until the
Fourteenth Amendment in 1866, which made United States citizenship automatically confer state citizenship as well.)

In addition, the Naturalization Act passed by only one vote in each
house, because pragmatic Federalists interested in wooing newcomers
joined Republicans in resisting it They also succeeded in defeating a
proposed constitutional amendment sponsored by Harrison Gray Otis

that would have barred voting and officeholding to all but the native-born. High Federalists like Otis were purists who scorned to cultivate voters or behave like a party at all. Government belonged in the hands of the wise and virtuous, and *any* organized "factional" challenge to it was simply subversion by another name.

Subversion was the prime target of the two other laws affecting aliens that passed in the period of maximum tension with France. One was the very severe Alien Enemies Act of July 6, which allowed the president to take measures for apprehending, restraining, or deporting citizens or subjects of a hostile nation during an invasion or a declared war. Never invoked at the time because there was no such declaration, it is still the basis of America's treatment of enemy aliens during an official state of war. But the Act Concerning Aliens of June 25 was operative immediately. It was passed under cover of the argument that mighty France, the toppler of little European republics like Holland, Switzerland, and Venice, might be preparing the same fate for America and had a peacetime corps of agents in the United States—in twentieth-century terms a fifth column—ready to do its work.

The act gave the president the right to expel any foreign-born resident not yet naturalized whom he considered "dangerous to the peace and safety of the United States" without specific charges or a judicial hearing. An alien caught in the country after being ordered out could be jailed for up to three years and permanently barred from future citizenship. If he sneaked back in after expulsion and was caught, he could be imprisoned for as long as the president thought it necessary to the public's safety. As originally passed by the Senate the sentence was hard labor for life. Another surveillance provision, later dropped, required Americans to report to federal authorities any visit to their homes, however short—say, for a dinner party—by a foreigner. Vice President Jefferson, forced to watch the debates in powerless silence from his high-backed red presiding officer's chair, privately called this Senate version "worthy of the eighth or ninth century."[22] On the other hand, ex-President Washington, no longer Jefferson's friend, was of the opinion that a law was needed because aliens "in many instances are sent among us . . . for the express purpose of poisoning the minds of our people and to sow dissensions among them . . . thereby endeavoring to dissolve the union."[23] Yet the Union could be in peril in more than one way. When the amended bill passed the House, the opposition votes were almost completely southern and the support overwhelmingly from New England. That showed a further coinciding of party and sectional lines more threatening to unity than any foreign conspiracy. Jefferson was even ready to try making Virginia a defiant refuge for victims of the measure.

Potentially dictatorial as it was, the Alien Act was never actually enforced against anyone. Adams was reluctant to use it and only authorized proceedings against one man, a refugee French general, Victor Collot, who managed to hide out from arresting officers until finally allowed to leave peacefully on his own in 1800. Still, framers of the act probably expected the mere threat of deportation to silence radicals in the community of immigrant intellectuals like the French historian Constantin Volney, or Joseph Priestley, the "discoverer" of oxygen, living on a Pennsylvania farm after his flight from England. In particular, the Federalists were after pro-French journalists of foreign birth like Callender. But Callender took the escape hatch of naturalization, and of course, antialien legislation was not an available weapon against native-born writers like Bache.

To get at such agitators there was the Sedition Act, signed by President Adams on July 14, coincidentally the ninth anniversary of the storming of the Bastille, which was the actual beginning of the French Revolution. Whereas antialien laws could technically be defended by the Federalists as justifiable on national security grounds, this last of the "emergency" measures was the one that most seemed to support the complaint of a Republican congressman that the Federalists were trying to "excite a fervor against foreign aggression only to establish tyranny at home."[24] As first introduced by a Maryland senator, its intentions were savage and would have named France an enemy nation and executed anyone guilty of expressions that might provide her aid and comfort. Those provisions fell by the wayside, but the Senate, where Federalists held twenty votes of thirty-two, left intact a catchall definition of "seditious libel." A person who in speech, printing, or writing circulated an opinion *"tending to induce a belief* . . . that the government, in enacting a law, was induced to do so by motives hostile to the Constitution, or the liberties and happiness of the people," could be tried and, if convicted, thrown in jail for up to five years and fined as much as five thousand dollars, a huge sum in 1798. Other punishable offenses were statements "tending to justify the hostile conduct of the French government" and attempts to defame the president and other federal officials by "declarations *directly or indirectly tending* to criminate [*sic*] their motives in any official transaction."[25]

The House, despite a 58–48 Federalist edge, could not swallow this wholesale ban on almost any criticism. To get the bill through, some safeguards had to be added. The prosecution would have to prove that the offending statement was maliciously intended. The truth of the allegation (which in English law at the time made no difference) could be offered as a defense. And the jury, properly instructed, could decide whether the law had actually been violated, instead of being confined to the facts alone. Even with these liberalizing provisions, the act was passed by only three votes, 44–41, and was ticketed to expire automatically on March 3, 1801.

Even in that diluted form it clearly made the First Amendment a dead letter and was seen by Jefferson—who called the whole period a "reign of witches"[26]—as a further step on a dark road to absolutism, already marked by the milestones of a big army and high taxes. Now came an experiment in censorship. "If this goes down," he wrote in November to his Virginia friend John Taylor, "we shall immediately see attempted another act of Congress, declaring that the President shall continue in office for life."[27] It was a fear that propelled his crucial political moves that fall.

✳

REPUBLICAN SUSPICIONS of the Sedition Act's long-range purposes were made more plausible by the actions of secretary of state Pickering, who became the chief enforcer. He hunted for Jacobin heresies in each day's papers with Javert-like zeal, and he expected United States district attorneys to do likewise. Merely to doubt the wisdom of the Sedition Act itself was ground for suspicion. "Those who complain of legal provisions for punishing intentional defamation and lies as bridling the liberty of speech and of the press," Pickering stated, "may with equal propriety complain against laws made for punishing assault and murder as restraints upon the freedom of men's actions."[28] Objection to being muzzled marked an editor as dangerous to society.

The actual impact of the first crusade against free speech was unimpressive. Like later outbursts of repression in American history, it caused some real suffering, but its long-term effect on public opinion was murky. Over time American sympathy for France did dry up, but that had more to do with the collapse of the Revolution into Napoleonic dictatorship and empire than with the scare tactics of Sedition Act prosecutors. And in the short run the political results for Federalists in 1800 were negative. They painted themselves as disinterested public servants fighting against the divisiveness of parties. But when all the victims turned out to be Republicans, despite the fact that many Federalist spokesmen also freely scolded President Adams for not being warlike enough, the law's defenders looked like partisan bullies and drove even more voters to think Republican. The warning of a dubious Alexander Hamilton that "if we push things to an extreme we shall . . . give to faction *body* and solidity" proved true.[29]

The actual trials ranged from the silly to the solemn and created a roster of martyrs. One of the former involved Luther Baldwin, who was drinking with a friend in a Newark, New Jersey, tavern when John Adams passed through town on the way to Quincy and was given a cannon salute by local militia. "There goes the president," said Baldwin's companion; "they are firing at his ass." Baldwin, described as "a little merry," answered that he did not care "if they fired through his ass." Tried under common law by the state, he got off with a hundred-dollar fine and no jail time.[30]

The trial of Representative Matthew Lyon, on the other hand, was unmistakably political. Lyon was an Irishman who had worked his way up from an immigrant indentured-servant boy to a Vermont landowner, become clubby with the best families in the state, and married the governor's daughter. In local politics, however, he was loud in defense of "the people" against the "aristocrats"—making him exactly the kind of self-made American democrat able to rise in an open and changing society such as the Federalists feared would be destabilizing. Lyon had recently escaped being tossed out of Congress for spitting on Representative Griswold without losing his combativeness. Back home between sessions (where congressional immunity did not apply), he published in his paper, the *Farmer's Library,* a letter accusing Adams of a "continual grasp for power . . . [and] an unbounded thirst for ridiculous pomp" and suggesting that he should be in a madhouse.[31] His punishment was more severe than Baldwin's—four months in jail and a thousand dollar fine. But his jailers handed him a martyr's crown. Congressman or not, he was clapped in midwinter into an unheated cell exposed to the elements and served by a reeking open toilet—ordinary eighteenth-century conditions for the low-life felons with whom he shared these quarters. Admiring Republicans in Vermont and Virginia raised the money to pay his fine. Virginia's Senator Stevens T. Mason personally rode all the way north with collected cash in his saddlebags, and Lyon's return to his House seat was triumphantly celebrated in Philadelphia. What was more, he ran for reelection in December while still behind bars and swamped his opponent by two thousand votes.

Other prosecutions were equally counterproductive. In September 1799 an indictment was brought against Jedidiah Peck, a New York assemblyman from upstate Otsego County. His offense was circulating a petition calling for repeal of the Alien and Sedition Acts. Peck was taken to New York City for trial, and at each stop in the five-day trip the sight of him, manacled and in the custody of a federal marshal, sparked anti-Federalist demonstrations. His case was dropped in 1800, and he was easily reelected to his seat.

Unsurprisingly, given the tenor of the political rhetoric in the press, three journalists, all from New England, would run afoul of the censors. Thomas Adams, of Boston's *Independent Chronicle,* was indicted by a Massachusetts court for "libeling" members of the state legislature by criticism. (State libel and sedition laws, often more severe than the national statute and especially so when administered by Federalist judges, were also a threat to the outspoken.) Thomas Adams died of illness before being brought to trial, but Abijah Adams, who was merely his brother's bookkeeper, got a month in jail. The presiding justice in the case, in his charge to the jury, took the opportunity to denounce Jacobins and their friends in America, who were "worse than infidels" and helpers in "a traitorous enterprise." Anthony Haswell ran the *Vermont Gazette* and opened its pages to reprints from the *Aurora* and appeals for funds to pay Matthew Lyon's fine. For that he himself was given jail time and a fine—two months and two hundred dollars. Charles Holt edited the New Haven *Bee*, and among his 1799 targets was the army mobilizing under the command of Alexander Hamilton. "Are our young officers and soldiers to learn virtue from General Hamilton?" asked Holt. "Or, like their generals are they to be found in the bed of adultery?" For this and other disdainful views of the armed forces, Holt was indicted in October as a "wicked, malicious, seditious and ill-disposed person," and eventually he got six months of prison time and a two-hundred-dollar fine. The punishments of Adams, Haswell, and Holt all occurred in the spring of 1800 and were successful campaign issues for local Republicans, while their papers continued, unterrified, to secure Jeffersonian beachheads in Federalist New England.[32]

The case of David Brown began as rowdy low comedy but had a brutal outcome. In Dedham, Massachusetts, a liberty pole appeared one morning in March. From it hung a placard: NO STAMP ACT, NO SEDITION AND NO ALIEN ACTS . . . DOWNFALL TO THE TYRANTS OF AMERICA; PEACE AND RETIREMENT TO THE PRESIDENT: LONG LIVE THE VICE PRESIDENT AND THE MINORITY. Outraged Federalists gathered and managed, after a mêlée with local Republicans, to chop it down. It was soon learned that the symbol was the work of Brown, ex-sailor, ex-Revolutionary War soldier, self-described European traveler, and conductor of hundreds of interviews to gauge public opinion in Massachusetts, a man who preached politics to local crowds, gave readings from his own pamphlets, and lived on whatever handouts he could collect in return. Brown believed that "the occupation of government is to plunder and steal" and that the entire federal (and Federalist) establishment in Philadelphia was "a tyrannic association of about five hundred out of five millions" for the purpose of grabbing the public's money.[33] He was obviously a kind of down-at-heels village anarchist, but he was in the wrong village, for Dedham was the home of High Federalist Fisher Ames (though also of his arch-Republican brother, Nathaniel, to show how politics was even invading the family circle), and Ames's friends soon saw to it that Brown was arrested. His case came up in June before the Circuit Court of the United States, and once again his luck was bad, because the man on the bench was Marylander Samuel Chase of the United States Supreme Court. (At that time Supreme Court justices traveled the "circuit" of federal judicial districts to try cases outside the capital.)

Chase had no sense of humor or proportion where a suspected Jacobin was concerned. He was in his late fifties and had left a trail of controversy behind him in his passage through law, politics, and the marketplace, starting when he was a young attorney, rioting with his fellow Sons of Liberty against the Stamp Act and was denounced by the mayor of his native Annapolis as "a foul mouthed and inflaming son of discord." He was a signer of the Declaration of Independence but in 1778 fell into disgrace by using privileged information obtained as a member of the Continental Congress to attempt a killing in the flour market. More failed business ventures followed. Then Chase returned to his legal career and switched over to the Federalist side. Washington named him to the high court in 1796 on the advice of Secretary McHenry that he was less dangerous inside the fold than out.

In his new status as a youthful radical turned into a reactionary elder, Chase had stated: "There is nothing we should more dread than the licentiousness of the press." It was a "certain means of bringing about the destruction of the government."[34] He made a frightening figure on the bench—full-bodied and tall, with a heavy thatch of white hair and a brownish complexion that earned him the name of "Bacon Face." Poor Brown was in fact awed, and switched his plea from not guilty to guilty, hoping to avoid irritating the judge by averting a parade of witnesses who would repeat his inflammatory words. Chase called them to testify anyway, to determine the "degree" of guilt. At sentencing time Brown pleaded repentance. Chase then pounced on the culprit and asked him, in that case, to prove it by naming names. Who had helped him? Brown, aghast, refused to answer, explaining, "I shall lose all my friends." Thereupon Chase handed down the heaviest punishment laid on any violator of the Sedition Act, a fine of $450—five to ten times the yearly cash income of a farm family—and a full eighteen months in prison. Brown seems to have compounded his guilt in Chase's eyes by being of the wrong class. When an accessory actually was unearthed and convicted, a wealthy farmer and town official named John Fairbanks, Chase took *his* expressed remorse into account and gave him a mere six hours imprisonment and a five-dollar fine.[35]

Chase would preside with equal notoriety over two other Sedition Act trials, those of Pennsylvania editor Thomas Cooper and of James Callender, neither of which reached the courtroom until 1800. These two were among the biggest fish prosecutors netted. Three who got away included John D. Burk, the Irish-born editor of the New York *Time Piece*, brought to book for invoking his readers' "*derision and contempt*" for the president.[36] Aaron Burr put up his bail and suggested a compromise—that Burk be allowed voluntary departure from the country. On getting permission, Burk instead went into hiding in Virginia as a "college principal." (He surfaced again in a few years as an alleged adulterer and was later killed in a duel provoked by a tavern insult.)

Benjamin Bache, certainly the major target of Pickering's wrath, also escaped punishment by law. A sadder fate awaited him. Even before the Sedition Act passed he was indicted late in June 1798 on a common-law charge of seditious libel. While out on bail and still fighting, he contracted yellow fever. On September 8, five days after the birth of his fourth child and one month before his trial was to begin, Bache died at twenty-nine. Ten days later John Fenno, too, was dead of the plague, his son succeeding him as publisher of the *Gazette of the United States*.

Duane took over the *Aurora* after a brief suspension and in the following year married Peggy Bache. He became the inheritor of Pickering's malice but was not easy to bring down. On a February Sunday in 1799 he showed up with several friends at St. Mary's Roman Catholic Church and began posting petitions against the Alien Act. A crowd assembled to rip them down, and a street fight ensued. When the black eyes and bloody noses were counted up, however, it was not the attackers but Duane and several friends who were charged with causing a "seditious riot." The jury, however, acquitted them with less than an hour's deliberation. In May a gang of about thirty, apparently including some army officers, broke into the *Aurora* office, dragged the editor into the street, and beat him and his teenaged son severely before he was rescued by supporters. Then in July he was finally indicted for sedition after publishing the charge that John Adams himself had complained of "British influence" in the appointment of federal officials.

Duane was untroubled because he actually was holding proof of the accusation's truth. Some years before, Adams *had* written just such a letter to an assistant of Hamilton in the Treasury. In it he charged the two Pinckney brothers in London with trying to get help from the British court in winning jobs for themselves. The assistant, Tench Coxe, had since become a Republican and delivered the letter to Duane. Its release would have been politically devastating to Adams, and the case was dropped by presidential request. Having twice escaped the law's grasp, Duane next took on the Senate Federalists early in 1800 by leaking a plan of theirs to rig the presidential election in case it ended in a tie, which everyone realized was a possibility. That got him hauled before a special Senate committee, and what happened afterward became part of the battle record of the campaign, still to be unfolded.

Since Republicans had no share in making or administering the Sedition Law, they were unable, at least on the national level, to hit back at Federalist gadflies. But Benjamin Rush, arguably the most distinguished nonoffice-holding Republican in Philadelphia, managed to rid the city of William Cobbett. During a yellow-fever outbreak in 1797, Cobbett had vigorously condemned Rush's bleeding-and-purging regime in a series of highly personal diatribes. Rush sued him for libel in the Pennsylvania state courts—which Republicans controlled—and won a five-thousand-dollar judgment in 1799. Cobbett, cleaned out, had to abandon *Porcupine's Gazette* and retire first to New York and then in June 1800 back to England.

In all, the relative handful of prosecutions did not add up to an Inquisition or a Reign of Terror, and moderate Federalists, including John

Adams when he signed the legislation, never expressed any such intentions. But the Sedition Act was threatening enough to Republican ideals, and to the Constitution, to bring on a vigorous counterattack from the two dormant Virginian fathers of republicanism. In the summer of 1798 James Madison and Thomas Jefferson were supposedly inactive politicians. Madison had left the House of Representatives for his plantation home, Montpelier, and Jefferson, though vice president, was spending as little time in the capital as possible. But now both took up what they saw as a desperate challenge.

✻

THERE WAS a sequence of events. On his way home from Philadelphia at the start of July, Jefferson stopped to call on Madison at Montpelier for a friendly Blue Ridge summertime reunion and unquestionably a discussion of how to stop the rush toward what Jefferson would insist in retrospect was "the rapid march of our government towards monarchy."[37] They separated then for three months during which they exchanged no letters because they did not trust Federalist postmasters not to open them. In October Madison made a trip to Monticello for more conferring in the midst of harvest bustle. On November 13 the legislature of Kentucky formally adopted a set of resolutions condemning the Alien and Sedition Acts as unconstitutional and possibly unenforceable within Kentucky's borders and asking the lawmaking bodies of other states to come on board with similar expressions of resistance. Shortly before Christmas the legislature of Virginia did so with resolutions of the same nature but slightly different wording.

The papers that reported the resolutions did not say, because they did not know, that Jefferson had drafted the Kentucky Resolution and that Madison was the author of Virginia's. Jefferson and Madison guarded the secret of their collaboration on the project so well that it was not penetrated for another ten years, a record that politicians in later and more leak-prone environments might envy. There were reasons for the concealment. It would be unseemly for Jefferson, as vice president, to lead the charge against administration policy. And for either man to put a personal stamp on the Virginia and Kentucky Resolutions would give them a flavor of local partisanship instead of national importance. Besides, the strong decentralizing implications of both sets, namely, that states might decide for themselves which federal enactments to observe, were a reversal of Madison's strong nationalism of 1787, which might be cited against him in public debate.

Jefferson and Madison did not have in mind simply a reexamination of abstract issues of sovereignty. Intentionally or not, they were finding some new issues for 1800 after the setbacks of 1798. The Republicans could no longer rely on arguments for closer ties to France. They were beaten on that field so long as American and French warships were hunting for each other. Traditional warnings against militarism would not play well either during the delirium of the war fever. But there was shrewdness in repeating the call for a return to first principles, a message that could even appear to transcend party. The Constitution needed strict construction to keep government in check. Wasn't the whole eight-year-old Republican movement only a reaction to Hamilton's stretching of the Constitution out of shape with ideas like "implied powers" that let Congress create a bank, pour money into the pockets of a financial elite, or lay taxes and duties that gouged one section and enriched another? And now, what were these oppressive new Alien and Sedition Acts but more exploitation of constitutional elasticity—such as "providing for the common defense" by jailing or exiling objectors to war preparations? And if presses were padlocked for criticism of government, how could any freedom be safe? The right of "freely examining public characters and measures," as Madison put it, was "the only effectual guardian of every other right."[38] Finally, who could better defend these rights than the state governments? They were closer to the people they represented; had led the Revolution; had actually created the nation by agreeing to the Constitution as a compact among themselves to set up a central authority but only with strictly limited powers. The time was ripe to halt federalism's rush toward arbitrary rule. That was a standard behind which to rally voters in their thousands.

The trouble was that the language of the Virginia and Kentucky Resolutions was also elastic. Exactly what did Jefferson's draft mean when, after demonstrating that the Alien and Sedition Acts were not based on any powers specifically granted to Congress or the president—that is to say, they were unconstitutional—he went on to claim that "a nullification . . . is the rightful remedy"; that "every State has a natural right . . . to nullify of their own authority, all assumptions of power within their limits?"[39] The Kentucky lawmakers actually took that out of the version they approved in 1798 and simply called for repeal of the unconstitutional laws. Madison, too, realized the potential dynamite in seeming to say that each state could judge for itself which national laws to apply, which would be a certain recipe for disunion. Time proved him correct thirty years later when South Carolina tried literally but unsuccessfully to nullify a tariff law of 1828, and that effort turned out to be a mere prelude to secession another thirty-two years down the road. He himself insisted that the Virginia Resolution should not take the dangerous tack of recommending a "remedy" but only ask other states to agree that there was no constitutional basis for the hated acts.

Jefferson himself was no seceder, either. Madison, who never saw his friend's draft of the Kentucky Resolution for lack of time, had earlier noted "a habit in Mr. Jefferson, as in others of great genius of expressing in strong and round terms, impressions of the moment," to wit in rhetorical flourishes that made inspiring propaganda but sometimes bad politics and history.[40] It was why Jefferson often submitted ideas to Madison's cooler judgment. What Jefferson really felt was confidence that in the long run the people would judge correctly. At the beginning of June he had assured a correspondent that with "a little patience" they would see the reign of witches pass, and the people, "recovering their true sight, restoring their government to its true principles."[41] Even though he was convinced a few months later that action was necessary as well as patience, he never thought of force as an option, especially as General Hamilton would have liked nothing better than an excuse to use his army to threaten Jefferson's home state, falsely rumored in the Federalist papers to be gathering arms. Hamilton even had a plan in mind that he confided to Senator Theodore Sedgwick of Massachusetts. "When a clever force has been collected, let them be drawn towards Virginia for which there is an obvious pretext, then . . . act upon the laws and put Virginia to the test of resistance."[42] Jefferson advised Virginians against taking that bait. He had a warning for anyone thinking of armed struggle. "This is not the kind of opposition the American people will permit. But keep away all show of force, and they will bear down the evil propensities of the government by the constitutional means of petition and election."[43]

Election was the key. Madison was persuaded to get back into the game by running for and winning a seat in the Virginia legislature in April 1799. Jefferson himself, returned to Philadelphia for the final winter session of the Fifth Congress, became busier than ever with stage-managing opposition and began to look like the candidate he would soon become. Letters needed to be written and money collected. "Every man must lay his purse and his pen under contribution." Copies of the Virginia and Kentucky Resolutions were circulated, as well as pamphlets—at least one batch personally mailed by Jefferson with the caution "Do not let my name appear in the matter."[44]

So the Virginia and Kentucky Resolutions became important as the kickoff of the Republican 1800 "campaign," such as it was. They were not the first step on the road to civil war except in Federalist editorials and in the historical hindsight that is never available to the generation actually living through a national experience. In 1799 the resolutions were actually counterproductive. They opened up fears of disunion, even if ill-founded, that worked against efforts to repeal the Alien and Sedition Acts, which might otherwise have had a chance. House Republicans tried repeal in the expiring Congress and failed, though on a close 52–48 vote. According to Jefferson, Federalist members did not argue but merely drowned out their opponents with coughs, conversation, and laughter. No other states answered the invitation to join Virginia and Kentucky's protests, some because they probably shared Aaron Burr's expressed view that "in the honest love of Liberty, [they] had gone a little too far."[45] Several legislatures actually passed counter-resolutions. In off-year elections, the Federalists moreover picked up some congressional seats in the South, fattening their lead in the House, due to meet in December, to 64 out of 106.

In the short run, the advantages going into 1800 seemed to be with the Federalists. But there were forces working against them, too. John

Adams's peace mission had fractured the party. The fading away of the threat of a Franco-American war meant that there was more room for resentment against high taxes (and the Alien and Sedition Acts) to bloom. More than that, the European war itself was entering a temporary period of remission—there would even be a brief peace in 1802—which meant that domestic issues would come to center stage once more and the Republicans could more easily shed the handicap of pro-Jacobin radicalism. Basic issues erupting in the first decade of actual American political life were still to be settled. The Constitution provided the machinery but not the answers—which, like it or not, depended now on what party electorates would say in the context of concrete, moment-to-moment controversies. What was the proper balance between national and state powers? Between city and countryside, farm and factory and countinghouse? Should the frontiers be pushed outward, and for whose benefit? Should the network of world trade be nourished, and at whose expense?

And above all, when one party or another had gained the victory, what would the losers do?

PART V

CAMPAIGN
AND CONSCIENCE,
1800–1801

CHAPTER 12

The Climax and the
Drawn Battle of 1800

FOR PHILADELPHIANS, the holiday season of 1799 was more reflective and somber than merry. The moment was one of transition, of farewell to the spotlight. In this concluding year of the eighteenth century, the twenty-fourth of the independence of the United States, the city would celebrate its final Christmas as a national capital. The seat of government would move southward in mid-1800 to the District of Columbia. Never again would a president and Congress sit in the shadow of Independence Hall where freedom had been proclaimed in 1776 and constitutional government ordained in 1787. The government of Pennsylvania, too, was transferring to a new location in the west. That was where the future lay.

As if to give the town some official excuse to mourn the passing moment, news came from Mount Vernon on December 17 that George Washington had died three days earlier. The Senate of the Fifth Congress voted to wear black for the remainder of its session. The First Lady canceled her regular receptions for ten days and asked that black gloves be worn by ladies attending thereafter. And bells tolled in measured melancholy each day until Friday, December 27. Then they were joined by the solemn drums of a slow military procession down the brick streets, honoring the departed general.

A playwright could not have brought together so much dramatic evidence of a closing era. Saying official good-bye to Philadelphia were President Adams and Vice President Jefferson, who had met there as kindred spirits and learned to be "Americans" together. Now they were about to contest each other as political enemies, with even their long personal friendship temporarily frozen. Likewise spending their final office-holding months in the City of Brotherly Love were federal appointees and members of Congress who had there framed the Constitution in concert——and who now were convinced that their onetime associates had basely betrayed the document's underlying principles. Was the spirit that had brought such men together in 1776 and 1787 dying, too?

The election of 1800 would hold the answer. It would be different from any election that followed, first because it pitted the president and vice president against each other, and far more so because it was conducted under the burden of a Sedition Act that could put men in jail for criticizing the president. It would be unlike the three that had gone before it, since political life no longer simply accepted the existence of two parties but was dominated by them. Yet each one still shunned the label. The philosophy of the Federalists in power, which in their eyes justified the Sedition Act, was that they were "the government." And government needed to be sustained by all uncorrupted patriots if the social order was not to collapse altogether. With equal fervor, the Republican "outs" spoke as if they were a temporary coalition to rescue "the government" from those who would reconvert it to monarchy and corrupting favoritism. Both groups still paid homage to the idea that "faction" should not become a regular factor in choosing leadership. But faction, however denied, had only grown more intense with each passing year of the 1790s.

*

THE DESTINY of the country was at stake, but the dramatic implications of the election were muted by the existing election system. In modern times there is a steady, suspenseful countdown toward the single November day on which a president and Congress are chosen. High-powered media coverage is punctuated by crises and turning points as the candidates respond immediately to swift-moving events. There was no such tight scenario in 1800; even the electoral process was nothing more than a patchwork of scattered pieces.

The people would choose a new House of Representatives, one third of the Senate, and a president, but not directly, or at the same moment, or in the same way. The Constitution left it to the states to set their own rules about "time, manner and place," subject to congressional changes, of which there were none yet. The only uniform date in 1800 was Wednesday, December 3, when the presidential electors had to meet within their states and cast their ballots. The day for congressional elections varied from state to state, generally but not always falling in the final quarter of the year—and in some cases even early the following year. Special vacancies caused by death or resignation could be filled at any time.

Only the House of Representatives was chosen by popular vote. Senators were appointed by the state legislatures. So too, in ten of the sixteen states in the Union, were electors for president, meaning that the outcome was heavily influenced, if not determined, by which party won control of those bodies. Election days for state officials were spread throughout the year. New York's, which was absolutely crucial, came in April 1800. Pennsylvania's, also critical, was held in October, but part of the Pennsylvania Senate had already been chosen in 1799. A party that hoped to win the presidency, then, had to make an early start on promoting its state legislative candidates.

Even victory in a state election did not absolutely guarantee the state's electoral vote to the winners. State legislatures had two houses, which had to agree on exactly how to pick the electors, whether by joint vote of both or a majority in each. In two cases in 1800, those of Pennsylvania and South Carolina, that was not settled until the very last days before the December 3 deadline.

There was still another issue for state laws to settle, especially in those states that allowed direct voter choice of electors. (These were

Virginia, Rhode Island, North Carolina, Maryland, Kentucky, and Tennessee.) Should there be a single, statewide slate of electors for each candidate? Or should there be one elector named for each election district in a state? The answer mattered hugely. If a party was sure of even a slender statewide advantage in numbers, then it gained from the choice of a general ticket of electors, because the winner got all the state's electoral votes—equal to the size of its delegation in Congress, as is the case in modern times. But a minority party with islands of strength inside a state could pick up some electoral votes if the electors were chosen singly by districts. The first victory of 1800 went to the Republicans in Virginia in January. Federalism, though still a minority sentiment throughout the state, was strong enough in several areas to have sent Federalists to Congress in 1798. So the Republicans in the legislature, ably organized by Madison, pushed through a general-ticket voting law, making it certain that all of the state's twenty-one electoral votes would fall completely into the Jefferson column.

What a modern reader needs to keep in mind is the central importance in 1800 of the contests to win the state houses. Some of these began even before Federalist and Republican congressional caucuses named their presidential and vice presidential candidates in May. In most states, voter courtship began soon after the candidate announcements, ran through the summer, and culminated on various days in September or October when those eligible would travel to scattered polling places. There they would announce their preferences aloud or else, in open view, drop a paper ballot in a box. Collecting and counting the statewide returns might take several days or more. Large-scale election management, from beginning to end, was still a new project, smelling of fresh paint.

The actual electorate was small. The number of eligibles was limited, and the percentage of those who turned out is partially guesswork. Separate tallies for presidential electors (where chosen by the people) were not always kept, and all the statistics for 1800 are fragmentary. One scholar who has carefully examined congressional vote returns has found that 31 percent of Massachusetts's eligible white males took part, and only 14 percent of Connecticut's. Maryland showed a more robust participation, with an average of 44 percent for twenty reporting counties, the low being 19 percent and the high an impressive 71 percent. In Virginia only about one quarter of the white male population voted.[1] When James Madison was elected to the Fourth Congress, in March of 1795, a voter noted in his diary: "I went to the Court House, it being the day for Election of Representatives for Congress. But few people met, the number who voted did not amount to 30, all for J. Madison."[2]

Yet to judge by the passion poured into the campaign, the voters of 1800, however few in number, truly believed that their choice mattered, and that nothing less was at stake than the future direction of the youthful republic—toward either greater freedom or greater control. Or, as they would have put it, toward either anarchy or despotism. Political participation was still in the hands of propertied elites, but there is no reason to think that their anxiety was unrepresentative of the nation as a whole. Despite the slow and ambiguous process of the actual election (or perhaps on account of it), the year was pervaded by a steadily deepening atmosphere of fateful, perhaps even bloody showdown. The last shots of the American Revolution had been fired only nineteen years earlier, and news from France was a steady reminder of how any revolution might end in terror and dictatorship.

✻

THE STAKES were even higher than the contestants realized. The Second Census showed the signs of demographic explosion. The population had increased 30 percent, from a little under 4 million to a little over 5.25. Almost all of it was rural, and some 85 percent of it was white. Of the nation's slightly more than 1 million blacks, 857,000 were slaves living in the South, though there were still some 36,000 slaves (and 83,000 free persons of color) in the Northeast. The biggest growth had been in Kentucky and Tennessee, whose populations, taken together, had nearly tripled in the decade—from 110,000 inhabitants in 1790 to 325,000 in 1800. Ohio had gone from having virtually no settlers in 1790 to 45,000, and would become a state in 1802. The ratio of foreign-born to native-born dwellers was not yet recorded.

An industrial revolution was beginning, too. Working steamboats had actually run on the Delaware River and New York City's Collect Pond—it was only a question of time before they would take over internal navigation. Eli Whitney, moving beyond the cotton gin, was developing a system of mass-producing muskets by assembling them from finely machined interchangeable parts, a technique that would eventually transform all manufacturing. In Wilmington, Delaware, Oliver Evans was operating a fully automated gristmill. American makers of glass, leather, hats, paper, gunpowder, and shipping and farm tools were already exploring how to replace scarce labor with machinery powered by flowing streams. Steam power would not be far behind. In Pawtucket, Rhode Island, Samuel Slater had already built the first American factory to spin cotton thread by machines. Slater, disguised, had smuggled the jealously guarded plans for them from his native England, stored in his prodigious mechanic's memory.

Intellectual and cultural change was bubbling, too. There were 903 post offices in 1800 compared with just 75 in 1790, and as many as 200 newspapers that they were helping to exchange among communities. Bookselling showed promise of becoming big business when, in the very year of the election, Mason L. ("Parson") Weems rushed into print his own topical bestseller, *The Life and Memorable Actions of George Washington*. It contained the famous tale of the cherry tree and went through fifty-nine editions in the following half century. At least seven new colleges had been started in the 1790s.[3] Evangelical Christianity flourished, too. Methodist and Baptist congregations multiplied at a dizzy pace, and "revivals of religion" rocked places as seemingly diverse as elite Yale College and raw frontier Kentucky, where, in 1801, thousands of people came together to pray, shout, and sing at a mammoth camp meeting in Cane Ridge.

The winners in 1800 would be taking control of a country at the dawn of modernization. That, too, made the election unlike any other.

✻

THE OVERTURE to the coming events was Pennsylvania's state election in October 1799. The big Commonwealth had a little of everything—a great Atlantic seaport, an Allegheny Mountain frontier, a large number of German, Irish, and other foreign-born residents, a variety of religious communities, and a mixed though mainly general-farming economy. A cross section of the whole country, it was a fair predictor of national trends. Each of the two candidates for governor was destined to play a key role in the ensuing year, and each was an example of how parties had begun to reach for "balance" in their tickets. Senator James Ross, a rich young lawyer, was named by the Federalists. They hoped he would attract some votes from around Pittsburgh, in the strongly Republican western part of the state, because it was his home. Thomas McKean, the Republican choice, was the state's chief justice and had a long record of law practice—he was sixty-three. Though a staunch party loyalist, he had many useful connections in the Federalist strongholds of Philadelphia and nearby Wilmington, Delaware. McKean's Scots-Irish background predisposed him to favor the anti-English mind-set of Republicanism, and his position on the Pennsylvania bench didn't prevent him from openly displaying his politics. In 1798, for example, state prosecutors tried to indict William Cobbett for allegedly libeling the Spanish minister to the United States. McKean, presiding over a grand jury, not only testified against the Federalist gadfly but practically ordered the jurors to bring in the indictment—which they refused to do. McKean also appeared in person to spring the disheveled and bloodied William Duane from arrest after the February 1799 riot in which Duane, leading an anti–Alien Act protest, had been mobbed.

After the nominations by citizens' committees meeting in their respective wards, the barbs began to fly. A typical Federalist blast touted Ross as "perfectly free from the influence of those perfidious and sacrilegious principles of Jacobinism." Federalists were also reminded: "You stand behind the last dyke of your happiness, constitution and laws . . . Defeat plunges you into endless and irretrievable ruin."[4] Meanwhile, a characteristic pro-McKean "address" in the *Aurora* ran: "It is well known that the *Republican* party are attached to . . . a constitution of equal rights; free from all hereditary honours and exclusive privileges; where the officials of Government are responsible for their conduct," whereas "the *Federalists* . . . think the government should have *more* and the people *less* power. To this party . . . we are indebted for all our late taxes . . . for a Standing Army [and] an extensive Navy."[5]

Election day in Philadelphia, October 8, saw a good turnout, even though the town was once again beset by yellow jack. McKean edged out Ross in the city with 3,649 to 2,800 votes. In the state overall 70,706 votes were cast—twice as many as in any previous election for governor— and the Republicans had 38,036 of them, according to the *Aurora*'s figures published on October 12.

William Cobbett decamped to New York, gloomily warning that McKean's choice "as Governor of . . . undeniably the most influential state in the union" foreshadowed "the complete triumph of Democracy."[6] Happy Philadelphia Republicans paraded through the streets to serenade McKean by torchlight, and in Lancaster the party threw a feast in which four hundred toasting celebrants consumed no less than 780 pounds of beef, smaller quantities of ham and turkey, two hogsheads (between 120 and 200 gallons) of local beer, and another 36 gallons of wine and brandy.

McKean's election was a boost to forward-looking Republican organizers in Pennsylvania (already known as "the keystone in the democratic arch").[7] Long before the term "spoils system" was coined, McKean practiced and believed in it. In his own later words to Jefferson, where two potential jobholders had "equal talents and integrity," political wisdom dictated "preference to real republicans . . . a friend before an enemy . . . for it is not right to put a dagger in the hands of an assassin."[8] The election machinery would be in Republican hands. McKean, meanwhile, appointed John Beckley, tireless as ever in pushing the Republican cause in the northern states, to two court clerkships in Philadelphia. Beckley had been hard pressed financially after the Federalists ousted him from the post of Clerk of the House of Representatives in revenge for his work in snatching Pennsylvania from them in 1796. Now he had a base from which to try again, and he would use it well.

But Republican celebration was premature. Pennsylvania's 1800 electoral vote was not yet sewn up. The law prescribing the manner of choosing electors would need renewing by the newly elected legislature. The Republicans had won control of the assembly, but the Federalists held an edge in the state senate. The two chambers wrangled, stalled, and blocked each other throughout January. Finally, at the month's end, they adjourned in deadlock. The popular Republican majority in the state was temporarily thwarted and forced to wait until the legislature reconvened in the autumn.

✻

DEFEATED BUT DEFIANT, Senator Ross returned to Congress and opened the next act by dropping into the hopper a bill that, in essence, could allow the Federalists to steal the presidency if they could cast doubt on the validity of any electors' votes. It provided that in deciding "disputed elections of President and Vice-President," the Senate and the House should each choose a six-member "Grand Committee," which could no longer thereafter be dissolved or changed. It would be chaired by the chief justice of the Supreme Court. Since the Congress that would open in December 1800 would still be the one chosen in 1798, with Federalists in control of both chambers, and since Chief Justice Ellsworth was an Adams appointee, this grand committee was certain to be a Federalist-dominated body. It would meet behind closed doors, rule on any challenge whatsoever to the qualifications of electors chosen in each state, and make a final determination, with no appeals allowed, on which votes should be counted. It would effectively replace the Constitution's method of choosing a president with a secret election by a Federalist-ruled caucus.

The Ross bill itself was a stealth measure, since the senate's debates were not then open either to the public or to reporters. But South Carolina senator Charles Pinckney—the clan member who had turned Republican—slipped the details to William Duane, who published them in the *Aurora* on February 19.[9] Enraged Federalists who had been unable to convict the Republican gadfly under the Sedition Act the preceding year now got a second chance to bring him down. The Senate called Duane before a quickly created Committee on Privileges to answer for the sin of printing "false, scandalous, defamatory, and malicious assertions, and pretended information, respecting the . . . Senate."[10] No legal basis or precedent for the summons existed, but Duane dutifully showed up on March 24 and asked if he might be represented by counsel. The two lawyers he had on his side were no ordinary attorneys but talented Republican immigrants starting long and illustrious careers. One, Thomas Cooper, was an Oxford-educated scientist, lawyer, doctor, and writer who would himself soon be jailed under the Sedition Act. The other was Alexander J. Dallas, born in the West Indies, a sometime student at the University of Edinburgh, an amateur dramatist, an editor, a reporter and compiler of court decisions, and at that moment the secretary of the Commonwealth of Pennsylvania. The senators wanted no debates with this high-powered pair. They told Duane that Cooper and Dallas could appear with him but would not be allowed to challenge the jurisdiction of the Senate as prosecutor, judge, and jury, or try to establish the truth of the story as a defense.

Both men refused to appear at all when so handcuffed, and Duane himself went into hiding on February 26 to escape seizure for contempt by the sergeant at arms. He stayed concealed for a couple of months, sneaking editorial copy to his assistants at the *Aurora*, until Congress adjourned and left town. During the proceedings against him, his friend Jefferson had been forced unhappily, as the Senate's presiding officer, to be a pro forma participant. But he and the Republicans got the last word. As president in 1801 Jefferson dismissed a federal case against Duane. More important, the Ross bill failed. It was killled in the House after Federalist hard-liners, of all people, could not agree on a final version. And so February 1800 passed.

✳

THE ROSS BILL and the attack on Duane were deeply troubling to Madison and Jefferson. The Federalists were obviously ready to twist the Constitution and terrify critics if that was what it took to stay in control. At the beginning of March, Madison wrote to Jefferson that the Ross measure "bid defiance to any possible parchment securities against usurpation."[11] Jefferson needed no persuading. He had already sent a letter to his son-in-law declaring: "The enemies of our Constitution are preparing a fearful operation."[12] Confirming his anxiety was Thomas Cooper's Sedition Act trial on the basis of a handbill he had composed against John Adams. It was held in Philadelphia on April 19 under the formidable Judge Chase, with Pickering and other administration officials sitting in the courtroom looking on. It was a clear warning to other fault-finding journalists of what they faced. Just as disturbing as the guilty verdict and six-month jail sentence was Chase's loaded charge to the jury. He told them that Cooper's intention to "dare and defy the government" was "the boldest attempt . . . to poison the minds of the people."[13]

Chase was also in unrestrained form two weeks later when he pronounced sentence of death on John Fries, found guilty of treason for interfering with federal arrests of tax resisters, though no blood had been shed or property damaged. "It cannot escape observation," said Chase, "that the ignorant and uninformed are taught to complain of taxes, which are necessary for the support of government, and . . . permit themselves to be seduced by insurrections."[14] And once again, in May, Chase had what was for him the obvious pleasure of sentencing a "seditious" journalist. This time it was the freelance pioneer of negative campaigning, James Callender, who had composed in Richmond a malignant personal attack on John Adams entitled *The Prospect Before Us.* Chase gave him nine months in jail and a two-hundred-dollar fine.

For Jefferson, this mounting evidence of Federalist plotting to seize absolute power with the help of a partisan judiciary underscored the urgency of a Republican victory in the election. This time he would not be a reluctant candidate. He still avoided writing overtly political letters to the press or even to private correspondents for fear that they would be intercepted and published, but he kept himself unmistakably at the head of the Republican table. He had his direct contacts in the Senate Chamber, and Albert Gallatin could relay information and suggestions to and from like-minded fellow Representatives in the House one floor below. Marache's boardinghouse, where Jefferson was staying during the congressional session of spring 1800, served as informal Republican national headquarters. Preparations included getting Republicans in each state to agree on their candidates for state legislators and electors,

getting the names out to the public through handbills and advertisements, setting up meetings, putting material into the newspapers, finding leading citizens to promote the ticket, and getting the cooperation
of state officials where possible. To be certain that all was done in a
timely and coordinated fashion, networks of correspondence and over-
sight had to be established. In Virginia, for example, where James Monroe was now the governor, he appointed three commissioners in each
county to supervise the choice of electors. In two thirds of those counties at least two and sometimes three of the commissioners were also
members of the county Republican committee.

No one showed a better mastery of the nuts and bolts of party organization, or more energy in endless work demands, than Aaron Burr
in New York. That was lucky for the Republicans, because on April 29
there would be a state election in which victory was absolutely indispensable to the further progress of their cause.

✳

THE ELECTION WAS for a legislature that would meet in the fall
and name all of New York's presidential electors. The Federalists controlled the outgoing one, but if the Republicans could retake it, New
York's twelve electoral votes would be in Jefferson's column, and they
were desperately needed. Jefferson was well positioned to get most if
not all of the southern and western states, but Adams seemed fairly certain to sweep New England again. The election could swing either way
on the outcome in the middle states. If New York was lost, Jefferson
would need to win both Pennsylvania and New Jersey, which he
thought unlikely. And within New York itself, the key to control in the
closely divided state was the thirteen-member bloc in the assembly allotted to the city and county of New York. Those thirteen were chosen
on a countywide general ticket, as Burr explained to Jefferson in January. Jefferson relayed to Madison his own belief that "if the *city* election
of New York is in favor of the Republican ticket, the issue [i.e., of the
entire election] will be republican."[15]

Burr used every one of his persuasive arts to build a city slate
packed with familiar and respectable names. He talked reluctant and

retired six-time governor George Clinton into running. He also won agreement from Brockholst Livingston, whose family name guaranteed recognition, and General Horatio Gates, remembered as the man who accepted Burgoyne's surrender at Saratoga. Other state notables completed the list, which was then approved at a caucus that Burr rigged with professional skill. His instructions to one of the "Burrites" were: "As soon as the room begins to fill up, I will nominate Daniel Smith as chairman and put the question quickly. Daniel being in the chair, you must nominate one member. I will nominate one . . . [and others will follow] and, in this way, we will get them nominated. We must then have some inspiring speeches, close the meeting and retire."[16]

Afterward, Burr continued, there must be more caucuses of "active and patriotic Democrats [*sic*] both young and old," ward meetings, speakers, and "frequent meetings at Tammany Hall until the election." Collecting money played a part, too, though a small one by later standards. No detail was overlooked, no rest allowed, and when the actual voting took place, over three days, Burr himself spent one ten-hour stretch at a polling place, where electioneering was then permitted, and a young henchman, Matthew Davis, put in a fifteen-hour stint without eating.

The results were worth it. Though Hamilton, too, had worked hard, he had been outgeneraled again by Burr. The Republicans carried the city by a 445-vote majority. Superiority in the legislature went with the victory. When the news reached Philadelphia, congressional Federalists were plunged into gloom. Hamilton himself was so stunned that he dropped any pretense of high-mindedness and tried to enlist Governor John Jay in a tainted scheme to nullify the result by a piece of ex post facto lawmaking.

Hamilton and his father-in-law, Philip Schuyler, suggested to Jay that the expiring legislature, whose term ran out on July 1, be called into emergency session to rewrite the election statute and provide for choice of electors by district instead of conferring them all on Jefferson. "I am aware," Hamilton wrote, "that there are weighty objections . . . [but] in times like these . . . it will not do to be over-scrupulous . . . Delicacy and propriety ought not to hinder the taking of a *legal* and *consti-*

tutional step to prevent an atheist in religion, and a fanatic in politics, from getting possession of the helm of state."[17] In short, the people were not entitled to their choice. The former chief justice of the United States was not a man to be convinced by any such logic. He filed Hamilton's letter with the endorsement "Proposing a measure for party purposes which it would not become me to adopt" and continued on with his upright career.

✳

NEW YORK'S ELECTION set up shock waves that rocked Philadelphia in May, as the small cadre of federal workers packed up for the following month's move to Washington. With adjournment in sight, both the Federalists and Republicans in Congress held their caucuses to agree on presidential and vice presidential candidates. Jefferson was the automatic choice for the Republicans, but for second place a New Yorker would obviously provide important sectional balance. And Aaron Burr's work there gave him a claim almost impossible to deny.

With Aaron Burr, though, nothing ever happened quite straightforwardly. Not all New York Republicans liked or trusted Burr, so Albert Gallatin asked James Nicholson of New York City, his father-in-law, to sound out old Governor Clinton for the vice presidency. Clinton gave an equivocal answer, and the emissary next tried Burr. Burr grumbled that he needed promises of better support from Virginia than he had gotten in 1796 and affected to hesitate but allowed himself to be coaxed. Nicholson sent back word (changing Clinton's "maybe" to a "no"), and on May 11 the caucus named Burr. The political wedding of Virginia and New York for 1800 was completed, but it was a chilly marriage, and that coolness would become important eight months later.

On the same day, the Federalists made Adams their official choice, then looked to South Carolina again for a vice president. It was an especially important choice because the state, long the anchor of southern Federalism, was now hanging in the balance. Once more a Pinckney was named. This time it was Charles Cotesworth, still on active duty as the commanding general of the United States Armed Forces in the southern sector. Brother Thomas the treaty maker and vice presidential candidate of 1796 was now in the House of Representatives; Cousin Charles the renegade who turned Republican was in the Senate. Nothing better shows how the elite Federalist families of 1800 considered the national government an almost personal creation that it was their duty to administer and to protect.

Congress adjourned on May 14, and the nationwide political battle began in earnest. But already the Federalists had suffered another setback. John Adams had finally fired Alexander Hamilton's loyal allies in his cabinet. Hamilton answered with an open declaration of war on Adams, and in a relatively short time the party was split.

✳

THE FINAL TWO YEARS of his presidency had been hard on Adams. The steady diet of insults in the *Aurora* and other Republican papers had taxed his limited patience, and his own party had treated him almost as outrageously. He had been forced in 1798, with the connivance of the secretary of war, to tear up his own plans for the high command of the army and swallow Hamilton. Then Federalist hardliners had blasted him mercilessly after his February 1799 decision to send a new peace mission to France. His own secretary of state had stalled for eight months in getting the envoys on the way. By the end of 1799 he knew that McHenry, Pickering, and Treasury secretary Wolcott were working against him and on behalf of Hamilton. Still he kept them on for the sake of unity, and possibly to avoid offending George Washington, who had appointed all three.

The general's death lifted that inhibition and cleared the way for Adams to be his own president. What may have brought him to action on the cabinet was the bad political news from New York and the aggravating knowledge that his son Charles was seriously ill. On May 6 the Adams temper boiled over. During a conference with McHenry, Adams mentioned having heard that Hamilton was trying to undermine him among New York's Federalists. McHenry was taken aback and, according to his own later version of the conversation, said he had "heard no such conduct ascribed to General Hamilton." This obvious polite falsehood stung Adams into fury. He shouted: "I know it, sir, to be so. . . . You are *subservient* to him. It was you who biased General Washington's mind . . . and induced him to place Hamilton on the list of major generals before Generals Knox and Pinckney." Then he burst into a stream of anti-Hamilton denunciation. That "intriguant," that man "devoid of every moral principle—a bastard and as much a foreigner as Gallatin," he roared at McHenry like a Yankee farmer blistering a hired laborer, was his enemy. McHenry, shaken, offered his resignation and got the reply "Very well, sir." Then, somewhat apologetically, Adams added, "I have always, I will acknowledge, considered you as a man . . . of the strictest integrity."[18]

Four days later he asked for Pickering's resignation. Pickering was tougher than McHenry, as well as more reluctant to give up the salary. He refused, forcing Adams to take the responsibility of firing him. He left without repentance, ironclad in his conviction that a cabinet member, far from being obliged to quit if he could not support his chief, had a "duty to prevent, as far as practicable, the mischievous measures of a wrongheaded President."[19] Soon afterward Adams replaced Pickering with John Marshall and named Massachusetts senator Samuel Dexter, like himself a Harvard graduate and lawyer, to fill McHenry's vacancy. Adams, for whatever practical or personal reasons, did not dismiss Oliver Wolcott from the Treasury. Wolcott would go on collaborating with Hamilton for the rest of the year, then leave on his own initiative under a barrage of campaign-inspired accusations of questionable financial practices.

On May 14 Adams signed the orders disbanding the "New Army" of 1798 as provided by law. On May 22, he pardoned John Fries and the two associates waiting to be hanged with him. Adams was perfectly assured in his own mind that they were not guilty of treason but at worst of a riot best forgotten. Within a space of two weeks he had gotten back at the High Federalists by disposing of the remnants of their inflated 1798 war scare and dumping Pickering and McHenry. He left Philadelphia with obvious satisfaction, went down for a ceremonial welcome to unfinished Washington, then "raced" home for summer in Quincy, averaging fifty miles a day. The next move in Federalist infighting would have to come from the other side, and it did not take long.

No sooner had McHenry been ousted than Alexander Hamilton, fuming, wrote to Massachusetts representative Theodore Sedgwick on May 11 swearing that nothing—even losing the election—could be worse than another four years of Adams. His exact words were: "I will never more be responsible for him by my direct support, even though the consequence should be the election of Jefferson. . . . If we must have an enemy at the head of the government let it be one . . . for whom we are not responsible." He predicted that "under Adams, as under Jefferson, the government will sink."[20] Between him and the Adams family the hostility was mutual. Abigail wrote to their son Thomas Boylston that sooner than see a "military man" brought in by Hamilton, she would prefer to "vote for Mr. Jefferson"[21] (a purely theoretical statement in an age when women could not vote).

The military man in question was General Pinckney. Hamilton immediately set about taking the election away from Adams, flouting the clear intention of the congressional caucus, by unleashing a full-blown pro-Pinckney effort, reminiscent of his "southern strategy" of 1796. He hoped to persuade every Federalist elector to give Pinckney one of his two votes, while encouraging some of them to deny Adams the other. That would put Pinckney ahead of Adams in the final count. If Pinckney picked up some more votes from independents, or even (as a favorite son) from South Carolina Republicans, he might become president himself or vice president to Jefferson. "The plot of a Spanish play is not more complicated with underplot," Fisher Ames observed to a Federalist colleague.[22] But there was nothing subtle in Hamilton's attacks. He spent the month of June on a military "inspection" tour of New England shortly before returning to civil life, during which he met with other Federalist Adams-haters to collect negative information. He also tried to prod Adams into public combat by writing him an insolent letter demanding that Adams admit or deny calling him the head of a "British faction" in this country.[23] Hamilton hoped that Adams would explode and justify the charge that he was "liable to gusts of passion little short of frenzy."[24] Adams was smart enough to ignore the bait and sent no reply.

✴

THE STORMY MONTH of May provided another asset to the Republicans as the campaign gained momentum. On the tenth, four days before adjournment, Congress passed the Land Act of 1800, regulating sales of the public domain. It was named for its principal sponsor, the delegate to the House of Representatives from the Northwest Territory, William Henry Harrison. Harrison, only twenty-seven, was the son of a distinguished Virginia planter and signer of the Declaration of Independence. After dropping medical study (under Benjamin Rush) he joined the army, fought the Indians with General Wayne, and made his home in the West, near the future Cincinnati. The passage of the act, which made it easier to buy a western farm, was made possible by the vigorous efforts of Albert Gallatin, by then the key Republican member of the House. Gallatin, raised in small and mountainous Switzerland, especially relished Jefferson's proposition that "the happiness of this country . . . would be found to arise . . . from the great plenty of land in proportion to the inhabitants."[25] He and Harrison, both aristocrats-turned-politicians, between them gave western commoners what they were clamoring for—easy access to ownership of that "great plenty." The minimum purchasable tract was set at 320 acres and the price at two dollars an acre, but payments could be stretched over four years at 25 percent a year, which meant that a frontiersman able to scrape together $160 could make a short trip to one of four conveniently located land offices set up in Ohio and leave with a clear title to independence. Federalist policy had aimed to convey public lands in large and expensive parcels to private investors, which would bring more money more quickly into the Treasury and also slow down the rush to the West. By identifying themselves as the friends of the family farmer against the rich speculator, the Republicans had not only locked in the votes of Kentucky and Tennessee but gained a distinct edge among farmers everywhere who were considering a move to the West.

There were long-range results, too. The Harrison Act spurred an immediate westward rush that brought increased pressure to make more Indian land available by whatever means. Harrison went on to be named governor of Indiana Territory in 1802, from which base he coerced and conned the Shawnee and other Native American peoples into signing over millions of acres to United States ownership for relative pittances. When two of the Indians' leaders, Tecumseh and the Prophet, rallied them to resist the process, fighting ensued. In 1811 Harrison beat off an attack led by the Prophet on an American encampment on Tippecanoe Creek, near today's Lafayette, Indiana. Though a very indecisive "victory," it helped to make Harrison president of the United States twenty-nine years later and it furthered what became a great national objective of the nineteenth century, to eliminate the Native American presence from the Promised Land of white Americans. The political outcome of the 1800 elections would quicken the pace of what many history books liked to call the march of democracy. But the original inhabitants of the land would not be included in the parade.

Some ninety days after Congress adjourned, an event took place that involved another unrepresented group in the national mix, and that threatened to have an impact on the outcome in Virginia. During the spring months a slave named Gabriel, property of a Thomas Prosser who had a plantation and kept a tavern six miles from Richmond, was making secret preparations. Twenty-four years old and an impressive six foot two, he was described as "a fellow of courage and intellect above his rank in life,"[26] who probably had heard of Toussaint-L'Ouverture's career, still in progress. With the help of his wife, two brothers, and a sturdy slave friend, he managed to hide a number of swords and bayonets crudely fashioned from farm tools and several hundred bullets. He also got word to an undetermined number of blacks on neighboring farms of his plan to gather a force just outside Richmond, march in to capture more arms and ammunition, and spark a general uprising. He intended to have them carry a silk flag inscribed DEATH OR LIBERTY. But rumors began to spread, and on the muggy afternoon of August 30 two frightened slaves betrayed the "conspiracy" to their owner, who rushed to tell Governor Monroe that the attack was set for that very night.

Monroe, busy as he was helping to run the Republican campaign, dropped everything, called out local militia, and had cannon hauled into place at defense points. Combat never started because a torrential thunderstorm broke out and made it impossible for the drenched rebel force collected at the rendezvous point (estimated at anywhere from 150 to 1,000) to reach the city over a washed-out bridge spanning a swamp. The next day militiamen began a manhunt and made dozens of arrests. Gabriel had fled but was captured on September 25. He would be interrogated, tried, and hung, with fifteen others, less than two weeks later, on October 7.

At least one Virginia Federalist newspaper tried to find campaign material in the event. It was all the fault of "vile French Jacobins, aided and abetted by some of our own profligate and abandoned democrats," the editor charged. "Liberty and equality have brought the evil upon us."[27] There was explosive material in the accusation that "Jacobinism" led down the path to a black republic like Haiti, possibly enough to give the Federalists more Virginia votes. But there was no serious follow-up effort to paint the Republicans as, to use a modern term, "soft on slavery." Gabriel's revolt could have led to an airing of the topic in 1800 and made slavery part of the ongoing debate over the young country's future. But southerners in both parties preferred to leave the touchy subject under the rug, where the Constitutional Convention had swept it.

✳

ON THE NIGHT of Gabriel's doomed uprising, the campaign was in full cry. By the time his body swung from the gallows, it was nearing its end. The summer and fall months swirled and bubbled with partisan activity as decision time approached. It was widely assumed that New England would be predominantly Federalist and the South—except possibly for South Carolina—Republican, so the crucial battles were in the middle states. In Maryland the state legislative election fell in September and the issue on the table was whether the winners would pass an election law allowing choice of electors by district, which would help the Republicans, or by a general ticket, which would favor the Federalists.

Republicans organized political meetings wherever crowds were gathered—at horse races, cockfights, and more respectable events like

Methodist quarterly meetings. Candidates would mount empty barrels and "harangue the Sovereign people—praise and recommend themselves at the expense of their adversary's character."[28] The results justified the party's effort. When the new legislature met in September choice by district won, and Jefferson would eventually collect half of the state's ten electoral votes.

New Jersey, too, was a battlefield throughout September, distracting men from the work of harvest time. The Republicans toiled diligently at perfecting an organization, creating committees in as many townships and counties as possible to name and publicize candidates. The indirect nature of the presidential-choice machinery produced sometimes elephantine, publicly adopted resolves. One ran: "Knowing as we do that the men who shall be returned to the next Legislature will . . . choose the Electors of President and Vice-President of the United States, we ought to give our suffrages for those characters in nomination who will vote for Electors that will join in placing at the head of the American Government men who have distinguished themselves . . . in advancing . . . the preservation of our Republican Government. Such men are THOMAS JEFFERSON and AARON BURR."[29]

In New Jersey, however, things went awry for the Republicans. The state constitution gave lightly populated Federalist counties equal representation with more populous ones, many of which were Republican in 1800. On the strength of this imbalance, the Federalists gained a slight majority in the legislature when the votes were tallied and, in contravention of statewide majority sentiment, gave all seven of the state's electoral votes to Adams.

The remaining undecided states were now more important than ever. In Pennsylvania, where the legislative election was set for October 14, John Beckley worked tirelessly from his office as clerk of the Philadelphia Mayoral Court, setting up committees of correspondence to keep Republicans informed of whom to vote for and why. In addition, he composed a pamphlet titled *A Vindication of the Public Life and Character of Thomas Jefferson* and saw to it that four thousand copies were addressed—by hand—and mailed, a thousand each to recipients in Pennsylvania, New York, Connecticut, and Maryland. He apologized sadly to James Monroe, his Virginia counterpart, that the piece was not as polished as it might be because he was "oppressed by sickness myself and the death of an only child."[30] Gallatin was also hard at work on an essay for popular distribution on how the Federalists had mismanaged the national debt. Governor McKean, meanwhile, busily contributed his share to the drive for every possible vote.

South Carolina, another vital and doubtful state, had an ardent Republican manager in Senator Charles Pinckney, for whom politics had become a family feud as he worked against his cousin Charles Cotesworth Pinckney. Some Carolinians called him "Blackguard Charlie" after his switch to the Republican side. In October 1800, with the new legislature soon to be chosen and election fever nearing its peak, he wrote to Madison: "I have incessantly laboured to carry this Election here and to sprinkle all the southern states with pamphlets and essays and everything I thought would promote the common cause." He must have been doing a good job, since a Charleston resident complained to the city's newspaper: "We have never been so pestered with politics as we are at this day."[31]

As the autumn leaves fell, Republicans were also busy in New England. Though it was assumed to be immovably in the Federalist column, they were building bases for the future. Their incessant activity among new classes of voters irritated Yankee conservatives. Already in 1799 Fisher Ames had grumbled by mail that the "jacobins," as he called them, were "trained, officered, regimented and formed to subordination in a manner that our militia have never yet equalled . . . every threshing floor, every husking, every party at work on a house-frame . . . the very funerals [were] infected with bawlers or whisperers against the government."[32] Now, with the climax in 1800 closing in, he lamented again that what a Connecticut paper called the "detestable practice of electioneering" was spreading like a contagion, with "men of the first consideration condescend[ing] to collect dissolute and ignorant mobs of hundreds of individuals, to whom they make long speeches in the open air."[33] But for all their disdain, Federalists were not backward about organizing their own slates, or using their advantage as incumbents to win supporters through patronage.

Aaron Burr, alone of all four major candidates, was in no way shy about undertaking the "detestable practice" and openly worked for himself. He made an October foray into New England, concentrating on Connecticut, to consult local leaders on the care and feeding of Republican networks, and also to urge his own claims with New England's Republican candidates for elector. Describing the trip to Madison and Jefferson, he warned that they must be sure that he got all of the Republican electoral votes in the South—that he would need every last one. And so the early autumn passed.

✯

SEPTEMBER BROUGHT an international event that could have helped Adams. His peacemaking gamble in the undeclared war with France had worked. Napoleon received Adams's three American envoys with civility and made a deal with them that reflected his own wish for a temporary peace. The Convention of 1800, signed on October 3, more or less ratified a draw. Diplomatic relations were restored, but the 1778 treaty of alliance was no longer in force. French shipping would get a deal in American ports as good as the best offered to any other nation, and in turn France would recognize America's neutral right to trade in noncontraband goods with whomever she chose. The sticky question of indemnity for the many millions' worth of cargoes already seized by the French would be deferred. The news did not reach American ears, however, until November 18, late in the game for Adams to get credit for it.

October brought bad news for the Federalists as Hamilton's campaign to destroy John Adams peaked. His ever-ready pen had poured out a scorching "letter" of twenty thousand words for circulation in pamphlet form urging Federalist leaders to abandon Adams. It contained a long list of presidential blunders and outbursts, furnished to Hamilton by his cabinet spies, all allegedly proving that Adams lacked presidential stature because of "great and intrinsic defects in his character" that included "disgusting egotism . . . distempered jealousy, and . . . ungovernable indiscretion of temper."[34] Hamilton recklessly confided his manifesto to the mails against the advice of those who had seen it. Just as they warned, a Republican postmaster opened a copy, which eventually fell into the hands of Aaron Burr. The text appeared late in October in Republican papers, one of which took note that it contained the "most gross and libellous charges against Mr. Adams ever yet to be published."[35] Lesser men had been sentenced to jail under the Sedition Act for lesser offenses.

Hamilton's blunder was mountainous—as if a party chairman in a twentieth-century campaign had gone on the air to denounce his own candidate. Federalists liked to see themselves as wise and virtuous solons. He made them look like a crowd of squabbling prima donnas. Even his admirer, George Cabot, sadly told him that "some very worthy and sensible men say you have exhibited the same *vanity* . . . which you charge as a dangerous weakness in Mr. Adams."[36] And Hamilton's closest New York ally, Robert Troup, wailed to Rufus King, then the American minister in London: "I cannot describe . . . how broken and scattered your Federal friends are. . . . Shadows, clouds, and darkness rest on our future prospects."[37]

Once more a curious, self-destructive streak had surfaced in a man whose calculating mind was one of the country's all-time best. Logic played no part in Hamilton's assault on Adams. He had fewer basic ideological conflicts with him than with Jefferson, whose prospects he must have known his pamphlet would boost. Adams and Hamilton alike admired the British form of rule and detested "Jacobins." Both favored an authoritative central government with a strong executive; both recognized the flaws in human nature that made self-rule so hard. Yet somehow, they purely detested each other. Adams had known what it was to watch in frustration when he was buried in the vice presidency and Hamilton was Washington's right-hand man. But his own vanity did not seem to suffer as much as Hamilton's when outside the circle of power. For Hamilton, the loss of his private channel to the cabinet through McHenry and Pickering left a vacuum that his New York income, influence, and social standing could not fill.

It was a sign of how, in a tight coterie of ex-revolutionists leading a new experiment in government, personal feuds could have wide and sometimes tragic repercussions. It also showed to what a dangerous point the bitter quarrels of a decade had brought America in 1800. Abigail Adams saw in the course of that single year "abuse and scandal enough to ruin and corrupt the minds and morals of the best people in the world." Granted that her tolerance for vigorous dissent was limited, there was something electrifyingly grim in her reaction to the non-stop assault and battery of the press: "God save the United States of America."[38]

She had good reason to feel that way, for as the final days of the election season approached, slander became more and more outrageous. There was, for example, the charge that Thomas Jefferson was an atheist. Perhaps the background noise of the French Revolution accounted for its surfacing in 1800. If Americans had not been aware of the Jacobins' war with the church, there might have been no issue in Thomas Jefferson's own distrust of religious establishments, nor in his easygoing 1782 remark in his *Notes on Virginia* that it made no difference to him whether his neighbor affirmed one god or twenty, since "it neither picks my pocket nor breaks my leg." But the 1800 equivalent of the Christian Right took this as a manifesto against the Almighty. One "Christian Federalist," as he signed himself, asked how anyone could fail to see that if Jefferson were elected, the morals that shielded the citizen from assassination, his wives and daughters from seduction, and "our religion from contempt and profanation [would] . . . be tramped on and exploded."[39] Another put his choice simply as: "Shall I continue in allegiance to God and a religious President; Or impiously declare for Jefferson—and no God!"[40]

On the other side, accusations flew that Adams yearned for a royal title. He was only guilty of expressing, in the *Discourses on Davila* published ten years earlier, the hard-boiled conclusion that limited monarchy might in the long run be the most realistic government for a vain and shortsighted humankind. It might have been forgotten if the intervening decade had not experienced a world war between European monarchs and a French republic that they wanted to destroy. But with a month to go before the electors met, Tench Coxe, a Federalist who had defected to the Republicans, affirmed in the *Aurora* that in 1794, while working in the Treasury Department, he had heard from New Hampshire senator John Langdon that Adams had "expressed himself

in favor of an hereditary President of the United States."[41] More colorful was a rumor that Adams had plotted to marry one of his three sons
to a daughter of George III to begin an American dynasty and had been
thwarted only by George Washington, who had showed up from Mount
Vernon in full uniform and sword and threatened to run him through if
he tried. The liveliest story of all was that Adams had sent General
Pinckney to England aboard a United States naval vessel to bring back
four pretty girls to share with him as mistresses. That one brought out
the sense of humor that Adams rarely showed in public. He wrote to a
friend: "I do declare upon my honor if this be true General Pinckney
has kept them all for himself and cheated me out of my two."[42]

But the savage war of words was not a laughing matter, especially to
the Federalists. "Our country is so divided and agitated," Oliver Wolcott told Hamilton, "as to be in some danger of civil commotions."[43] A
conservative newspaper in Wolcott's native Connecticut took it one
step further in saying that there was "scarcely a possibility that we shall
escape a civil war." And down in South Carolina, seventy-six-year-old
Christopher Gadsden, a hero of the Revolution and friend to both
Adams (whom he was supporting) *and* Jefferson, anticipated Lincoln's
Gettysburg Address by sixty-three years in linking the fate of freedom
everywhere to its survival in America. "It is impossible the union can
much longer exist," he wrote in a newspaper essay. "But . . . if such a
republic should be self-destroyed . . . then adieu (in all probability) to
any attempt for such governments in future."[44]

*

AS THE FINAL DAYS APPROACHED, speculation simmered in
every newspaper report and every letter that passed among the principal actors. Rumors were plentiful (including one, dating back to July,
that Jefferson had died). Guesses could be made when one party or the
other won a state election, but finality would come only on that December morning when all the electors met in their separate states to announce their choices. These did not have to be kept secret, so the
actual results would then be revealed to Adams and Jefferson as fast as
horseflesh and mail pouches could carry them to Washington, where

both men had repaired for the opening of Congress. That could be a matter of weeks in the case of the western states. The formal opening and counting of the ballots before Congress would come on February 11, 1801.

In a number of states, individuals or groups could escape the tightening restraints of party control and run as "independent" Federalists or Republicans. But the proof that politics was now a highly organized game and getting more so week by week was in the final electoral-college result. The 138 electors actually chosen were faithful to their Republican or Federalist tickets. In contrast with 1796, when seventy-eight electoral votes had been scattered among candidates other than the "official" choices, every elector but one chosen in 1800 submitted the names of Burr and Jefferson or Adams and Pinckney. The exception was a Rhode Islander who gave his vote to John Jay, and he was presumably following instructions to make sure that Pinckney and Adams were not tied. Discipline ruled. But this, of course, was not known yet, so the uncertainty and suspense were compounded.

State results through the beginning of October gave early but not decisive signals. The New England states were safe in the Adams column for a total of 39 of the 70 electoral votes needed to win. Federalist hopes were boosted by victory in New Jersey, which promised 7 more. With New York and Virginia on his side, Jefferson had 32 to start with. Then, on October 11, an apparent huge victory for the Jefferson camp was recorded. Pennsylvania's election turned into a Republican sweep. They won 10 of 13 congressional seats and 55 of 78 seats in the assembly. Pennsylvania's 15 electoral votes would bring Jefferson to within 22 of victory, and the remaining Republican-friendly states of the South and West alone had 27 between them.

But the triumph quickly turned hollow. Pennsylvania's senate, unlike its assembly, was not renewed annually; its members sat for four years. With holdovers from previous years, the Federalists still held a 13–11 edge in the upper chamber. In full defiance of the obvious political sentiment of the state, they refused to approve a Republican electoral slate. Governor McKean was furious at the "arts, calumnies and baseness" deployed by his enemies. Threats and promises were exchanged and furious bargaining went on behind closed doors, but day after day passed, December approached, and McKean could not deliver his state to Jefferson.

In the meantime a similar battle was going on in South Carolina. In that atypical state, slowly turning from federalism to republicanism, personal, local, and family loyalties were still stronger than party. As a result, when the new legislature finally sat down in November to pick electors, there was a new development—a proposed joint slate of Thomas Jefferson and Charles Cotesworth Pinckney. Neither party could count on a majority, so the idea was to appeal to a handful of undecided legislators holding the key. These included Carolina Republicans far more willing to vote for Charles Cotesworth Pinckney than for Aaron Burr, and dissident Federalists who were unenthusiastic about Adams and would take fellow southerner Thomas Jefferson if they could have Charles Cotesworth Pinckney with him. Given the uncertainty of the overall national vote, it was even possible that their votes could bring Charles Cotesworth Pinckney in first and make him president.

But cousin Charles Pinckney would have none of this. He had worked too long and too hard to get a straight Republican electoral vote from his home state, and he would not be denied.

In both Pennsylvania and South Carolina the stalemates persisted as the hours ticked away to the electoral deadline of December 3. If no one budged, neither state would have its electoral vote counted at all. This was unthinkable to the leaders in both. In the final weekend, the ice broke in Lancaster and Columbia. On Saturday, November 29, McKean surrendered and made a deal. He would accept a slate of electors with eight Republicans and seven Federalists. Meanwhile, Charles Pinckney kept on fighting, pulling every wire and calling in every chit in his possession, working frantically to hold the Republican lines firm. And, like Aaron Burr in New York, he succeeded. On December 2 the compromise ticket failed and South Carolina pledged all eight of her electors to Jefferson and Burr.

If the congressional vote had been held on a single day that autumn, it would have shown that the country had gone Republican. The Federalists had been routed in both houses. The Seventh Congress—not due to meet until the end of 1801—would have a five-vote Republican majority in the Senate and sixty-five representatives to the Federalists' forty-one.[45] But because of the ungainly electoral system, this impressive political "revolution" would not become clear until early in 1801. And even if it had been known, it would not have affected the vote of the electors already chosen. The race for president, despite public sentiment, remained a tight one.

At last, after the long months of campaiging, false starts, and innuendo, the electors gathered in their sixteen distantly separated states for the "real" election of December 3. In the unfinished Executive Mansion and in a boardinghouse at the foot of Capitol Hill, John Adams and Thomas Jefferson waited for news of what their long-mingled destinies held for them in the new century. Now it was no longer a matter of rumor, report, hopes, and anxieties. By December 8 the count was in from New Jersey and Pennsylvania, with its disappointing result for Jefferson. Next came news of Maryland's even split between the two candidates. More totals arrived in bundles of papers that were snatched eagerly from the post riders' hands. North Carolina, also voting by the district system, had divided its electoral vote: eight for Jefferson, four for Adams. Little Delaware and Rhode Island were in Adams's column as well. But where was South Carolina, on which everything seemed to depend? On the sixteenth, the defining word arrived—South Carolina cast eight Republican votes.

The western states had yet to be heard from, but Adams correctly expected nothing from them, and he still stood five short of the magic seventy. That day the *Aurora* correctly predicted Adams's sixty-five votes to Jefferson's seventy-three, and rejoiced: "Our Country and our form of government are rescued from the talons of Monarchists."[46] The rival *Gazette of the United States* made a grudging concession. Thomas Jefferson, it said, was "highly likely" to become the next president, "a circumstance much regretted by the Editor of this Gazette and all real Americans."[47]

December 16 was an especially bleak day for John Adams. He learned that he had lost the election—and also that a week earlier, in

New York, his son Charles, aged forty, had died of a combination of dropsy, liver infection, and "consumption," all basically due to alcoholism, which was in turn due to (and responsible for) his failure to earn a living at the law. The pressure of being an Adams son had proven too much. "Let the eternal will be done," John Adams wrote to Charles's brother Thomas, two years younger. Like King David mourning his son Absalom, John Adams declared "would that I had died for him," but then added, as King David did not, "if that would have relieved him from his faults as well as his disease."[48]

A week later, tasting the full bitterness of knowing that his influence in public affairs was ended, Adams expressed fear for the fate of the country. "What course is it we steer," he asked Elbridge Gerry by post, "and to what harbor are we bound?"[49]

The answer was even more uncertain than the outgoing president believed, for the election was not over. When the final tallies were reported from Kentucky and Tennessee, an unexpected complication had developed. Pinckney had gotten the requisite one vote less than Adams. But the Republican managers had not made certain that one of their electors "threw away" a second vote on someone other than Aaron Burr. Part of the reason was the solid commitment to Burr that the South would not let him down again. That had combined with fear that in a really tight race a single lost vote could reshuffle the order of finish to create a monumental error. From any perspective, however, the tie was a thunderclap. Aaron Burr, the wild card of the game, was in a dead tie with Thomas Jefferson. Jefferson, Adams, and Pinckney were known quantities, consistent and open in their views and behavior for three decades past. Burr was the man of intrigue and mystery, of charm, style, and risky investments, of managerial talent and deep silence as to his political philosophy. Reflecting on it, John Adams saw something almost tragic after three decades of nation making. "All the old patriots, all the splendid talents, the long experience, both of Federalists and Anti-Federalists, must be subjected to the humiliation of seeing this dextrous gentleman rise like a balloon filled with inflammable air over their heads."[50]

There was still another ironic twist to give Adams a harsh last laugh.

A Republican Congress would easily have broken the tie in favor of Jefferson. But whether he or Burr would become the third president would be decided by the lame-duck House of Representatives elected two years earlier. It was still controlled by the Federalists, now a divided party but with one powerful wing still looking for guidance to Alexander Hamilton. They would want his advice on where to stand between Burr and Jefferson, two men he loathed as much as he did John Adams. Adams got some private amusement out of the turn of fortune. "Mr. Hamilton has carried his eggs to a fine market," he noted in a country-boy image. "The very two men of all the world that he was most jealous of are now placed over him."[51]

But it was no laughing matter. What if Hamilton and his Federalist cohorts were to look for another strategy, and use the tie as an excuse for rewriting the rules and invalidating the election altogether? Then the country might be at the devil's mercy. The election and the crisis were far from over.

CHAPTER 13

The Crossroads of
February 1801

AMID BITTERNESS and mutual suspicion, both sides now looked to the young Constitution for guidance on how to handle the tie. On paper it seemed clear enough. The winner was supposed to be the person who had the greatest number of electoral votes, providing they were a majority of the whole number. But, said Section 2, "if there be more than one who have such majority, and have an equal number of votes, then the House of Representatives shall *immediately* choose by ballot *one of them* for President" (emphasis added). For the Federalists in the dying days of 1800 that meant there was little time for speculation on what had toppled them, or for continuing their feuds. When the ballots were officially tallied in the presence of Congress in February, the election would move "immediately" into the House. If the party planned any concerted action to affect the result, the mail coaches would have to be kept busy. The same held true for Republicans concerned with countermeasures.

There was danger in the air. The Constitution further declared that the voting in the House should be by state, with each state delegation having a single collective vote, and a majority of all the states—meaning nine states out of the sixteen then in the Union—necessary for election. But it did not command the representatives to ratify any preexisting understanding by voters as to who should be president and who vice president. More important, it made no provision for what could happen if no decision was reached when the sitting president's term expired. Presumably the Federalist Sixth Congress, in its expiring session, would have to legislate an on-the-spot answer that would be in tune with the Constitution. But the Federalists were the party identified with a loose interpretation of the Constitution. No one knew what *they* might do. And the Republican leaders since 1798 had become strong defenders of the right of states to resist "usurpation." No one knew what they might do to answer a Federalist move that would keep Jefferson out of the presidency.

It was a situation made for dealing and maneuvering among allies of Jefferson, Burr, Hamilton, and Adams; for extremists to threaten and concerned moderates to confer—for intrigue, and for maximum tension. The final winter days of federalism's grip on power saw all of those elements in plenty.

✳

IN THE LAST TWO WEEKS of December the players began to assume their roles and positions. From the moment the final returns were known, both sides were aware of the possibilities. Jefferson lamented to Virginia governor Monroe on December 20 that thanks to the lack of "foresight" on the Republicans' part, "we remain in the hands of our enemies."[1] Those enemies had a pair of options opened to them by the tie. They could support Aaron Burr in the voting, and since they controlled six state delegations, and two state delegations were evenly divided so that their votes would not count, Federalists could keep Jefferson indefinitely from getting the needed nine. Then, on March 4, they could push through some law to keep the government in their control. Jefferson had an idea of what that law might be and on December 19 he got off a letter of warning to Madison, who was spending the winter at Montpelier, nursing rheumatism and coping with the final illness and death of his father. The shy little party strategist did not want to be on the scene in Washington because it would look as if he were too eagerly awaiting an appointment from the new administration, which he would obviously get. With aching joints, he read Jefferson's ominous prediction. "The federalists . . . openly declare they will prevent an election, and will name a President of the Senate *pro tem* by what they say would be only a *Stretch* of the Constitution." Then, as he explained in a follow-up message, they would "transfer the government by an act either to that official or to the Chief Justice or Secretary of State."[2]

Such an annulment of the people's choice would be the worst-case scenario for the Republicans and the happiest outcome for the Federalists. But the Federalists also had a fallback position. They might make a deal with Burr. He had never been ardent in denouncing their principles, since principles were rarely on his tongue. If he pledged postelection cooperation with them and in return they stayed with him solidly, then some Republican congressmen might be persuaded to switch a winning number of votes to him in preference to continued stalemate and constitutional crisis. It would be a form of political blackmail, but to those Federalists who especially hated Jefferson, it was an acceptable idea. Talk about it must have been floating in Washington circles at an early date, since the new British minister, Edward Thornton, reported it to London on December 27.

> The federal party in the House of Representatives seem determined to support the choice of Mr. Burr to be the President of the United States—provided he is willing to agree to certain conditions. . . . He is regarded by some of them as a man possessing talents at least equal to those of Mr. Jefferson, with greater energy and consistency of character—of unbounded ambition, little scrupulous about the means of attaining his object, and therefore easily induced to sacrifice a party who have supported him . . . only with a view of securing his interest in the state of New York.[3]

Jefferson was aware of the scheme, too, which depended on driving a wedge between himself and Burr, a relationship that had always been cool. When a tie seemed likely but wasn't yet confirmed, he sounded out Burr's intentions in a letter intended to show the sensitive New

Yorker his goodwill but at the same time to remind him that he had been intended for a distinctly noninfluential second place. "While I must congratulate you, my dear Sir," said Jefferson, "I feel most sensitively the loss . . . of your aid in our new administration." Burr's becoming vice president, he regretted, would leave "a chasm in my arrangements which cannot be adequately filled up." Burr answered with a matching artfulness. He got the point and would "never think of diverting a single vote" from Jefferson, but if his help would be missed that much, he would be willing to "abandon the office of V.P. if it shall be thought that I can be more useful in any active station."[4] If this hinted at a deal—Burr to get out of the way in return for a significant job for which he would quit the vice presidency after election—the hint was not taken up. In any case, Burr *appeared* to take himself honorably out of any potential complicity with the Federalists in a letter that he wrote on December 16 to Maryland representative Samuel L. Smith, a Republican merchant from Baltimore who, as Burr's friend, asked him to clarify his position. "It is highly probable," Burr answered, "that I shall have an equal number of votes with Mr. Jefferson; but if such should be the result, every man who knows me ought to know that I should utterly disclaim all competition. Be assured that the Federal party can entertain no wish for such an exchange." And, he concluded, Smith could be his "proxy" to report these sentiments "should the occasion require."[5]

But nothing about Aaron Burr's career was ever entirely clear or uncontroversial. Sometime early in January, when a tie was no longer just "probable" but a certainty, there was a change in tone. Burr got a letter from a vehemently anti-Jefferson South Carolina Federalist, Representative Robert Goodloe Harper, who urged him not to be so quick to stand aside. "I advise you to take no step whatever," said Harper, "by which the choice of the House of Representatives can be . . . embarrassed. Keep the game perfectly in your own hands but do not answer this letter or any other that may be written to you by a Federal man, nor write to any of that party."[6]

There is no evidence that Burr ever did have contact thereafter with Federalist managers. But there *is* testimony that he had second thoughts about holding to his "no-competition" pledge. He supposedly wrote to Samuel Smith that still another Republican had asked if he would thwart the Federalist plan by simply threatening to resign if chosen president with their help. Burr told Smith he had rejected such an "unreasonable, unnecessary and impertinent" suggestion, which might be taken as an admission that he did not feel qualified for the job.[7] Next, it was said, Smith set up a secret meeting with Burr in Philadelphia at which Burr was asked what would happen if the Federalists persisted in voting for him to the bitter end. His answer was: "We must have a President and a constitutional one. . . . Our friends must join the federalists and give the President" (meaning "give the country a President," meaning himself). Jefferson, he said, could be vice president.[8] The trouble is that this saga of betrayal is based on hearsay, inscribed by Jefferson in that book of recollections that he called his *Anas* fully three years later, when his distrust of Burr had considerably swollen. There is corroboration from a letter by another Republican, but he was not there either and his letter was composed two years after the event.[9] All that can be said definitely is that Burr did "keep the game perfectly in his own hands," which meant keeping a smoke screen now two centuries old around his true thinking. In any case, following the meeting, he went back to Albany to pursue business in the state legislature and to celebrate the wedding there of his beloved eighteen-year-old daughter, Theodosia, on February 2, to Joseph Alston of South Carolina.

As December drew to a close, Jefferson worried that the only possible constitutional outcome that would preserve the Republican victory might actually be an agreement for the ticket to be flipflopped—he himself returned to the vice presidency and Burr made the president. He would have been astonished to know (as later gossip may have informed him) that he had a major ally inside the Federalist party, who was working at his celebrated hardest to keep that from happening. That man was Jefferson's inveterate enemy, Alexander Hamilton.

From the moment the results were known, Hamilton's mind was made up. On December 16 he wrote to Oliver Wolcott, who was in Washington getting ready to leave the Treasury Department on December 31, saying: "Jefferson is to be preferred. . . . As to Burr, there is nothing in his favor. . . . He is bankrupt beyond redemption, except by the plunder of his country. . . . He is truly the Catiline of America." (Catiline, an alleged plotter against the Roman Republic in 63 B.C., was a familiar villain to educated statesmen of 1800, who often spoke as if they were wearing togas.) "Early measures must be taken to fix on this point the opinion of the Federalists."[10]

From the New York office where he was resuming his law practice after his second tour of duty in the army, ex-General Hamilton poured out a stream of letters to Federalist friends in Congress. At first he seemed to feel that Burr should be encouraged to stay in the race to "lay the foundation of dissension" in the top ranks of the Republicans.[11] But the rising fury of Hamilton's accusations discouraged even the remotest idea of doing anything that could conceivably put Burr in the executive residence. He told Gouverneur Morris, now the junior senator from New York, that Federalists would be "mad" to make a Burr presidency possible, for it would "only promote the purposes of the desperate and profligate."[12] He wrote to Speaker of the House Theodore Sedgwick, of Massachusetts, that putting Burr at the head of the nation "would disgrace our country abroad. . . . His ambition aims at nothing short of permanent power and wealth in his own person. For heaven's sake, let not the federal party be responsible for the elevation of this man!"[13] John Rutledge of South Carolina was warned that "Mr. Burr is one of the most unprincipled men in the United States. . . . You cannot render a greater service to your country than by exerting your influence to counteract the impolitic and impure idea of raising Mr. Burr to the chief magistracy."[14] And to Delaware's James A. Bayard went a long indictment on December 27. "Be assured, my dear sir, that this man has no principle, public or private. . . . [He is] a voluptuary by system—with habits of expense that can be satisfied by no fair expedients . . . and of an ambition that will be content with nothing less than *permanent* power in his own hands." Burr's constant indebtedness, Hamilton argued, would make corruption "indispensable" to him. He would seek out a war with Great Britain just to have an excuse for seizing power in the manner of Napoleon, whom he admired (exactly the charge brought against Hamilton by *his* opponents when he was looking for a war with France in 1798). There wasn't a "discreet" man of either party in New York who did not "think Mr. Burr the most unfit man in the United States for the office of President. Disgrace abroad, ruin at home, are the probable fruits of his elevation."[15]

And what about Thomas Jefferson? Hamilton believed that he would be "the least of two evils," or so he told Gouverneur Morris. He struck a pose of rectitude. "If there be a man in the world I ought to hate," he confessed, "it is Jefferson. With Burr I have always been personally well. But the public good must be paramount to every private consideration." Jefferson was a better choice for the Federalists than trying to thwart the election by law. That would be "a most dangerous and unbecoming policy."[16] He expressed himself more fully to Bayard in words that qualify for a world record in damnation-by-faint-praise. "I admit that his politics are tinctured with fanaticism . . . that he has been a mischievous enemy . . . that he is crafty and persevering in his objects . . . nor very mindful of truth, and . . . a contemptible hypocrite." All the same, Hamilton argued, unlike Burr, whose head was full of daring schemes, Jefferson was "as likely as any man I know to temporize— to calculate what will be likely to promote his own reputation; . . . and the probable result of such a temper is the preservation of systems . . . which, being once established, could not be overturned without danger to the person who did it."[17] In sum, Jefferson was more likely to honor a deal than Burr, and the outlines of such a deal were in a communication from Hamilton to Pennsylvania's Senator Ross. Let the Federalists vote for Jefferson after getting "assurances" from him that he would preserve "the actual [i.e., existing] system of finance and public credit," along with neutrality abroad, the "support and gradual increase of the navy," and the "preservation in office of our friends, except in the great departments," meaning the top cabinet posts to which he should be "at liberty to promote his friends."[18] If Jefferson stood behind the national debt, protected overseas trade, stayed out of a war with the British, and left all but the top Federalist administrators alone, Hamilton would be satisfied.

Of all these pleas by Hamilton to what remained of his partisans, the most important was to James Bayard, who was Delaware's sole representative. As such, he would cast the state's vote all by himself, and one state could (and in fact would) make the difference. Bayard was a still-youthful lawyer of thirty-three, who appears to have enjoyed his crucial role. Well born to a Philadelphia surgeon, well married to the daughter of the chief justice of Delaware, a Princeton graduate and trained by Jared Ingersoll, one of the most prestigious members of the Pennsylvania bar, Bayard would be at the center of a swirl of negotiations as the crisis continued to develop, and would become the main character of its final episode.

How much influence Hamilton's letter had with Bayard, or with any of the recipients, is hard to guess. Certainly his divisive behavior during the campaign itself could not have increased his weight in party councils. Only inflation of the evidence allows for the conclusion that he "swung" the final choice. But there is less mystery about his motive. Admiring biographers are inclined to give credit to his interest in "the public good," and praise him for burying old feuds and recognizing that Jefferson's claim to lead young America was far superior to Burr's. "Hamilton Puts Nation Above Personal Feelings" makes a good story. But considering the violence of his language against Burr, it is also possible that in December 1800 he simply hated the man who had recently beaten him in New York State more than any of his enemies—more than Jefferson in 1792, more than John Adams whom he was out to destroy only a few months earlier. That he got on "personally well" with Burr in the small world of Albany and New York City courtrooms and dinner tables, or that they did not attack each other by name in the local papers they both read, did not reduce Hamilton's animosity. The very frequency of the contacts may even have inflamed him more. Mingled with Hamilton's keen intellect were streaks of passion, bad judgment, outsider resentment, and jealousy that surfaced when someone else got ahead of him. He was, in the much later observation of John Quincy Adams, "of that class of characters which cannot bear a rival."[19] One day that intemperance would cost Hamilton his life.

John Adams was a spectator of the year-end maneuvering but would play no recorded part or express no preference, though he certainly thought more highly of Jefferson than of Burr. So did Abigail, despite her fretting (as a minister's daughter) over Jefferson's lack of faith in "the Christian system." Both were still in mourning for son Charles, and that deepened the gloom of defeat that darkened the entire month. Adams kept his election thoughts to himself and instead worried about the larger question that was looming. The day before New Year's Eve he wrote to Thomas, now the only one of his "boys" living in the United States, that the final achievement of "both the extreme parties which divide us, will be a dissolution of the union and a civil war."[20]

✶

WHEN THE NEW YEAR of 1801 dawned in Washington, it came to a city that in six months had already become obsessed with politics—mainly because there were few other distractions for the all-male community huddled in the boardinghouses. Gallatin wrote home to wife Hannah that without their families on hand, "a few [members of Congress] drink and some gamble, but the majority drink nought but politics."[21] Sessions were held in the unfinished Capitol. Only the north or Senate wing, of white stone, was ready for use. The House met either in one of its back chambers or in a temporary brick structure simply known as "the Oven." No one could escape gossip about the election. Jefferson, keeping the Senate in order in his well-mannered Virginia way, must have overheard Federalist talk that blistered his ears.

January was a time of wary waiting before the scheduled official count. While the party leaders thought over their moves, there was business to transact, and some of it would later become stamped with the suspicion that was the signature emotion of the crisis. There was no problem in getting the "convention" with France ratified. It failed to get the needed two thirds in the Senate on January 12 but was easily approved a few weeks later after grumbling anti-Adams Federalists managed to speed up the settlement of American shippers' damage claims. However, a new Judiciary Act, which passed the House on January 20, got into a more controversial arena. It rather sensibly relieved Supreme Court justices of their time-consuming obligation to "ride the circuit" of federal district courts to hear cases, thereby allowing for the reduction of the high court from six members to five. It provided for permanent three-judge circuit courts and also rearranged the districts to accommodate the growth in population and lawsuits. All in all, it opened up twenty-three new posts to be filled by John Adams with Federalist judges appointed for life. As Adams put it in a letter to John Jay, a job like that was "as independent of the inconstancy of the people, as it is of the will of a President."[22] Particularly an incoming president. Jefferson understood as much. "I dread this above all," he commented, because appointments of such a nature would "render difficult to undo what is done."[23]

Though the act clearly had a political benefit for the opposition, House Republicans did not put up much of a fight. Afterward, though, in campaign after campaign, outraged Republican spokesmen would denounce the Federalist "plot" to keep a lock on the government by controlling the judiciary for another generation. They floated the story—colorful but untrue—that in the final hours of March 3 Adams sat at his desk signing the commissions of these "midnight judges" and other last-minute appointees. Fear of conspiracy was rank in the air. On the evening of March 20 a fire broke out in the offices of the Treasury Department. Some records were burned and others carried away in haste by the secretary. The same thing had happened in November in the Department of War, and the darker-minded Republicans at once speculated in print that both blazes were set so that incriminating evidence of fraud in military procurement could "disappear."

The biggest setback to republicanism from a long-range viewpoint occurred almost unnoticed on that same January 20 when Adams submitted the name of Secretary of State John Marshall to be chief justice in place of Oliver Ellsworth, who had quit for reasons of health. It surprised both parties but generated little argument. Marshall was a second choice—John Jay had gotten the offer and turned it down—but was a respected moderate among the Federalists, and Adams had appreciated his loyalty. Republicans knew of Marshall's distaste for Jefferson but weren't yet aware of its strength. They could not know that when Hamilton had recently asked Marshall for help in avoiding a Burr presidency, Marshall had declined, saying that he had "almost insuperable objections" to Jefferson's pro-French "foreign prejudices" and serious doubts about his moral purity.[24] Those "objections" would make some turbulent later history when Marshall took his place on the bench. His confirmation came easily at the start of February.

✳

MEANWHILE, the maneuvering went on. The Republican unofficial "high command" of Jefferson, Madison, Monroe, and Gallatin began to consider their options in the face of the blunt truth that the House could deny them the presidency. Madison had an idea on January 10. It was within presidential power to convene Congress in an emergency. Both Burr and Jefferson already had the needed majority in the electoral college to have won fairly, so one or the other was already entitled to the office. What if the two of them jointly issued a call for the new Seventh Congress to meet in special session on March 5, immediately after the Sixth expired? That would eliminate the nine-month interregnum until December's regularly scheduled convening of Congress, and the Republican Seventh would make short work of breaking the tie in Jefferson's favor. It was, Madison admitted, "not strictly regular" under the Constitution, but less irregular than other suggested remedies.[25]

Some of those other remedies were weighed, presumably in January, by floor leader Gallatin after conferring with House Republicans. He put them in writing to Jefferson. If the Federalists tried to "usurp" the presidency, it was absolutely necessary to resist. But how to do so without civil war? Gallatin suggested a kind of paralyzing noncooperation. Republican members could hang together in voting against any change in the method of naming a president. States with Republican governors and legislatures could refuse to obey any orders from a "temporary" president put in place by the Federalists. Republican senators could boycott whatever meetings the Senate held to deal with the situation if there were no president by inaugural time. A special convention of delegates from Republican states could meet to consider still more choices such as proposing a fresh election. Gallatin's orderly and diligent mind ran through other possibilities too, weighing the possible results of each. They included trying to enlist President Adams to veto any act of "usurpation," or issuing a warning to any "usurper" that he would face legal punishment "as soon as regular government shall have been established." The common denominator of whatever was done, however, would be to stick to the established rules—to block the Federalists from any reach for power "not strictly warranted by the forms and substance of our constitutions" (state and national), and to make sure that unconstitutional means should not be "adopted by *us* in any case."[26]

There were a few Republicans ready for rougher expedients as the clock ticked down to the voting hour. Governor McKean in Pennsylvania was nursing a plan that he did not reveal until after everything was over. Under it, if any Federalist had tried to occupy the presidential chair after March 4, thereby allowing "bad men" to "destroy . . . our general Government," McKean would have commanded all state officers to follow only orders emanating from Burr or Jefferson. Then, having already gotten hold of "arms for upward of twenty thousand" plus "brass field-pieces, *etc., etc.*" and the militia alerted, an order would have been issued "for the arrest and bringing to justice [of] every member of Congress and other persons found in Pennsyl[vani]a who . . . [had] been concerned in the treason."[27] McKean's language of "arrests," "treason," and "arms" sounded as if he had a French Revolutionary variety of violence in mind. And then there was also the shadow of secession. On January 15 one Republican representative wrote a constituent that in case of a "usurpation"—by now the standard Republican term—"Virginia would instantly proclaim herself out of the Union."[28]

Statements like that, circulating in Washington's rumor mills, shook less belligerent Republicans into reminding themselves that it would be both peaceful and constitutional to take Aaron Burr. They also may have prompted Albert Gallatin to some second thoughts. Gallatin knew and liked Burr from the brief time they had spent together in the Senate in 1794, when Burr had defended him against the Federalists' successful attempt to throw him out on a technical flaw in his election. Gallatin's New York in-laws, too, moved in circles friendly to Burr. Gallatin would lose no opportunity for personal preferment in a Burr administration, if that should come to pass. And so, on February 3, Gallatin wrote Burr a letter, which Burr received in Albany on February

12, the day after the balloting had begun. Exactly what was in it will never be known for sure, because it has never been found and probably was destroyed. Only Burr's circumspectly worded answer remains. But one of Burr's close associates in Albany, Peter Townsend, later told a New York businessman confidant (who put it in his diary) a provocative human-interest story of how Burr behaved after reading it that February day.

If the diary's version is accurate, Burr asked Townsend and John Swartwout, another of his trusted fellow members of the New York Assembly, to come to his rooms, where he shared Gallatin's message with them. Gallatin was truly alarmed at the prospect of a continued deadlock, a Federalist attempt to seize control, and a fight that would be disastrous. But three Republican representatives from New York, Maryland, and New Jersey were ready to switch from Jefferson to Burr, and that could make him the president, certainly a far better outcome. But Burr needed to be on hand himself to "secure" the three votes. He must leave for Washington *immediately* if he wanted to save the country. Burr asked Townsend and Swartwout what they thought, and both responded that he should get on the first available conveyance and rush south.

Then, the story concludes, they went back to the legislature and returned to find him packed. But, Townsend reported, "at the critical moment his heart failed him [and] he remained at Albany."[29] Instead he answered Gallatin almost soothingly that his own information was different—Jefferson already had the votes to win on the first ballot. (Burr had no way of knowing that circumstances had *already* proven him wrong. Had telephones been available, the course of history might have been changed.) However, he added somewhat murkily, if that did not happen and the Federalists tried to confer the presidency on some temporary officer chosen by them, then "my opinion is definitely made up." And, moreover, it was already known to two of the three wavering Republicans. But was his mind "made up" to accept the presidency or join in some other plan? There is no certainty. All Burr said in conclusion was that he would shortly start for Washington via New York, where he could be reached after February 21.

Gallatin would, years afterward, deny that he had ever written anything intended to undercut Jefferson. But if there is any truth in Townsend's account, Burr was in the interesting position of being wooed—as, constitutionally, he was perfectly entitled to be—by peacemaking negotiators of both parties. Bayard was still apparently looking for some kind of promise of cooperation from Burr that could be reported to his fellow Federalists if any were inclined to ditch him early in favor of some more drastic move. One of Bayard's colleagues got increasingly annoyed as no promises came, even after voting had begun, and grumbled to a correspondent: "Had Burr done anything for himself, he would long ere this have been President."[30]

Washington, meanwhile, approached February 11 in a state of alarm and uncertainty. "Rumors are various and intrigues great," said Gouverneur Morris, who had learned a good deal about intrigue as the American envoy to France from 1792 to 1794. It was "impossible to determine which of the two candidates will be chosen."[31] One of those flying scare stories was that Federalists were getting ready to invalidate a number of Jefferson's electoral votes on technical grounds, which could make Adams the winner after all. A Virginia representative wrote to Monroe that in such a case, since Pennsylvania already had "22,000 prepared to take up arms," Monroe should move to get Virginia and Pennsylvania, plus New York and all the southern states, into a convention, presumably to split off from New England. Though he added that he thought "the Feds will yield," he was a good barometer of the sullen pretempest atmosphere.[32]

So Wednesday, February 11, finally arrived, and the curtain went up at last.

✻

ALMOST SYMBOLICALLY, an actual storm broke on the appointed day. One of Washington's infrequent heavy snowfalls blanketed rutted streets and raw lumber in white as both houses of Congress gathered at midday in the Senate Chamber. Vice President Jefferson solemnly opened the certificates from each state and passed them to the clerks. The official announcement confirmed what everyone knew, and then, amid the clatter and shuffle of chairs being moved, the House of Representatives withdrew to the room set aside for it to choose "immediately" either Burr or Jefferson as president. All but one of the 105 representatives were on hand. The prize for dutifulness clearly belonged to thirty-year-old Joseph Hopper Nicholson of Maryland. Though dangerously ill of some unspecified sickness, he had himself carried, on his bed, two miles through the snow. Placed on the floor in an "antechamber," he would prop himself up with the help of his wife and scrawl Jefferson's name on a piece of paper each time his turn to vote came up. He had little choice as a dedicated Republican, because the Maryland delegation was exactly divided—four Republicans including himself, and four Federalists. They canceled each other out, so that Maryland was recorded as nonvoting. But Nicholson's absence would have let the Federalists give the state to Burr. He simply could not afford to stay away. Vermont, too, had an evenly split delegation—one Federalist and one Republican, the Republican being Matthew Lyon, the former prisoner of the Sedition Act. And so, when the first ballot was taken, the results stood: eight states for Thomas Jefferson, six for Aaron Burr (four New England states, South Carolina and Delaware), and two not counting.

The House had resolved to ballot continuously until it had a result, with no interruptions for other business. So a second vote was taken. Then a third, and a fourth and fifth. Some individual members shifted from Burr to Jefferson but not enough to tip any state. The early darkness of midwinter fell, and the roll calls droned on in the glow from fireplaces and candles. A short break was taken after the seventh ballot, and another after the fifteenth, so that the members could snatch whatever food they sent for from the boardinghouse kitchens. As the hour grew later, the exhausted lawmakers accommodated themselves as best they could between votes. Some snored, head down at their desks. Others sent out for bedding, which they spread on the floor for naps. Bleary-eyed and stubbled after more than twelve hours of talk and argument and no fewer than twenty-seven ballots, they all agreed to a recess at 3:00 A.M. until the following noon. Friends and relatives waiting for news could at last go to bed, too. Margaret Smith, wife of the Republican editor of Washington's *National Intelligencer,* testified that she never closed her eyes the night long.

The nearest thing to a Republican command post was Governor Monroe's office in Richmond. He had arranged for a chain of express riders to start out on the ninety-mile trip at hourly intervals. When the first marathon day and night were over, Gallatin scribbled a few words reporting the count and then added a note of alarm. Was it true that some people had taken up arms in Richmond already? He hoped not. "Anything [like] a commotion would be fatal to us."[33] It was not true, but rumors kept reaching the members, isolated in their uncompleted building. Thousands of people were pouring into Washington ready for violence if there should be a "usurpation." Partisans were arming in Philadelphia, in Baltimore. In John Adams's recollection many years afterward, extremists "saw not the precipice on which they stood. . . . To dispatch all in a few words, a *civil war* was expected."[34]

When they reconvened on Thursday afternoon, February 12, only one ballot was taken. Only two more occurred on Friday the thirteenth. The reason was partly fatigue, but beyond that the combatants were pausing between rounds to wait for the results of dealings that were in progress. The Federalists were sticking with Burr all the way. Some were ready to settle for him as president. Others were zealots who only wanted to sabotage the process and provoke a showdown when time ran out. But if all the Republicans were just as stubborn, there seemed no hope of avoiding the collapse of the government. By now, a worried James Bayard began to see only one possible escape route. The Federalists would have to blink first and take Jefferson—but Jefferson needed to make it easier by some promises that would quell Federalist anxieties. Bayard started to explore possibilities. On Friday night he talked to John Nicholas, a Virginia House member. Would Nicholas, he asked, "consult" with Mr. Jefferson to see how his mind stood on some accommodation? No, Mr. Nicholas replied, he would not, but he could give Bayard a pretty good idea of what Jefferson was thinking. That was not good enough, said Bayard, and soon turned to another possible intermediary, Maryland Republican Samuel Smith, who was a confidant of both Jefferson and Burr.

On Saturday, when there were three more inconclusive votes, Jefferson himself met Adams while walking on Pennsylvania Avenue, and they discussed the situation. What wouldn't a historian give to have been the proverbial fly on the wall as the two old friends-turned-enemies, recognizing the threat to the country for whose creation they had risked their lives, sparred to see who would retreat. Jefferson began (as he remembered it) by saying that he knew that a Federalist plan existed to elect a president pro tem of the Senate and make him Adams's successor on March 5. Wouldn't Adams promise to take that option away by announcing that he would veto any such measure? Because if enacted, he went on, it would "produce resistance by force, and incalculable consequences." Jefferson's stance now was to threaten the Federalists with the prospect of rebellion, possibly coupled with a call for a new convention to reorganize the government. "The very word convention gives them the horrors, " he wrote the next day to Monroe, in view of the "present democratical spirit of America."[35]

But Adams, like Jefferson, was an ex-diplomat and knew how to bargain and bluff. His response, in Jefferson's description, was that Jefferson himself could solve the problem "by a word in an instant" declaring that he "would not turn out the [F]ederal[ist] officers nor put down the navy, nor spunge [i.e., expunge] the national debt." There is no evidence whatever that Adams had consulted on these terms with anyone, or taken any part at all in Federalist strategy, but they were clearly the three items that most concerned all the party's members, Hamilton included.

But on Saturday Jefferson was not ready to compromise. Finding Adams's "mind made up," he reminisced, "I urged . . . no further [and] observed that the world must judge as to myself of the future by the past."[36] Then he left, trailing a slight cloud of ambiguity as to exactly what cues the Federalists were supposed to pick up from the consideration of his record that he seemed to be inviting.

That night, with a little breathing room afforded by the Sunday recess planned for next day, Bayard talked to Samuel Smith again. Now Smith claimed that he had talked to Jefferson without letting Jefferson know his purpose, and merely raised in general terms the subject of what might happen to the civil service in a new administration. And Smith had happy news for the Federalists. Jefferson had told him that "he did not think that such office[r]s ought to be dismissed on political grounds only." That was good enough for Bayard, who then told Smith that he would "give the vote" that put Jefferson over on Monday. The turning point of the five-day standoff had finally been reached.

However optimistic Bayard's promise had been, at Monday's Federalist caucus he would meet with a storm of protest and find his resolution weakened. In the teeth of mutterings and shouts, he made his case. There was no sign of Burr and no word from Burr either that he would accept the presidency or offer the Federalists any kind of reward for their cooperation. And there was no sign of a break in Republican ranks, either—so the best possible alternative was to take Smith's word for what Jefferson had said and end the struggle. "The clamor was prodigious," he testified, and "the reproaches vehement. . . . Some were appeased; others furious, and we broke up in confusion."[37] The confusion lasted through another two ballots on Monday with no result as Bayard still cast Delaware's vote for Burr, unwilling to break ranks with his fellow Federalists while he still had a chance to persuade them. In the evening more alarms swept the capital. The lobby of the House had to be cleared of a noisy, angry crowd. Stories circulated that some Federalist members had received written death threats, while stones had come crashing through the windows of others.

Whether those episodes, if they happened, were the convincers no one knows. But after further Federalist caucuses, on the afternoon of Tuesday, February 17, on the thirty-sixth ballot, the irreconcilables gave in. The Federalists in the Maryland and Vermont delegations agreed not to vote, thereby letting those two states go Republican. Bayard himself cast a blank ballot, and so did the Federalists in South Carolina. The final result, then, was two states—Delaware and South Carolina—abstaining, ten for Jefferson, and four, all in New England, for Burr.

The will of the electorate was fulfilled. Thomas Jefferson would become the third president of the United States.

✻

LEFT BEHIND were unanswered questions, still buzzing after two hundred years. The first, naturally, concerns Burr. Jefferson, in time, and some of Jefferson's biographers became convinced that Burr had thumbed his nose at "his" party and clandestinely connived with the Federalists to make himself the president. He had it in his power to have made a crisis-shortening, honest statement that he would not serve if elected and would not be used by anyone to thwart the people's choice. Instead, his critics charge, like the high-flying gambler and self-promoter he always was, he kept himself available, hoping and expecting that the game would break his way.

Burr's defenders see it otherwise. He was a pragmatist and not a doctrinaire. Removing himself as an option would not necessarily have prevented the Federalists from forcing a constitutional confrontation, while staying in the race meant that the country had a last-resort alternative to civil war. He was willing to play that part as a patriot, but *only* in the last resort, just as he had told Samuel Smith in the Philadelphia meeting that was his only known conference with other Republicans on the subject. In any case, if he had simply wanted the grand prize, it was his to take. All he needed to do was to jump into a carriage and race day and night to Washington as Gallatin suggested, and nail down the support of those Republicans ready to join him. Did his heart fail him, as Peter Townsend believed? Was he afraid of what a mean figure he would cut if he openly challenged Jefferson and lost? Or was he, uncharacteristically, disdaining deals in a gentlemanly way and leaving things to Fate? The unresolved debate goes on. Whatever the truth, Burr got the worst of it—neither side really trusted or respected him thereafter. He himself felt especially abandoned by the Republicans, given the huge contribution to victory made through his unstinting efforts in New York. At forty-five, he was at a political peak, one step away from the throne that the two vice presidents before him had already mounted. Yet he was, or soon would be, a political outcast. Few men of more teasing complexity ever played in the theater of American elections. And in the parlor game of counterfactual (or "What if?") history that the professionals sometimes play, there is no more mind-bending challenge than trying to imagine what a Burr presidency would have looked like.

And what of Jefferson? There is nothing on record to contradict his denial that he made any promises to the Federalists, directly or indirectly as Bayard suggested. His position was always that he refused to go into office "with his hands tied." But Jefferson always claimed to be unmotivated by politics, yet he somehow kept on top of political developments, suggested strategies and arguments, and made decisions that helped to organize, within eight years, a broad-based political movement that wrested power from the well-dug-in Federalist elite. In his self-contradictory way, he would resist taking credit for such political skills by insisting on his own definitions. The victory now in his hands, he would assert, was not a partisan one but a restoration of the betrayed principles of the American Revolution. But how he would use it would have inevitably partisan results. And no one knew, as the sun set on February 16, just what that use would be. It was a worrisome question.

Margaret Bayard Smith wrote to a kinswoman that after the result was known, "the dark and threatening cloud that had hung over the political horizon rolled harmlessly away, and the sunshine of prosperity and gladness broke forth." Changes of government that in other times and places had "most generally been epochs of confusion, villainy and bloodshed . . . in this our happy country take place without any species of distraction or disorder."[38]

But would that be the case? The election machinery had, finally, "worked." But the new president was taking office after six years in the shadow of imminent war, two years of jailings, deportations, and treason trials, one year filled with charges of immorality and atheism brought against one party, and of readiness to destroy popular government charged to the other. Would those brawling, consensus-shattering emotions really subside enough to make peaceful transition possible? The road ahead did not look any less dark or dangerous to plenty of thinking Americans who were actually living through the remaining weeks until inauguration day.

CHAPTER 14

The Republican President

THE CALCULATED MODESTY of Jefferson's inaugural, the first ever held in Washington, underscored his will to make an opening statement about his "republican revolution." The simple walk to the Capitol with a minimum escort (coupled with John Adams's noiseless departure by public coach, of which Jefferson was presumbly unaware) made the day the overture to a new order of things in the national capital. True, there were splendid Republican rejoicings in other cities—in Philadelphia, for example, where an eye-popping procession included an "elegant" schooner, the *Thomas Jefferson,* on a flatbed carriage drawn by sixteen horses representing the sixteen states, each with a rider dressed in white.[1] But the new president, who did not even move from his boardinghouse to the executive mansion for two weeks, intended deliberately to signal that his administration would have no monarchical trappings. Twelve years earlier George Washington had counted on at least some display of pomp to show the dignity of the new government. Now, in changing times, Jefferson was using the power of symbolic behavior—especially by the chief executive—to underscore that a Republican regime would operate with "republican" simplicity. As the first "modern" president chosen in a hotly contested election between parties, he was emphasizing a clean break with the Federalist past.

That was exactly what worried his recent opponents. How sharp would that break be? More important, how much would it threaten them? Answering that question in a way that would calm the storms of recent weeks without giving up any essential principles was the project that kept Jefferson busy working over drafts of his inaugural speech, which he wrote absolutely and entirely on his own in the interim between February 18 and March 4. He got it finished in time to hand it over to S. H. Smith, the publisher of what would become the administration's semiofficial newspaper, the Washington *National Intelligencer.* It was in print either on or soon after the day on which he read it to the Congress and the audience packed in the gallery, speaking from the well of the Senate, after Vice President Burr had shaken his hand in welcome and Chief Justice Marshall had sworn him in. It was just as well that the text was (or would soon be) available, since the testimony is that while the graying president, almost fifty-eight, was still a tall and commanding figure behind the reading desk, he spoke so softly that he could not be heard in the back rows.

But if the delivery was unimpressive, the content was sensational. The address was as extraordinary as the inauguration ritual itself was mundane by design. It remains one of the two or three best, best-known, and most oft quoted inaugural speeches in American history thanks to its literary grace, its ripe expression of where Thomas Jefferson's political thought had arrived nearly twenty-five years after he wrote the Declaration of Independence, and its summary of what he believed he had just achieved and what he was about to do. Most significant of all, it was reassuring—and it pointed the way to the American future.

*

JEFFERSON BEGAN by unfurling the red, white, and blue banner. He felt humbled, he said, by the responsibility that his administration would have for "the honor, the happiness, and the hopes of this beloved country." And what a country it was!

A rising nation, spread over a wide and fruitful land, traversing all the seas with the rich productions of their industry engaged in commerce with nations who feel power and forget right, advancing rapidly to destinies beyond the reach of mortal eye.

There the opening themes sounded. The United States was already a success story, with an even more brilliant "destiny" ahead—so promising that no living person could foresee its final glory. She was also special—a virtuous contrast with those nations that strutted in their power and forgot to do right, although she could trade with them without necessarily corrupting herself—a statement that was a friendly nod to the merchant class suspicious of Jefferson. And America's people were hardworking. That was what he meant by their "industry," though it could also be taken as still another friendly nod to manufacturers. Jefferson's plain intention at that moment was to be inclusive, as his next and possibly most crucial point showed. *All* Americans were partners in the national enterprise and needed always to keep that in mind. "Let us . . . fellow citizens," he implored (using the same term of address that Washington initiated), "restore to social intercourse that harmony and affection without which liberty and even life itself are but dreary things."

By implication Jefferson was admitting the divisive bitterness of the just-ended campaign. But he explained that the rancor was not the fault of good-hearted Americans—only the echo of the revolutionary turmoil in Europe. That was what had driven the wedge.

During the throes and convulsions . . . the agonizing spasms of infuriated man, seeking through blood and slaughter his long-lost liberty, it was not wonderful that the agitation of the billows should reach even this distant and peaceful shore; that this should be more . . . feared by some, and less by others, and should divide opinions as to measures of safety.

So it was taking sides in the wars of the "ancient world," as he called Europe, that had led to all the trouble. But what a mistake it would be to continue a "political intolerance" that would be "as despotic, as wicked, and as capable of as bitter and bloody persecutions" as the age-old religious intolerance that America had gloriously "banished from our land." Then came the most celebrated words of the speech, clearly addressed to the fears of the moment:

> But every difference of opinion is not a difference of principle. We have called by different names brethren of the same principle. We are all republicans, we are all federalists. If there be any among us who wish to dissolve this Union, or to change its republican form, let them stand undisturbed as monuments of the safety with which error of opinion may be tolerated, where reason is left free to combat it.

In the printed version, *Federalist* and *Republican* were capitalized, making it sound as if the president was giving his blessing to both parties, a healing if somewhat unrealistic interpretation. But in his hand-written version the labels were not in capitals, and the message was more general. Most Americans, Jefferson was insisting, were moderates. They were united in their commitment to preserving both the state *and* national governments in the "federal" system provided by the Constitution, and they were agreed that America should turn her back on monarchy forever and keep a "republican" character. There might be extremists on both sides—some who wanted to go back to pre-1787 undiluted state sovereignty; others to the days before 1776 when a king ruled. But it wasn't necessary to stifle these minorities with Alien and Sedition Acts, or to punish them in any way. There would be no reprisals against losers. Reason would be left free to win its inevitable victory.

Jefferson was showing the Federalists who dreaded him as a dangerous revolutionary that he was not so dangerous. But he made no secret of supporting a "revolutionary" proposition as his well-crafted phrases rolled on. Conservatives throughout history had argued that only authority kept governments in business—only the strength of entrenched bureaucracies, police forces, standing armies, established religions, and privileged leadership classes kept states from crumbling into anarchy. According to Jefferson, they were wrong.

I know, indeed, that some honest men feel that a republican government cannot be strong, that this government is not strong enough.
But would the honest patriot, in the full tide of successful experiment, abandon a government which has so far kept us free and firm,
on the theoretic and visionary fear that this government, _the world's
best hope,_ may . . . want energy to preserve itself? I trust not. _I believe
this, on the contrary, the strongest government on earth._ I believe it the only
one where every man, at the call of the law, would fly to the standard
of the law, and would meet invasions of the public order as _his own personal concern._ [emphasis added]

It was freedom that made a government strong, not the reverse.
America's future would be based on the radical idea that free people
would, without coercion, preserve a government of their own choosing.
That was something new in the human story, and it made the American
"experiment" meaningful to peoples everywhere. That was what the
election victory, the peacable "revolution of 1800," meant. It carried a
universal message to a globe still overwhelmingly run by crowned
heads.

Sometimes it is said that man cannot be trusted with the government
of himself. Can he, then, be trusted with the government of others?
Or have we found angels, in the form of kings, to govern him? Let history answer this question.

It was a bold, shining declaration of democratic faith, though Jefferson's word of choice at the time was "republican." Having struck that
note, Jefferson went back to the conciliatory tone. He sketched out
bright prospects ahead for everyone, and even soothed any readers who
were ruffled by his remarks against "religious intolerance."

Let us, then, with courage and confidence, pursue . . . our attachment to union and representative government. Kindly separated by
nature and a wide ocean from the exterminating havoc of one quarter of the globe . . . possessing a chosen country with room enough

for our descendants to the thousandth and thousandth generation, entertaining a due sense of our equal rights . . . to honor and confidence . . . resulting not from birth but from our actions . . . [and] enlightened by a benign religion, professed . . . and practised in various forms, yet all of them inculcating honesty, truth, temperance, gratitude, and the love of man; acknowledging and adoring an overruling Providence, which, by all its dispensation proves that it delights in the happiness of man here, and his greater happiness hereafter—with all these blessings, what more is necessary to make us a prosperous people?

When he came to answering his own question, Jefferson sounded somewhat less like the detached statesman and more like the old political enemy of Hamilton's plans for an interventionist and expensive government. What more was necessary?

Still one thing more, fellow citizens, a wise and frugal government, which shall restrain men from injuring one another, shall leave them otherwise free to regulate their own pursuits . . . and shall not take from the mouth of labor the bread it has earned. This is the sum of good government.

There it was, an enduring American creed. It wasn't entirely of Jefferson's own invention, but neither was the Declaration of Independence, and in both cases the cadences were so beautiful that they became an unconscious, unexamined, and rarely challenged part of the nation's thinking, handed down through the generations long after the actual circumstances of 1800 had drastically changed. America was the darling of a divine providence that wished the human race well. Because America was sheltered from Europe's strife and hatreds by the boundless ocean, her people were free to write a brand-new page in the annals of human progress, and the whole world would be watching. The hopes of liberty everywhere rode on the success of the American experiment.

On social specifics, Jefferson's words suggested that opportunity was limitless "to the thousandth generation" because of America's roominess. So individuals had an equal chance to show their inborn talents and would be judged, one by one, on their achievements and not their family pedigrees. As long as law and custom did not draw artificial class distinctions, there would always be an open door for merit. In their domestic politics, the American people would look first to their local and state governments to serve their local needs and protect their freedoms. In their relations with the world through the national government, the compass would always point to "peace, commerce and honest friendship with all nations—entangling alliances with none." (Jefferson, even more than Washington, was the father of American isolationism.) And government at all levels should be held strictly to a few functions of defense and the protection of rights. Under those conditions it couldn't become either oppressive or expensive, and tax collectors would need to take only the minimum bite from productive society.

Finally, the American consensus on these points was so complete that peaceable dissent could be tolerated and even encouraged. Freedom of thought was the key to constant improvement.

Two hundred years later it's easy to pick holes in this idealized design, find the weak spots where it expressed more hope than historical truth, jab at how serenely Jefferson dropped slaves, women, and Indians from his definition of "Americans," or show how cranks of every sort have used his "glittering generalities" to advance their ends. But doing that overlooks the energizing power of such a generous estimate of human and national potential. America today may not be what Jefferson judged it would be, but it is almost certainly better than it might have been if Americans over two centuries had not intermittently tried to live up to the image that he painted of them. His words on that March day became one of the best legacies of the 1800 election.

✳

JEFFERSON HIMSELF CLAIMED to have invented nothing. His own idea of the "revolution of 1800" was that by peaceful persuasion he had simply brought the country back to the original intentions of the Revolution of 1776. The High Federalists had steered the new ship of state off course, but as Jefferson wrote to another signer of the Declaration of Independence just two days after inauguration, "We shall put her back on her republican tack and she will show by the beauty of her motion the skill of her builders."² Nor would he have agreed with the historians who afterward decided that "revolution" consisted in putting the seal of approval on permanently organized competing parties. Jefferson still thought that once the people got a taste of true republicanism, all future quarrels would be differences of opinion, not principle, to be settled among republican brethren on a case-by-case basis. Federalist heresies would quietly vanish. Or, in his words a year and a half after the election, he would "by the establishment of republican principles sink federalism into an abyss from which there shall be no resurrection."³

Luckily for peace and quiet, in March 1801 Federalist leaders were not aware that they were expected to disappear. That was, in fact, just what they had nervously anticipated from the man who had once said (though in private letters when not in power) that "a little rebellion now and then" was a good thing and that the tree of liberty needed occasional watering in the blood of patriots and tyrants.⁴ Instead they heard a promise of continuity. Hamilton took the words as "a pledge to the community that the new President will not lend himself to dangerous innovations, but in essential points will tread in the steps of his predecessors."⁵ John Marshall, who had written to Charles Pinckney that very morning of March 4 that Republicans were "speculative theorists and absolute terrorists," added a grumpy but relieved postscript in the afternoon that Jefferson's speech was "in general well judged and conciliatory . . . giving the lie to the violent party declamation which . . . elected him."⁶ One Federalist newspaper said: "His public assurances . . . have inspired us with a hope that *he is not the man we thought him.*"⁷

Republicans, of course, were ecstatic, and as the address made its way across the country in the press, gratifying hosannas rang in Jefferson's ears. The typical impression was voiced by Benjamin Rush, always the enthusiastic optimist. Rush saw the Federalists already fading away. "You have opened a new era," he wrote to his old friend the new president. "Never have I seen the public mind more generally or more agreeably affected by any publication. Old friends . . . separated by party names . . . for many years shook hands with each other. . . . It would require a page to contain the names of all the citizens (formerly called Federalists) who have spoken in the highest terms of your speech."[8]

But the honeymoon with critics was inevitably short. No one yet knew the specifics Jefferson had in mind. The nearest thing to a concrete statement in the inaugural address was the pledge of peace with all nations—of neutrality, rather than a pro-French policy, as the Federalists had feared. But just exactly what did the man from Monticello (to which he headed for a vacation on April 1) mean by a "wise and frugal" government guaranteeing "equal and exact justice to all men of whatever persuasion?" What would be cut? What would be added? What Jefferson had said was wonderful. But what would this nonpolitical politician do?

Jefferson's only other experience of executive responsibility had not been promising. He was wartime governor of Virginia from June 1779 to June 1781. The state had been invaded, Richmond had been captured, and a British raiding party had chased Jefferson out of Monticello for a day. Serious accusations of mismanagement and lack of preparation lingered around his reputation.

But given this second chance to lead—and on a larger scale—Jefferson rose to the challenge and made another major contribution to the revolution of 1800. He took the presidency that George Washington had invented and gave it its modern form.

✷

THIS TIME the fortunes of war were on his side. The fighting in Europe had been winding down, and in March 1802, the Peace of Amiens was signed, ending hostilities between France and England. The "peace" was actually a mere breathing spell, and at the end of 1803 it fell apart. But for most of his first term Jefferson was free of the problems of neutrality and harassment on the high seas that had tormented Washington and Adams for seven straight years. He could concentrate on his debt-reduction program without much concern for defense costs;

and even better, the revival of trade with the West Indies and Europe, no longer hampered by blockades and seizures, boosted the economy and poured customs revenues into the Treasury.

Jefferson *did* have a small war to handle, however, with one of the maritime racketeers of North Africa. In May 1801 the pasha of Tripoli, dissatisfied with the timing and amount of American "tribute" payments, declared war on the United States. Jefferson the antimilitarist candidate had condemned the costly naval buildup under Adams. But Jefferson the president did not hesitate to take some of the warships launched by Adams and send them to patrol and fight in the Mediterranean. The miniconflict lasted four years before the pasha gave in, and it made hero's reputations for American commanders like Edward Preble and especially Stephen Decatur. In 1804 Decatur led a daring raid into the harbor of Tripoli and, right under the enemy's noses and cannon, set ablaze and destroyed a powerful American frigate that they had captured and were busy converting to their own use. Jefferson's action wasn't necessarily inconsistent or hypocritical—he had always favored resistance to the extortion of the Barbary States. But it showed, in the opening weeks of his presidency, that where the national interest was concerned, he would be pragmatic rather than ideological. He might condemn war and preach strict construction of the Constitution, but he promptly sent the armed forces into overseas battle entirely on his presidential initiative. As an ironic footnote, Jefferson, always friendly to government-sponsored free education, signed legislation in 1802 establishing an engineering school in New York State for worthy young men who hoped to become professional army officers. And so Jefferson, who always professed a "passion for peace," was the first president to send Americans "to the shores of Tripoli" and the one who helped to found West Point.

Jefferson also was the first occupant of the executive residence to carry out a complete, conscious, and clearly defined program of "reform." He hated Hamilton's idea that a controlled national debt was a national "blessing" that gave the bankers who lent money to the United States a stake in its success. Jefferson saw that path as a sure road to corruption, speculation, high taxes, and bureaucracy, all of them burdens on "republican" freedom. What he wanted was for a "frugal" government to get rid of the debt, and, with the collaboration of Gallatin, who became his secretary of the Treasury, he went at it promptly. They devised a plan to pay down the $83 million worth of federal certificates of indebtedness, plus the accumulating interest, inside of sixteen years by earmarking $7.3 million a year for debt retirement. But they only estimated anticipated revenues at $10.5 million annually, especially since Jefferson insisted on cutting out "internal" taxes like the hated levy on whiskey. That would leave a mere $3.2 million for the government to spend per year, instead of the $10.8 million it had laid out in 1800 or the $9.7 million of 1799.

The only way to manage was to make deep cuts, especially in the diplomatic and military services. Embassies to Portugal, Prussia, and the Netherlands were closed. Naval ships not serving in North African waters were "laid up"—in twentieth-century terms, "mothballed." And the army was slashed to three thousand men to defend the thousands of miles of America's frontiers. Jefferson believed, as most Americans did for nearly a century and a half to follow, that in an emergency such as an invasion, militia could do the job. As it happened, even these reductions never shrank expenses below $7.8 million in Jefferson's two terms. But tariff revenues were up, and a fresh surge of westward expansion (bringing Ohio into the Union in 1802) increased public land sales, so the nation's yearly income from 1801 through 1804 was better than anticipated—between a low of $11 million and a high of nearly $15 million, generating hefty surpluses. The debt was down to $75.7 million by 1805 and got as low as $45.2 million before the War of 1812 shot it up again. Best of all, from Jefferson's point of view, he could say in his *second* inaugural address in March 1805, "What farmer, what mechanic, what laborer ever sees a tax-gatherer of the United States?"[9]

Setting and enacting a presidential agenda required a novel degree of top-down management. Washington presented a public image of command, but he was willing to let his cabinet set the course of policy after open discussions like the councils of war. He listened attentively to conflicting positions, then made up his mind. By contrast Jefferson kept cabinet sessions to a minimum, preferring to have the department heads iron out disputes among themselves before meetings—he hated time-wasting arguments—and encouraging all of them to communicate any suggestions to one another through him. He operated not in Washington's way but rather more like the master of Monticello, taking reports from his various supervisors and overseers to make sure that his guidelines were being followed.

Presidential initiatives also had to be turned into legislation on the floor of Congress. President Washington had never attempted to build a personal cadre of supporters in the House or Senate, although Hamilton had done so with some success. But President Jefferson worked quietly through the network of friendly congressional Republicans that his endless letter-writing had woven during his days out of power. North Carolina's Nathaniel Macon, speaker of the house in the new Congress, was an associate who knew what Jefferson wanted and saw to it that the committee chairmen he appointed knew, too. Both Madison, now secretary of state, and Gallatin freely kept up and used the collegial contacts they had made during their own past services as representatives. In the Senate a Virginia loyalist, Stevens T. Mason—the man who had ridden all the way from Virginia to Vermont with the money for Matthew Lyon's Sedition Act fine—was a competent floor leader until his death in 1803. Jefferson did not need to bulldoze or plead to find party followers to steer legislation through parliamentary roadblocks. All the while, however, he denied that he was interfering with congressional prerogatives. The Federalist minority, powerless against the solid phalanx of Jeffersonians, strenuously disagreed. "The President has only to act and the majority will approve," one of them grumbled: "In each house a majority of puppets move as he touches the wires."[10]

One lever of presidential power that later became traditional was the use of patronage, the winning of a congressman's vote by appointing his nominees to office. Here, however, Jefferson was limited by his own self-imposed rules. He wanted to reduce, not enlarge, the number of federal offices to be awarded, and he was ambivalent about creating vacancies by firing incumbent Federalists. For one thing, he continued to feel that he was above partisanship and would fill posts only on the basis of merit. For another, as part of the conciliatory strategy suggested by the inaugural address, he expected to retain some deserving Federalist functionaries and convert them into good Republicans.

But in actual practice he made liberal exceptions. Adams's lame-duck appointments—those made after mid-December 1800, when the Federalist defeat was known—were fair game for removal, since they flouted the results of the election. So were Federalists impossibly rooted in their wickedness, those "whom I abandon as incurables," as he told Monroe.[11] And in some cases Jefferson, whether he liked it or not, had to consider the demands of loyal Republicans in the states for a clean sweep of Federalist customs, excise, and postal workers. Their views were summed up by a New York editor who asked: "If this should not be the case, for what, in the name of God, have we been contending?"[12] It was impossible to preside over the country's first change in administrations from one party to another and be deaf to claims for the spoils. Like presidents after him, Jefferson found that satisfying office seekers was a major aggravation, since every choice that made a friend also made enemies among those passed over. Yet the job, he said, "like the office of hangman . . . must be executed by someone."[13] In all, he transferred about half of roughly 330 "significant civil offices," according to one biographer,[14] into new hands. He insisted privately that only a tiny fraction of the changes were for political reasons. But each award tightened the connections of the Jeffersonian party machinery whose existence its leader denied. One plum appointment—as the first Librarian of Congress—went to the faithful Republican factotum John Beckley, who was also reelected to his old job as clerk of the House of Representatives.

In a pretelephone era, the only way that even a president could keep up with his official and political business was to spend long hours with a pen in his hand. Jefferson got up with the sun and stuck to his desk until one in the afternoon, with a brief recess for breakfast. Then he rode horseback for an hour or two in Washington's wooded or marshy lanes, often stopping to chat with townspeople high and low. Dinner was around 3:30 or 4:00 P.M., and he would often go back to writing for an hour or two after it was finished. But Jefferson's renowned table had its managerial uses, too. The new president enjoyed informal dinner parties of eight to ten, to which members of Congress were often invited. He began by trying to mix Federalists and Republicans but had to give it up after a while when the chill became too great—even though there was an understood rule against talking politics and he himself often steered the conversation to science, history, and literature. Still, even a "nonpolitical" evening among congressmen comfortably filling their stomachs with dishes of soup, rice, eggs, turkey, mutton, ham, veal, and beef, followed by ice creams, custards, fruits, and tarts prepared in the best French style and accompanied by the very best of imported wines (Jefferson's annual wine bill alone was about $2,400) could not fail to produce fond memories that would be helpful the next time a bill was introduced that carried a presidential recommendation. The diplomatic corps and the rest of Washington's official establishment enjoyed Jeffersonian hospitality, too, although some of the stuffier royal ambassadors were ruffled by the practice of guests seating themselves "pell mell," wherever was most convenient, rather than following a strict order of priority based on rank.

In all these ways, Thomas Jefferson was making his influence palpable in policymaking, even though he had always denounced the tendency to a strong executive. Unlike Washington, who had a different agenda, he worked hard at avoiding ceremony, and he was capable of startling visiting dignitaries by sometimes receiving them in slippers, vest, and corduroy breeches. He even made a point of not delivering his annual message to Congress in person because it struck him as too much like an "address from the throne" to Parliament. (He sent it up to Capitol Hill to be read by a clerk instead. The practice stuck until 1913. Nowadays, billed as the State of the Union address, it is a major public relations event.) For all that scrupulousness, though, Jefferson was turning himself and his majority leaders in Congress into a working team. In doing so, he was blurring the lines between the branches and laying down the foundations for the active kind of presidential leadership that later giants in the office like Jackson, Lincoln, and the two Roosevelts would emulate.

He could not so easily influence the third of the federal government's "separated powers," the judiciary, although he tried hard. He had never stopped fuming over the new judgeships created by the Judiciary Act of January 1801 and filled by Adams. To him it was a scheme by which his enemies had "retreated into the judiciary as a stronghold," from which, protected by lifetime tenure, they would keep up the fight against him.[15] The least he could do was to urge the repeal of the act, and no sooner had the Seventh Congress met in December than it took up the matter and, inside of two months, scrubbed it from the books. The "midnight judges" were not dismissed. Their jobs simply disappeared, and none took the risk of challenging the repeal in the Supreme Court. All the same, Jefferson could not throw out Federalist life-term judges already sitting before 1801, and above all he could not undo the appointment of John Marshall as chief justice.

Early in 1803 Marshall scored the first points in a careerlong battle with Jefferson by handing down the landmark decision of *Marbury* v. *Madison*. William Marbury was one of the midnight appointees, a justice of the peace named by Adams. Jefferson ordered Madison, as secretary of state, not to deliver Marbury his commission of office. Marbury petitioned the Supreme Court for a "writ of mandamus," an order that would force Jefferson to carry out the lawful intention of the outgoing president. The issue was clear. Was the president subject to the chief justice's orders like any other official? Could he be punished if he refused? Marshall's opinion shrewdly ducked a direct confrontation. It denounced the president for denying Marbury what he was legally entitled to—but then went on to say that the Supreme Court could not do anything to help Marbury because the 1789 law authorizing it to issue writs of mandamus had no basis in the Constitution, which specifically limited the kinds of cases that could be initiated in, rather than appealed to, the nation's highest court. And a statute that contradicted the Constitution, the highest law of the land, could not by definition be applied. Unlucky Marbury was without a remedy.

On the surface it looked like a surrender to Jefferson. Actually, however, Marshall was making the sweeping assertion that a law passed in good faith by congressmen and signed by a president, all of them also able to read and understand the Constitution, simply had no force and effect if judges on the bench concluded that it was inconsistent with the Constitution's provisions. That could happen whenever a plaintiff brought suit claiming that a national or, for that matter, a state law deprived him of some constitutional right. And therefore in practice, the final word on what the Constitution meant would rest with one of the three supposedly "equal" branches, the federal judiciary, the only one whose decision-making personnel could not be changed by elections. The doctrine of "judicial review" did not dovetail comfortably with the idea of popular government.

Confronted with this setback, Jefferson made an effort to counterattack by proposing the removal of Associate Justice Chase, famed for his intemperate outbursts in Sedition Act trials, on the grounds of his blatant partisanship. The House of Representatives duly impeached Chase in 1804. But in the Senate trial the following year, a two-thirds vote for conviction could not be mustered. Pro-Federalist harangues from the bench did not clearly qualify as a "high crime and misdemeanor," and even some Republican senators worried about using impeachment as a tool to force a wholesale change of judges every time there was a new administration. "Old Bacon Face" remained where he was, and historians generally agree that it was a fortunate decision for Marshall: if Chase had been ousted, Jefferson might have gone after the chief justice next. As it was, Chase's escape frustrated Jefferson's only really "revolutionary" attack on the status quo and guaranteed that "republicanism" would have to learn to live in a permanent though often stormy relationship with a lifetime-tenured judiciary and judicial review. The best Jefferson could do against the judges was to drop the prosecution of still-pending cases under the hated Sedition Act, which had automatically expired anyway in 1801.

The courts never had a chance, however, to deal with Thomas Jefferson's most sweeping, unforeseen, transformative, and probably unconstitutional exercise of raw presidential power, the Louisiana Purchase.

✳

THE STORY is well enough known to require little repetition in detail. By the spring of 1802 it was known for certain that Napoleon had forced Spain, under the Treaty of San Ildefonso, to cede to France New Orleans and all of the vaguely defined territory known as Louisiana. He had then dispatched twenty-five thousand troops to the West Indies to retake Santo Domingo—that is, modern-day Haiti and the Dominican Republic—from Toussaint-L'Ouverture, after which they would move on to occupy the emperor's new New World possession. Instead of toothless Spain, the world's greatest military power would have an army stationed on the western frontier and would control the vital outlet of the Mississippi River. The gateway to the unsettled empire of land where Americans would fulfill their future promise "to the thousandth generation" would be closed forever, and the commerce of the existing states and territories beyond the Alleghenies choked to death.

Jefferson could not hide his anxiety, and he wasted no time on channels. He wrote directly, and not through Secretary of State Madison, to the American minister in Paris, New York Republican Robert Livingston. Something would have to be done and done quickly to avoid a disaster. "There is on the globe one single spot, the possessor of which is our natural and habitual enemy, " said Jefferson. Napoleon was stepping into that role, and from the moment the French flag was raised over New Orleans, "we must marry ourselves to the British fleet and nation," an appalling prospect of dependence.[16] Next, not trusting Livingston to handle the situation alone, the president dispatched his trusty longtime protégé, James Monroe, to join Livingston in Paris, and there to offer Napoleon a sum of ten million dollars—not yet appropriated and certain to shatter the austerity budget—to buy New Orleans and as much of the territory surrounding it as they could.

Once more, luck was on Jefferson's side. The French force in the Caribbean was decimated by yellow fever and black military resistance. It failed to subdue Toussaint-L'Ouverture's troops (though Toussaint himself was tricked into capture) during the winter of 1802–3. Napoleon was also beginning to prepare for the inevitable resumption of war with England and decided that he would prefer ready cash to a faraway North American province from which he could easily be cut off. He offered to sell the United States the entire, uncertainly bounded territory known as Louisiana, for fifteen million dollars, almost exactly the government's income for the previous year of 1802. The news reached Washington on July 4, 1803. The deal was consummated as fast as wind and wave could carry the president's approval to Paris. France's foreign minister was the great survivor, Talleyrand, who told Livingston and Monroe that they had "made a noble bargain" for themselves. They certainly had. The Louisiana Territory, after eventual agreement on its boundaries, turned out to stretch from the Mississippi to the Rockies and to include all or part of what would become fifteen states of the Union[17]—some 830,000 resource-rich square miles, bought at an estimated cost of three cents an acre.

Jefferson had not even waited for Napoleon's answer to the Livingston-Monroe proffer before authorizing Meriwether Lewis, his secretary, to prepare a "scientific" expedition through the region and on to the west coast of North America to see if a water route to the Pacific existed. He did that in April 1803, so anxious was he to find out more about that trans-Mississippi region that he once called "an empire for liberty." Lewis and his partner, William Clark, set off from Washington to begin assembling their exploring party just as word arrived that they would officially be on American soil for most of the trip.

Once he had his prize in hand, Jefferson had to deal with his own uncomfortable awareness that there was absolutely nothing in the Constitution authorizing his action—he had dealt with Napoleon as one "boss" to another, though of course he intended to go to Congress for approval and funding. He thought at first of submitting a request for a constitutional amendment along with the legislation to acquire Louisiana, but then he became afraid that it would lead to wrangling and delay. So he told his attorney general that "the less that is said about my constitutional difficulty, the better. . . . [I]t will be desirable for Congress to do what is necessary in silence."[18] There was no problem. The Republican majority quickly approved the sale, in spite of Federalist objections best put by the versatile John Quincy Adams, who had come back from diplomatic service abroad to practice law, become a professor of literature at Harvard instead, and was then elected to the Senate from Massachusetts. In Senator Adams's words, the purchase was "an assumption of implied powers greater . . . than all the assump-

tions of implied powers in the years of the Washington and Adams administrations put together."[19] Hamilton could hardly have stretched the
Constitution further. When it was necessary to provide some temporary
government for the area around New Orleans occupied mostly by
French-speaking Creoles, Jefferson, the denouncer of unrepresentative
government, had his Congress enact an ordinance that allowed him to
appoint a governor who would rule with the help of an unelected council. He submitted his draft to a Kentucky senator to be introduced without admitting his own authorship, well knowing that the Federalists
would be quick to attack his overnight conversion to rule by decree.

No serious public thinker, then or since, would disapprove the
Louisiana Purchase. It doubled the size of the United States overnight,
laid one foundation for her dazzling economic growth, and made the little republic an inland empire obviously earmarked for a great future
among the powers of the earth. But it was achieved because Jefferson,
believing he embodied the popular will, saw a personal chance to make
a move that was beneficial to the American nation—and unhesitatingly
made it. Because of his previous opposition to executive Caesarism, he
was in a better position to get away with it than either of the presidents
before him. In one sense, then, the wonders that flowed from the
"noble bargain" also became part of the legacy of 1800.

✴

THAT JEFFERSON WAS the people's choice could hardly be
doubted, even though there were no popularity polls, no "photo ops," not
even any photos. In fact, since the press lacked even the technique for
good reproduction of drawings, most Americans did not even know what
their president looked like. But the beginnings of a popular presidency
were already visible in the somewhat primitive public relations events devised by Republican supporters—like the twelve-hundred-pound cheese,
four feet in diameter and a foot and a quarter thick, presented to the president on New Year's Day 1802 by the farmers of Cheshire, Massachusetts.
Made from the milk of nine hundred "Republican" cows, it was carried to
Washington by sloop and wagon and eventually served to White House
guests after ripening in the unfinished East Room for over a year.

Travel conditions of the time precluded a heavy schedule of public demonstrations, however, which allowed Jefferson to continue his own personally preferred invisibility. At the same time, he was freely quoted by a friendly press and his name featured in Republican celebrations, so that he could acquire the popularity that allowed him to lead. He had his private definition of what popularity meant. He would not pretend to be all things to all men or count noses (even if it were possible) to decide what was right. That was the demagoguery that Federalists insisted was part of his nature. But as he put it, "He who would do his country the most good . . . must go quietly with the prejudices of the majority until he can lead them into reason."[20] To guide without seeming to be at the head of the column was the art of democratic administration. How well it worked and rubbed off on the party was shown by the 1802 off-year elections. Republicans increased their Senate lead to 25 seats out of the 34 now available, including Ohio's, and their House margin to 102–39.

By 1804 Thomas Jefferson had become a special kind of president. He was more than a unifying symbol, a republican monarch as Washington had been. He seemed to embody the collective self-image of Americans, to be the force to whom they looked to reflect and enact their wishes. It was a contradictory role for a shy thinker of aristocratic tastes, but it was only one of the intriguing contradictions of Thomas Jefferson. He was large enough, to use a phrase of Walt Whitman's from many years later, to contain multitudes.

As the next election neared, Jefferson made up his mind, like almost every incumbent first-tem president, to run a second time. There was one piece of preliminary business to dispatch, which was to avoid the horror of another tie—especially a tie with Aaron Burr, whose relationship with Jefferson and with the party had steadily chilled. In the first session of the Eighth Congress congressional Republicans introduced the Twelfth Amendment. It provided that electors should vote distinctly in separate ballots for a president and a vice president. Sent to the states in December 1803, it had received the needed thirteen ratifications by the next June and was in effect by September 1804. Only the Federalists resisted, mainly because the old system offered a better chance of electoral success, but also because they said it would put a seal on the insignificance of the Vice Presidency, which no promising politician would accept if he could help it.

In the campaign the Republican caucus named New York's canny veteran George Clinton, at that point a Burr enemy, to the vice presidential spot. The Federalists nominated Charles Cotesworth Pinckney for president and also chose a favorite son from electoral-vote-rich New York, Rufus King, for the vice presidency. There wasn't much to campaign about. Low taxes, peace, prosperity, and Louisiana gave Jefferson an enormous advantage, and the best that the opposition could do was to sling mud, itself a sign of how important the personal image of the president had become. But no scandals would overcome the good Republican record. The Jefferson-Clinton ticket won in the first political landslide of the new century, the first election under the Twelfth Amendment, and the second to take place within a two-party system that was already, though unofficially, a part of the machinery of self-government. To call it a two-party system in 1804 almost seems like an exaggeration. The president carried every state but Delaware and Connecticut and had 162 electoral votes to 14 for the Federalists, two of those coming from Maryland. The congressional vote was even more lopsided. In the House, grown to 141 members after the new census, the Republicans would have a 116–25 majority, plus 27 of 34 senators.

With that gigantic mandate, so different from the crisis of four years earlier, the "revolution" was ratified and sealed. The Republicans had not only taken power peacefully, but they had managed to virtually wipe out the opposition, at least temporarily, without a single act of violence against any man, without a weapon raised or a detention order issued. After the terrible days of threats and protests and prophecies of doom—after the mobs, the liberty poles, the broken windows, the flaming effigies—after the whiskey rebels and the sedition jailings—after all that, Americans had kept the republic.

All that remains is to listen for the echoes that are still reverberating.

Aftermath and Echoes

THE ELECTION of 1800 stands almost alone in United States history as a drama with the fate of the Constitution at stake. There was only one other like it. In 1860 the rampaging slavery question finally broke out of the cage where the politicians had tried to keep it for seventy-three years. Slaveholders swore that they would not accept the election of Abraham Lincoln. He won, eleven southern states seceded, and war followed. In 1800 the nation had escaped a breakup. In 1860 it was not so lucky.

Almost but not quite as perilous was the election of 1876. That one had to be settled by the whole Congress. Three southern states turned in double sets of electoral votes, each proclaimed as official, and each backed by a party charging that the others were fraudulent. Neither of the presidential candidates, Rutherford B. Hayes and Samuel Tilden, had a majority without at least some of them. There was talk on both sides of fighting rather than surrendering, but in the end a special commission of senators, representatives, and justices of the Supreme Court made a last-minute deal that gave Hayes the disputed votes and the White House in exchange for political concessions. This "Compromise of 1877" put the stamp of closure on the sixteen years of destruction and rebuilding that began with the Civil War.

One other presidential election—in 1824—was decided in the House of Representatives because neither Andrew Jackson, John Quincy Adams, nor Henry Clay, the three contenders, had a majority of electoral tallies. Jackson had the highest number, but a combination of Clay and Adams supporters gave Adams the victory. Supporters of Jackson raged that the people's choice had been corruptly denied, but they were compensated when Jackson won easily in 1828.

With those three exceptions, the forty-nine presidential contests that followed Jefferson's victory in the House were settled noisily, but without threats, in the voting booths. The precedent set by Federalists and Republicans in 1800 made that possible.

The election of 1800 was also, for all intents and purposes, the last to divide people and parties somewhat evenly between two warring European powers. Never again would "Anglomen" and "Gallomen" confront each other with hot words and raised fists. Though the Franco-British war resumed, American friends of the French Revolution were not inclined to defend Napoleon's imperial vision. And even Federalist admirers of His Majesty's government kept their opinions private when the British navy turned into a major tormentor of American ships. It began "impressing" (to wit, snatching) sailors from the decks of merchantmen and in one 1807 case took four sailors from a United States naval vessel, the USS *Chesapeake*, after forcing her to surrender with an attack that killed three and wounded eighteen. In the War of 1812 the United States did not take the side of France but carried on a private fight with the British.

After that there were no major European conflicts on anything like the Napoleonic scale until the great wars of 1914 and 1939. America did enter those wars after prolonged debate, but there was no great divide between partisans of Great Britain and Germany. The issue was basically between benevolent pro-British neutrality or intervention. Other American wars have been divisive at home. The one with Mexico in 1846–48 was denounced by abolitionists; the 1899–1901 campaign to conquer the Philippines drew resistance from anti-imperialists; and a large cross section of the population spoke out against the Vietnam War. But these crises did not involve choosing sides in fights among foreigners—and by luck or design, the advice of Washington and Jefferson to avoid demeaning and quarrelsome partiality to other countries has generally been followed in every election of the last two centuries.

There have been presidential elections that were crucial in ratifying a change in the country's political direction, like the landslide of 1936 for Franklin D. Roosevelt and the New Deal. Or earlier, in 1896 and 1900, when successive wins for William McKinley showed a popular will to industrialism and empire. But in those elections, the rules themselves were never questioned. Americans had at least that much trust in one another. The winners took the reins and the losers bided their time and waited for the voters to give different directions four years down the road. It was and is the best of systems, the gift that Americans of 1800 gave to themselves and to those peoples of the world who eventually caught up with their example.

✶

OTHER "BEQUESTS" of the 1800 campaign are less admirable, including the vice presidency under the Twelfth Amendment. A distinct vote for vice president prevented any more tie votes, but it did not solve the failure of the Founding Fathers to meet the basic problem of finding someone well enough qualified to become a good president at a moment's notice but modest enough to spend four or eight years in a trivial and meaningless post. Gouverneur Morris, in opposing the amendment, correctly argued that no politician with any reasonable career prospects would want the job, and it would become a kind of minnow bait dangled before loyal party members who could add some regional, ethnic, or other interest-group votes to the ticket. So it proved with rare exceptions, as shown by a long string of now obscure second fiddlers like Daniel Tompkins (Monroe), George Dallas (Polk), Hannibal Hamlin (Lincoln), Schuyler Colfax (Grant), Garret Hobart (McKinley), and Thomas Marshall (Wilson). Only the seven who succeeded by accident up to 1945 got into the history texts, and only two of those, Theodore Roosevelt and Harry Truman, had unexpectedly great presidencies.[1] Martin Van Buren, after completing a vice presidential term under Jackson, ran for the highest office and won in 1836. He was the first post-1800 vice president to do so. He would also be the last for more than a century—until Richard Nixon, who had been Eisenhower's vice president for eight years, managed it in 1968. Truman and Lyndon Johnson won terms of their own (in 1948 and 1964), but only after finishing out the presidencies of their deceased predecessors.

The vice president is often a stranger not only to the public but to his own president and cabinet. That led to the frightening situation on April 12, 1945, when Truman became instant commander in chief, decision maker, and world leader, knowing nothing about the atomic bomb or other war plans. Since then, prudent chief executives have shared more information with their "shadow" successors, and the stature of the "veep" has grown into that of an heir apparent. Of the nine vice presidents between 1952 and 2000, two (Johnson and Ford) succeeded by death or resignation and four became their party's presidential candidates. Two of those won their races.[2]

So the position is no longer a graveyard for ambition. Still, a century and a half's worth of political second-stringers standing a heartbeat away from the Oval Office was an unattractive outcome of the Burr-Jefferson deadlock in 1800.

And then there was the spoils system—the replacement of middle- and junior-ranking government officials with political friends and partners. Jefferson did it sparingly, but he was still the first to strengthen an incoming new party with such appointments. Thirty-two years later, in Andrew Jackson's time, a senator from New York gave the system its name with his remark on the floor: "To the victors belong the spoils." For years presidents were hounded by literally thousands of applicants for insignificant clerkships—an unwelcome souvenir of Jefferson's precedent—until the modern civil service system finally confined presidential appointive responsibilities to the highest levels.

※

IMPORTANT EVENTS were still in store for many participants in the 1800 election drama—enough to end the story with a wrap-up worthy of a Victorian novel. First, there were the two old friends turned to foes, Jefferson and Adams. For Jefferson, 1804 was the pinnacle of his public life, but it brought private heartache. In April his younger daughter, Maria, only twenty-four, died in childbirth like her mother before her. The grief-stricken president could never be reconciled to this latest loss.

Then followed a second term that turned into a calamity. The rekindled European war brought back all America's woes as a powerless neutral. France and England again tried to cut each other off from the granaries of the New World, with American ships as pawns and victims in the struggle. Looking for a peaceful solution, Jefferson decided to compel respect by denying to both parties—especially the British on their small island—the imported foodstuffs on which they depended. He got Congress to pass the Embargo Act of 1807, imposing a total ban on exports to belligerent territories. It was a sweeping suppression of commerce, a total back flip from the Republicans' limited-government philosophy. And it blew up in the president's face. Depression paralyzed the economy, idle ships rotted at the docks, unsold crops spoiled in the barns, and idle workers cursed the "Ograbme" (*embargo* spelled backward). Though Madison won the 1808 election, Jefferson's final months in office, which ended with him dejectedly signing the embargo's repeal, were tainted forever.

He returned to Monticello for the seventeen years left him. He farmed, entertained visitors with food, wine, and music, played with his eleven grandchildren, continued scientific experiments and endless improvements of the main house, pushed his state toward creating a public school system, and helped to found the University of Virginia. He coped unsuccessfully with his eternal debts and his growing list of illnesses. And he wrote letters, many of them to John Adams, with whom he resumed correspondence in 1811. For both old men the exchanges were invigorating. Though they addressed each other, each man seemed to write with an eye on explaining himself to posterity. The letters are still a pleasure for posterity to read.

The two old foes circled cautiously around the politics of the day and did not linger over recollections of the 1790s, neither wishing to imperil the repaired friendship. Otherwise they ranged through wide realms of history and literature familiar to both of them as omnivorous readers in several languages. Having at last struck back at his old enemies (other than Jefferson) through a number of communications to the press, Adams seemed relieved and at peace. His letters were more frequent, playful, and ironic. He stuck to his vinegary doubts about the goodness of human nature, while Jefferson, despite his personal burdens, did not lose faith in progress and the essential soundness of popular judgment.

On July 4, 1826, John Adams at ninety and Thomas Jefferson at eighty-three died within hours of each other. They left the world hand in hand fifty years to the day after seeing through the adoption of the Declaration of Independence. It is hard to shake the impression of some divine stage manager at work.

✳

NO WRITER of romances would have dared imagine the outcomes awaiting that other great pair of antagonists of 1800, Burr and Hamilton. By 1804 Burr had no political future. The Republicans—and Jefferson—were convinced that he was untrustworthy. He was cut out of decision making and patronage and certain to be replaced on the ticket. Still only forty-eight years old and full of appetites, Burr was not yet ready to vanish into the wings. He set his sight on the governorship of New York, to be decided that April, and he courted the state's Federalists, among whom he still had some standing.

But that brought the renewed opposition of Hamilton. He, too, nearing fifty, was in a cul-de-sac of blocked ambition, a man going nowhere, blamed by most of his party for losing the 1800 election through his senseless attack on Adams. But he had not lost all influence. When Burr ran and lost by eight thousand votes out of about fifty thousand cast, he and others were convinced that the fault lay with defections by Federalist voters thanks to a vigorous anti-Burr effort on Hamilton's part.

A few days after the election a private letter from a New York Federalist found its way into the *Albany Register.* It described a dinner party at which "General" Hamilton had called Burr a dangerous man, and the letter writer then added: "I could detail to you a still more despicable opinion" that General Hamilton has expressed of Mr. Burr. On reading this, Burr wrote to Hamilton asking him to "acknowledge or deny" that he had expressed a "despicable opinion" of him. Hamilton did not like dueling, especially after losing his son Philip to a duel a few years earlier. He answered with a request for particulars. Exchanges of notes went on, with Burr getting more peremptory in his demands that Hamilton repudiate all past attacks on him, and Hamilton trying to leave loopholes for compromise without surrendering his own "honor." Finally, the correspondence broke off, the challenge was sent, the seconds chosen, and the "interview" set for the morning of July 11, 1804, in Weehawken, New Jersey, on secluded woodland heights just across the Hudson River from Manhattan. Dueling was illegal in both states but rarely prosecuted if done discreetly.

The two men, so alike in some ways, so hostile in others, prepared for their last encounter. The night before, Burr wrote to daughter Theodosia asking her, if he should fall, to burn any of his papers whose publication would be embarrassing, especially from "female correspondents." Hamilton told a friend that he meant to "reserve his first fire" and see what Burr's response would be. Duels sometimes ended bloodlessly with both parties taking that course. But when the signal was given, two reports echoed off the cliffs. Hamilton's shot went high and wide and clipped off a tree branch over Burr's head. Burr's bullet tore through Hamilton's abdominal cavity and lodged in his spine. He died of internal injuries the next day. When the news inevitably broke, a furious public forced prosecutors and grand juries on both sides of the Hudson to indict the vice president of the United States for murder.

Burr would always swear that Hamilton had fired at him. Hamilton's second insisted that the general's shot was a reflex as his arm jerked upward when he was hit. Like so much about Aaron Burr, the truth will remain a mystery. He was rushed into hiding, then went to Georgia and Florida for the rest of the year. But though Aaron Burr, like Don Giovanni, might be a sinner, he would not show cowardice. He appeared in Washington to preside over his final term as presiding officer of the Senate. Ironically, one of his duties was to run the impeachment trial of Justice Chase, which by all accounts he did fairly.

His bizarre story wasn't yet over. In 1805 and 1806 Burr's travels and activities included various visits to the West to look over land investments, consult maps, meet with various movers and shakers, and draw castles in the air. And, it's alleged, to discuss various sinister schemes for raising a private army and seizing Florida and/or Mexico, leading a march on Washington, separating the West from the Union—rumors, conflicting testimony, and legends surround the facts. Whatever was going on, Jefferson decided that Aaron Burr was in fact a dangerous man who needed to be stopped.

On March 30, 1807, the fifty-one-year-old Burr was indicted for plotting treason against the United States of America. The trial took place in the Circuit Court in Richmond under Chief Justice Marshall, who took great pains to instruct the jurors that a guilty verdict required proof (which was unobtainable) of Burr's actual participation in a treasonable gathering. Mere involvement by correspondence and arrangements was not enough. This was practically a directed verdict of acquittal. The actual verdict was rendered after a long process, much to Jefferson's frustration and Marshall's pleasure at defeating him.

It was time for Burr to get away from arrest warrants, attorneys, and bill collectors. He sailed for Great Britain in 1809 and spent four years there and in France trying unsuccessfully to interest Napoleon in new projects to get a foothold in North America, to be led by Burr, of course. In 1812, when the indictments had expired, he returned to New York. He went back to his law practice and became a familiar figure in the courts, a genial old man still surrounded by a circle of young admirers and distrusted by proper people, still a polished gallant, still chronically insolvent. In July 1833 he married the well-fixed widow of Stephen Jumel, a New York businessman. Inside of a year she sued him for divorce for running through her estate. On September 14, 1836, Burr died on Staten Island, less than ninety days after the passing of his onetime Princeton classmate, James Madison.

*

WHETHER OR NOT John Marshall's appointment to the chief justiceship in January 1801 was a calculated effort by Adams to hold back the Republican tide, it did exactly that with enormous success. The Federalist Party went aground, but Federalist principles of national supremacy and encouragement to business were nailed into the Constitution during the third of a century—until 1835—that Marshall held the office. Personally easygoing and as democratic as any Blue Ridge farmer in his personal contacts, he was nevertheless a dominating fig-

ure on the bench. He wrote more than half of the eleven hundred opinions issued during his tenure. He was almost never on the dissenting
(i.e., losing) side and often persuaded his colleagues to make the decisions unanimous. He wrote a clear and nonlegalistic prose that, according to his opponents, began with a proposition he favored and then
irresistibly bent the law and the facts to fit.

States' rights took a backseat in one landmark Marshall decision after
another. A state could not rescind a fraudulent land grant[3] or change a
private college's charter of incorporation because both were "contracts,"
obligations that could not be "impaired."[4] A state could not tax a branch
of the Bank of the United States, because the Bank operated under a national government charter, which was superior to the state's taxing
power.[5] A state could not grant a transportation monopoly on a river that
separated it from another, because that cut into the exclusive national
power to regulate interstate commerce.[6] And the Constitution itself was
a compact not among sovereign states but between the national government and the entire people of the United States, whose collective will
was superior to that of any one state's populace.[7] Throughout the hundreds of Justice Marshall's opinions ran the thread of a strong, tight
sense of single nationhood, born in Lieutenant Marshall's experiences
on the battlefields of the Revolution. He did as much as his old commander, Washington, to make that sentiment a reality.

✳

JEFFERSON'S MAJOR AIDES in fashioning his victory were well
rewarded. Madison, who was a prime creator both of the Constitution
and the Republican Party, succeeded to the presidency in 1808 and was
reelected in 1812. The victory turned somewhat sour for him because
the War of 1812, which he was unable to avoid, was a failure. The Republican philosophy of small budgets and minimal government was not
designed for wartime. American history books for schoolchildren focus
on a few small naval victories and the defeat of a British invasion force
at New Orleans—which took place three weeks after the peace treaty
was signed in Europe but before the news could reach America. They
give less emphasis to the British capture, brief occupation, and torching

of Washington in August 1814. Madison literally had to flee for his life along with the rest of the national government. But he returned to finish out his term and live on to be an elder statesman of eighty-five, the last survivor of the Constitutional Convention.

Following Madison came two terms in the White House for James Monroe. Among them, Jefferson and his two chief Virginia lieutenants held the presidency for almost the whole first quarter of the nineteenth century. The third stalwart Jeffersonian comrade in arms, Albert Gallatin, left the Treasury Department and domestic politics in 1813 for a long and successful career as a diplomat. At seventy he settled down in New York City as a banker and civic leader, sponsor of New York University and the New York Historical Society, and, as a hobby, a pioneer in the study of American Indian culture. He was the last of the trio to pass on, in 1849, his eighty-ninth year.

When Monroe retired, he spent six years in Virginia but then moved to New York City, his wife's original home. In 1831, the year of his death, he, Gallatin, and Aaron Burr were all living there, in what was still a small place. There is a certain piquancy in imagining what memories of 1800 and 1801 those three onetime campaign teammates would have shared if and when they ran into one another.

※

THE LAST MEMBERS of the cast of 1800 whose influence lingers on were the Federalist and Republican Parties as a whole. In important and surprising ways they are with us still, although Jefferson's lopsided 1804 win left the impression that he had buried the Federalist heresy in a grave from which it would never be resurrected. Without a strong national leader after Hamilton was killed and Marshall moved up to the bench, the Federalist Party could not take advantage of the reaction against the embargo. Charles Cotesworth Pinckney, running for president a second time, got only 47 of 176 electoral votes. After that he abandoned politics to become a Charleston patriarch—college founder, chairman of the Bible and Library Associations, honorary militia commander. Brother Thomas did much the same and, like his mother, spent happy years experimenting with ways to improve Carolina's agricultural output.

The two gentlemanly, English-raised brothers represented southern federalism in its best but also in its final form. After 1808 the party was almost entirely a New England splinter group dominated by the likes of Timothy Pickering, who stubbornly swam against the democratic current. They also tarred themselves with disloyalty by bitter resistance to the 1812 war. And the end came quickly. The last Federalist candidate for president, Rufus King, got just 34 of 226 electoral votes in 1816. The last Congress to seat any members calling themselves Federalists—4 senators out of 48 and 26 representatives among 213—was chosen in 1822. The United States seemed to be a one-party (or, as Jefferson would have liked to think of it, a no-party) country.

But if the Federalist Party was dead, all of its ideas were not—especially Marshall's nationalism and Hamilton's program of nationally sponsored economic development. These lived on and found a home in former "enemy" ranks. A number of self-styled "national" Republicans abandoned Jefferson's economics for Hamilton's. They called for a central bank, federal support for road and canal building, river and harbor dredging, and other "internal improvements" to the transportation network—and a tariff to encourage manufactures. Eventually they coalesced into a National Republican Party, which, in the mid-1830s, renamed itself the Whig Party.

In the meantime there was a change of labels in the opposite camp. Thomas Jefferson's followers in the 1790s had only rarely referred to themselves as Democratic-Republicans, although many reference books try to avoid confusion by assuming otherwise. *Democracy* was, for many, an alienating word back then. But as the tide of "universal [that is, white, propertyless male] suffrage" rolled on in the new century, Jefferson's political legatees were not reluctant to use it—and finally began unabashedly calling themselves Democrats. By 1840, both Whigs and Democrats were holding regular nominating conventions and running modern-style campaigns. The two-party system was back.

Then, in the 1850s, the alignments were scrambled again by the question of whether slavery should expand into the vast continental area not yet organized into states, now stretching as far as the Pacific. The levers of the Democratic Party fell into the hands of southerners out of

step with the country's growing reluctance to give slavery a foothold on
the future via implantation in the territories. Northern and western Democrats, both from principle and political realism, protested that Jefferson's basic message of liberty was being betrayed. In 1854 hundreds of
them met with representatives of the Whigs, who had also broken up
over the issue, and of other groups pushing for "free soil," and created a
brand new organization. To show that they were the genuine and true
heirs of the revolution of 1800, they took the old Jeffersonian name for
the new alliance. The modern Republican Party was born. Six years later
it elected a former Whig, Abraham Lincoln, to the presidency.

Thanks to this convoluted line of political genealogy, today's Republican and Democratic Parties can both claim descent from Thomas
Jefferson's original creation.

In the 146 years since, both parties have played beanbag with the
ideas of Jefferson (and Lincoln). The Republicans have generally stood
for nationally supported probusiness policies, but when convenient
they have invoked Jeffersonian notions of a government that taxes
lightly, regulates rarely, and stays within narrowly defined boundaries of
authority. Liberal Democrats, in contrast, especially since the New
Deal, use Jefferson's commitment to freedom, progress, and equality to
justify social programs funded and administered by the federal government and designed to help minorities, the poor, and the disadvan-
taged—-Hamiltonian means, some might say, for Jeffersonian ends.
Neither party is completely consistent, and neither has paid much attention since 1945 to Jefferson's strongly antimilitaristic message.

There is consensus on the virtues of a strong government when it
comes to foreign and military policy. And, rhetoric aside, the polls and the
record show that both businessmen and individuals want an activist central government, provided that they control it through their votes and per-
ceive it as acting on their side. Yet they also want their local communities
and governments preserved, and their individual freedoms—the rights to
life, liberty, and the pursuit of happiness—guaranteed and kept intact.

Which means that it is still as true as it was on March 4, 1801, that
we are "all republicans, all federalists." The revolution is still at work.

Notes

PROLOGUE

1. Ralph Adams Brown, *The Presidency of John Adams* (Lawrence: University of Kansas Press, 1975), 207–8.
2. Ibid., 206.
3. John Ferling, *John Adams: A Life* (New York: Henry Holt and Co., 1996), 409.
4. Brown, *Presidency*, 207.
5. Brown, *Presidency*, 206; Ferling, *John Adams* ("Genteel Dwelling"), 296.
6. To Benjamin Stoddert, 31 Mar. 1801, quoted in Richard Rosenfeld, *American Aurora: A Democratic-Republican Returns: The Suppressed History of Our Nation's Beginning and the Heroic Newspaper That Tried to Report It* (New York: St. Martin's Press, 1997), 901.
7. *Dictionary of American Biography* (New York: Charles Scribner's Sons, 1933) s.v. 6, "L'Enfant, Pierre-Charles."
8. Stanley Elkins and Eric McKitrick, *The Age of Federalism: The Early American Republic, 1788–1800* (New York: Oxford University Press, 1993), 171; WPA Guide to Washington, D.C., 20, 60–63.
9. *WPA Guide*, 30.
10. Thomas Froncek, ed., *An Illustrated History of the City of Washington by the Junior League of Washington* (New York: Alfred A. Knopf, 1977), 87.
11. Bess Furman, *White House Profile* (Indianapolis: Bobbs-Merrill, 1951), 29.
12. Bob Arnebeck, *Through a Fiery Trial: Building Washington, 1790–1800* (Lanham, Md.: Yale University Press, 1962), 595.
13. Ibid., 574–75.
14. Constance M. Green, *Washington, Village and Capital, 1800–1878* (Princeton, N.J.: Princeton University Press, 1962), 21.

CHAPTER 1: PHILADELPHIA, SUMMER 1787

1. *The Federalist*, no. 10.
2. Jefferson to Adams, 30 Aug. 1787, in Lester J. Cappon, ed., *The Adams-Jefferson Letters: The Complete Correspondence Between Thomas Jefferson and Abigail and John Adams*, vol. 1, 1774–1804 (Chapel Hill: University of North Carolina Press, 1959), 196.

 3. *Dictionary of American Biography*, s.v. "Madison, James."

 4. Max Farrand, ed., *Records of the Federal Convention of 1787*, revised edition in four volumes, vol. 3 (New Haven and London: Yale University Press, 1966), 94.

 5. Ibid., 27, 33–34.

 6. Ibid., 167.

 7. Ibid., 176–79. The actual free population figures according to Rossiter's authoritative *The Grand Convention* were 378,787 for Massachusetts, 318,796 for New York, and 2,964,047 for the thirteen states as a whole.

 8. All of the facts concerning Hamilton's birth are a little murky. He gave his birthdate as 1757, but there is some arguable evidence that it was 1755. See James Flexner, *The Young Hamilton: A Biography* (Boston: Little, Brown, 1978), 18, 31–32.

 9. Ibid., 35.

10. Farrand, *Records*, III, 234. *"Il a un peu trop de pretentions et trop peu de prudence . . . a force de vouloir tout conduire, il manque son but."*

11. Ibid., 89.

12. Ibid., I, 282–93.

13. Ibid., 451, 490–93, 500.

14. William Peters, *A More Perfect Union* (New York: Crown Publishers, 1987), 95–96.

15. Ibid., 108, 123–24.

16. *Historical Statistics of the United States;* Farrand, *Records*, I, 592–93.

17. Ibid., II, 221, 273.

18. Ibid., III, 166.

19. John P. Roche, quoted in Rossiter, *Grand Convention*, 198.

20. Farrand, *Records*, I, 48.

21. Ibid., I, 80; II, 29, 31.

22. Ibid., II, 99, 101, 103.

23. Ibid., 501, 515, 537.

24. Ibid., 645.

25. US Const, Art VI, emphasis added.

26. Bill Moyers, *Report from Philadelphia* (New York: Ballantine, 1987), 29, 61, 70, 110.

CHAPTER 2: THE NATION IN 1790

 1. The actual figure, according to *Historical Statistics of the U.S.*, was 888,811 square miles for the United States' land and water area. The United Kingdom (including Northern Ireland) has, at this day, 94,216 square miles; France, 211,207; and Spain, 194,884. *Columbia Encyclopedia*.

 2. *Historical Statistics*. The figure for the North includes just under 182,000 living in Maine and Vermont, not yet states in 1790, and that for the South about 109,000 in fingers of settlement in Kentucky and Tennessee, likewise still not organized into states.

 3. Psalm 24.

 4. Kentucky was admitted in 1792, Tennessee in 1796.

 5. *Letters from an American Farmer*, quoted in Bernard A. Weisberger, *Many People, One Nation* (Boston: Houghton Mifflin, 1987), 59.

 6. Wayne E. Fuller, *The American Mail: Enlarger of the Common Life* (Chicago: University of Chicago Press, 1972), 45–47.

 7. Robert Dinkin, *Voting in Revolutionary America: A Study of Elections in the Original Thirteen States 1776–1789* (Westport, Conn.: Greenwood Press, 1982), 29–30, 42.

 8. Ibid., 88, 55.

 9. Eugene H. Roseboom, *A History of Presidential Elections* (New York: Macmillan, 1957), 4.

CHAPTER 3: WASHINGTON'S HOPEFUL FIRST TERM

1. Douglas Freeman, *George Washington: A Biography*, vol. 6, *Patriot and President* (New York: Charles Scribner's Sons, 1957), 166.
2. Ibid., 183.
3. Ibid., 193–94.
4. Stanley Elkins and Eric McKitrick, *The Age of Federalism: The Early American Republic, 1788–1800* (New York: Oxford University Press, 1993), 47–48.
5. John Ferling, *John Adams: A Life* (New York: Henry Holt and Co., 1996) 17.
6. Ibid., 129.
7. Elkins and McKitrick, *Age of Federalism*, 533.
8. Ferling, *John Adams*, 18–19.
9. Ibid., 129.
10. Ibid., 101.
11. Bill Moyers, *Report from Philadelphia* (New York: Harper Bros., 1960), 164.
12. Clinton Rossiter, *1787: The Grand Convention* (New York: W. W. Norton, 1987), 20.
13. *American Heritage Dictionary of American Quotations* (New York: Penguin, 1997).
14. Elkins and McKitrick, *Age of Federalism*, 49.
15. Freeman, *George Washington*, vol. 6, 195.
16. Richard B. Bernstein, with Jerome Agel, *Amending America: If We Love the Constitution So Much Why Do We Keep Trying to Change It?* (New York: Times Books, 1993), 34.
17. Ralph Ketcham, *James Madison: A Biography* (Charlottesville: University of Virginia Press, 1990), 290.
18. Of the two that were not ratified, one attempted to dictate permanently the ratio between population and representation. The other required that any increase in congressional salaries not take effect until an election had intervened. After two hundred years in limbo, it was ratified in May 1992 and is now the Twenty-seventh Amendment.
19. Alvin Josephy, *On the Hill: A History of the American Congress* (New York: Simon & Schuster, 1979), 55.
20. Elkins and McKitrick, *Age of Federalism*, 125.
21. Mary-Jo Kline, ed., *Alexander Hamilton: A Biography in His Own Words* (New York, Newsweek Books, 1972), 229, 232.
22. Josephy, *On the Hill*, 69.
23. Elkins and McKitrick, *Age of Federalism*, 142, 144.
24. Ibid., 310.
25. Ibid., 155. Jefferson wrote the story twice, once at a time guessed by scholars to be 1793 and again in 1818.
26. Noble E. Cunningham Jr., *The Jeffersonian Republicans: The Formation of Party Organization, 1789–1801* (Chapel Hill: University of North Carolina Press, 1957), 6.
27. Ibid., 5.
28. Jacob E. Cooke, "The Compromise of 1790," *William and Mary Quarterly*, Oct. 1970, cited and discussed in Elkins and McKitrick, *Age of Federalism*, 156–60, 782.
29. Ferling, *John Adams*, 318.
30. Joel Silbey, ed., "First Congress Under the Constitution," in *The Congress of the United States: Its Origins and Early Development* (Brooklyn, N.Y.: Carlson Publishers, 1991), 125.
31. Elkins and McKitrick, *Age of Federalism*, 229.
32. Kline, *Alexander Hamilton*, 243.
33. Elkins and McKitrick, *Age of Federalism*, 234, 237.
34. Freeman, *George Washington*, vol. 6, 348.

CHAPTER 4: THE CURSE OF FACTION

1. Ralph Ketcham, *James Madison: A Biography* (Charlottesville: University of Virginia Press, 1990), 324.
2. Noble E. Cunningham Jr., *The Jeffersonian Republicans: The Formation of Party Organization, 1789–1801* (Chapel Hill: University of North Carolina Press, 1957), 11.
3. Page Smith, *John Adams*, vol. 2 (New York: Doubleday, 1982), 799–801.
4. Cunningham, *Jeffersonian Republicans*, 11.
5. Merrill D. Peterson, *Thomas Jefferson and the New Nation: A Biography* (New York: Oxford University Press, 1970), 441.
6. James Morton Smith, ed., *The Republic of Letters: The Correspondence Between Thomas Jefferson and James Madison 1776–1826*, vol. 2, *1790–1804* (New York: W. W. Norton, 1995), 684–85.
7. Ibid., 445.
8. Ibid., 708–10; Ketcham, *James Madison*, 329–30.
9. Smith, *Republic of Letters*, 695, 706.
10. John Ferling, *John Adams: A Life* (New York: Henry Holt and Co., 1996), 306.
11. Cunningham, *Jeffersonian Republicans*, 20.
12. 26, 30 Apr. 1792, quoted in Philip M. Marsh, *Philip Freneau: Poet and Journalist* (Minneapolis: Dillon Press, 1967), 155, 158.
13. Ibid., 157.
14. Cunningham, *Jeffersonian Republicans*, 21.
15. Ibid., 24.
16. Ibid., 25.
17. Ibid., 26–27.
18. Peterson, *Thomas Jefferson*, 473–74.
19. Mary-Jo Kline, ed., *Alexander Hamilton: A Biography in His Own Words* (New York: Newsweek Books, 1972), 275–76.
20. Ibid., 267–70.
21. Smith, *Republic of Letters*, 715; Stanley Elkins and Eric McKitrick, *The Age of Federalism: The Early American Republic, 1788–1800* (New York: Oxford University Press, 1993), 292.
22. Cunningham, *Jeffersonian Republicans*, 31–32.
23. Smith, *Republic of Letters*, 814, 819–20.
24. J. H. Powell, *Bring Out Your Dead: The Great Plague of Yellow Fever in Philadelphia in 1793* (Philadelphia: University of Pennsylvania Press, 1949), 127.
25. Bernard A. Weisberger, "The Paradoxical Dr. Rush," *American Heritage*, Dec. 1975.
26. Ibid.

CHAPTER 5: MR. BURR LAUNCHES A MACHINE

1. Rush to Burr, 24 Sep. 1792; Beckley to Madison, 17 Oct. 1792, in Noble E. Cunningham, *The Jeffersonian Republicans: The Formation of Party Organization, 1789–1801* (Chapel Hill: University of North Carolina Press, 1957), 45–46.
2. Monroe to Madison, 9 Oct. 1792, in ibid.
3. Herbert Parmet and Marie B. Hecht, *Aaron Burr: Portrait of an Ambitious Man* (New York: Macmillan, 1967), 65–66; Milton Lomask, *Aaron Burr: The Years from Princeton to President, 1756–1805* (New York: Farrar, Straus & Giroux, 1979), 144.
4. Lomask, *Aaron Burr*, 103.
5. Nathaniel Hazard to Hamilton, 25 Nov. 1791, quoted in ibid., 142, 197; Parmet and Hecht, *Aaron Burr*, 87.
6. Lomask, *Aaron Burr*, 192.
7. Burr to Peter Van Gaasbeek, 27 May 1795, 23 Apr. 1796, Mary-Jo Kline, ed., *Political Correspondence and Public Papers of Aaron Burr*, vol. 1 (Princeton, N.J.: Princeton University Press, 1983), 210, 250.

8. Quoting Josiah Hoffman to Peter van Shaack, 26 June 1792, Parmet and Hecht, *Aaron Burr*, 79.
9. Ibid., 82.
10. William L. Smith to Ralph Izard, 18 May 1796, quoted in Kline, *Papers of Aaron Burr*, 267.
11. Lomask, *Aaron Burr*, 190.
12. George J. Lankevich and Howard B. Furer, *A Brief History of New York City* (New York: Associated Faculty Press, 1984), 65.
13. Kline, *Papers of Aaron Burr*, 420–21.
14. Quoted in Bayrd Still, *Mirror for Gotham: New York As Seen by Contemporaries from Dutch Days to the Present* (New York: New York University Press, 1956), 68–69.
15. Lankevich and Furer, *Brief History of New York City*, 65.
16. Rochefoucault-Liancourt, *Voyage aux Etats-Unis* [Albany, 1795], quoted in Arthur J. Weise, *The History of the City of Albany New York from the Discovery of the Great River in 1524, by Verrazzano, to the Present Time* (Albany, N.Y.: E. H. Bender, 1884), 421.
17. To Natalie Delage [Sumter] 2 Feb. 1800, Burr Papers, Microfilm ed.
18. Weise, *History of Albany*, 427.

CHAPTER 6: WEDGES OF SECTIONALISM

1. 2 May 1740, Elise Pinckney, ed., *The Letterbook of Eliza Lucas Pinckney, 1739–1762* (Chapel Hill: University of North Carolina Press, 1972).
2. N.d., 1741, ibid., 19.
3. Ibid., xxi–xxii.
4. George C. Rogers Jr., *Charleston in the Age of the Pinckneys* (Norman: University of Oklahoma Press, 1969), 124.
5. Samuel Eliot Morison, *The Maritime History of Massachusetts, 1783–1860* (Boston: Houghton Mifflin, 1941), 42.
6. *Dictionary of American Biography*, s.v. "Ames, Fisher" (vol. 1).
7. Ibid., s.v. "Pickering, Timothy" (vol. 7).
8. Weisberger, "Seeking a Real Tax Revolt," *American Heritage*, May/June 1991, 22.
9. Federal Writers Project, *Pennsylvania: A Guide to the Keystone State*, 298.
10. Thomas Slaughter, *The Whiskey Rebellion: Frontier Epilogue to the American Revolution* (New York: Oxford University Press, 1986), 121.
11. Ibid., 221.
12. Ibid., 123.
13. Ibid., 130, 135.
14. Weisberger, "Tax Revolt," 24.

CHAPTER 7: TERROR, TURMOIL, AND CITIZEN GENET

1. Joseph J. Ellis, *American Sphinx: The Character of Thomas Jefferson* (New York: Alfred A. Knopf, 1998), 158–59.
2. Merrill D. Peterson, *Thomas Jefferson and the New Nation: A Biography* (New York: Oxford University Press, 1970), 493.
3. Ibid., 516.
4. Ibid.
5. Stanley Elkins and Eric McKitrick, *The Age of Federalism: The Early American Republic, 1788–1800* (New York: Oxford University Press, 1993), 301, quoting Jefferson to Thomas Mann Randolph, 3 Mar. 1793.
6. Broadus Mitchell, *Hamilton: A Concise Biography* (New York: Oxford University Press, 1976), 318; this is the source used here for the entire story, covering pp. 318–23.
7. Ibid., 320.

8. Adams to Abigail, 24 Jan. 1793, 15 Dec. 1794, quoted in John Ferling, *John Adams: A Life* (New York: Henry Holt and Co., 1996), 320.

9. Ibid., 464.

10. Mitchell, *Hamilton*, 251.

11. Peterson, *Thomas Jefferson*, 385.

12. Ralph Ketcham, *James Madison: A Biography* (Charlottesville: University of Virginia Press, 1990), 339.

13. Adams to Rufus King, 11 Oct. 1792, and Ames to Timothy Dwight, 4 Oct. 1792, both quoted in ibid., 338.

14. Ibid., 339–40.

15. Peterson, *Thomas Jefferson*, 481.

16. Peterson, *Thomas Jefferson*, 461.

17. Gouverneur Morris, *A Diary of the French Revolution by Gouverneur Morris, 1752–1816*, vol. 2, ed. Beatrix Carey Davenport (Boston: Houghton Mifflin, 1939), 594–95.

18. Meade Minnigerode, *Lives and Times: Four Informal American Biographies* (New York: G. P. Putnam's Sons, 1925), 187.

19. Ibid., 191.

20. Ibid., 187.

21. *National Gazette*, 1, 5, 8, 12 June 1793 quoted in Douglas S. Freeman, *George Washington: A Biography*, vol. 7 (New York: Charles Scribner's Sons, 1957), 86.

22. Alexander De Conde, *Entangling Alliance: Politics and Diplomacy Under George Washington* (Durham, N.C.: Duke University Press, 1958), 221.

23. Jefferson to Madison, 7 July 1793, quoted in ibid., 285.

24. Minnigerode, *Lives and Times*, 205.

25. Freeman, *George Washington*, vol. 7, 112–13.

CHAPTER 8: JOHN JAY'S DIVISIVE TREATY, 1794–1795

1. Stanley Elkins and Eric McKitrick, *The Age of Federalism: The Early American Republic, 1788–1800* (New York: Oxford University Press, 1993), 246.

2. As reprinted in Samuel F. Bemis, *Jay's Treaty: A Study in Commerce and Diplomacy* (New Haven, Conn.: Yale University Press, 1962), 448–49.

3. Ibid., 141, 144.

4. Hammond to Grenville, 17 Apr. 1794, quoted in ibid., 276.

5. Elkins and McKitrick, *Age of Federalism*, 377.

6. Dumas Malone, *Jefferson and the Ordeal of Liberty* (Boston: Little, Brown, 1962), 152.

7. John C. Miller, *The Federalist Era, 1789–1801* (New York: Harper Bros., 1960), 143.

8. Elkins and McKitrick, *Age of Federalism*, 384.

9. Ibid., 386.

10. Miller, *Federalist Era*, 148.

11. Bemis, *Jay's Treaty*, 277, quoting Hammond to Grenville, 17 Apr. 1794.

12. Richard B. Morris, ed., *Alexander Hamilton and the Founding of the Nation* (New York: Dial Press, 1957), quoting draft of "Camillus" No. 2, July 1795.

13. Miller, *Federalist Era*, 168.

14. Malone, *Ordeal of Liberty*, 249.

15. Douglas S. Freeman, *Washington: An Abridgement in One Volume by Richard Harwell* (New York: Simon & Schuster, 1968), 671.

16. Ibid., 672.

17. Elkins and McKitrick, *Age of Federalism*, 425.

18. Readers who would like to follow the historical controversy can find a good discussion and excellent bibliography in Elkins and McKitrick, *Age of Federalism*, 425–31 and 838–39.

19. Freeman, *Washington*, 674.

20. Ibid., 666–67.
21. Miller, *Federalist Era*, 171.
22. Freeman, *Washington*, 697.
23. Quoted in Elkins and McKitrick, *Age of Federalism*, 441.
24. Freeman, *Washington*, 686, 690.

CHAPTER 9: JEFFERSON AND ADAMS'S FIRST ROUND, 1796

1. Page Smith, *John Adams*, vol. 2 (New York: Doubleday, 1982), 880.
2. Ibid., 890, 912.
3. Ibid., 880–81.
4. Stephen G. Kurtz, *The Presidency of John Adams: The Collapse of Federalism, 1795–1800* (Philadelphia: University of Pennsylvania Press, 1957), 80.
5. To Edward Rutledge, 17 Dec. 1796, quoted in Dumas Malone, *Jefferson and the Ordeal of Liberty* (Boston: Little, Brown, 1962), 83.
6. Same letter, this time quoted in Kurtz, *Presidency of John Adams*, 95.
7. Smith, *John Adams*, vol. 2, 882, 887, 894, quoting letters to Abigail.
8. Jefferson to Adams, 28 Feb. 1796, and to Philip Mazzei, 24 Apr. 1796, quoted in Malone, *Ordeal of Liberty*, 265–68.
9. Smith, *John Adams*, vol. 2, 904, 908.
10. Ibid., 901–2; Stanley Elkins and Eric McKitrick, *The Age of Federalism: The Early American Republic, 1788–1800* (New York: Oxford University Press, 1993), 520–21.
11. Malone, *Ordeal of Liberty*, 286–90; Adet's report to Paris is dated 31 Dec. 1796.
12. Smith, *John Adams*, vol. 2, 908.
13. A good breakdown is in Kurtz, *Presidency of John Adams*, 412–14.
14. Smith, *John Adams*, vol. 2, 909.
15. Kurtz, *Presidency of John Adams*, 209.
16. Malone, *Ordeal of Liberty*, 296, 299.
17. Elkins and McKitrick, *Age of Federalism*, 528.
18. Ibid., 428–29.

CHAPTER 10: X, Y, Z, AND THE FRENCH CONNECTION, 1798

1. Page Smith, *John Adams*, vol. 2 (New York: Doubleday, 1982), 881.
2. *Dictionary of National Biography*, s.v. "Liston, Robert."
3. Ralph Adams Brown, *The Presidency of John Adams* (Lawrence: University of Kansas Press, 1975), 42.
4. Ibid., 43.
5. *Dictionary of American Biography*, s.v. "Marshall, John."
6. George A. Billias, *Elbridge Gerry: Founding Father and Republican Statesman* (New York: McGraw-Hill, 1976), 262.
7. Ibid., 268; Albert J. Beveridge, *The Life of John Marshall*, vol. 2 (Boston: Houghton Mifflin, 1916), 286.
8. Beveridge, *John Marshall*, vol. 2, 260.
9. Billias, *Elbridge Gerry*, 271.
10. Ibid.
11. Beveridge, *John Marshall*, vol. 2, 285.
12. Billias, *Elbridge Gerry*, 282.
13. Harry Ammon, *James Monroe: The Quest for National Identity* (New York: McGraw-Hill, 1971), 159.
14. Mary-Jo Kline, ed., *Alexander Hamilton: A Biography in His Own Words* (New York: Newsweek Books, 1972), 355–56.

15. Gerald H. Clarfield, *Timothy Pickering and the American Republic* (Pittsburgh: University of Pittsburgh Press, 1980), 188.
16. Brown, *Presidency of John Adams*, 50.
17. Stephen G. Kurtz, *The Presidency of John Adams: The Collapse of Federalism, 1795–1800* (Philadelphia: Univeristy of Pennsylvania Press, 1957), 80, 296.
18. Stanley Elkins and Eric McKitrick, *The Age of Federalism: The Early American Republic, 1788–1800* (New York: Oxford University Press, 1993), 588.
19. Brown, *Presidency of John Adams*, 52, 54, 56.
20. Kurtz, *Presidency of John Adams*, 300.
21. Brown, *Presidency of John Adams*, 53.
22. Clarfield, *Timothy Pickering* (quoting Ames to Pickering, 4 June 1798), 192.
23. William M. Fowler Jr., *Jack Tars and Commodores: The American Navy, 1783–1815* (Boston: Houghton Mifflin, 1984), 36.
24. Ibid., 43.
25. Richard H. Kohn, *Eagle and Sword: The Federalists and the Creation of the Military Establishment in America, 1788–1802* (New York: Free Press, 1975), 2.
26. John C. Miller, *Alexander Hamilton: Portrait in Paradox* (New York: Harper Bros., 1959), 508.
27. Kohn, *Eagle and Sword*, 226.
28. To Elbridge Gerry, 3 May 1798, quoted in ibid., 230.
29. 22 Oct. 1798, quoted in Elkins and McKitrick, *Age of Federalism*, 606.
30. Miller, *Alexander Hamilton*, 477.
31. Ibid., 475.
32. Dumas Malone, *Jefferson and the Ordeal of Liberty* (Boston: Little, Brown, 1962), 427.
33. Elkins and McKitrick, *Age of Federalism*, 629.
34. Ibid., 617.
35. Ibid., 617–18.
36. Joseph Ellis, *Passionate Sage: The Legacy and Character of John Adams* (New York: W. W. Norton, 1993), 76.
37. Elkins and McKitrick, *Age of Federalism*, 618–22, quoting George Cabot to Rufus King, 10 Mar. 1799, and Theodore Sedgwick to Hamilton, 22 Feb. 1799.
38. 10 July 1799, quoted in ibid., 622.
39. Ibid., 638, quoting Uriah Forrest to Adams, 28 Apr. 1799.
40. Ibid., 640.
41. Kohn, *Eagle and Sword*, 212.

CHAPTER 11: GAGGING THE PRESS, 1798

1. Robert Rutland, *The Newsmongers: Journalism in the Life of the Nation, 1690–1972* (New York: Dial Press, 1973), 84–85, quoting Frederick Marryatt (1839) and Thomas Hamilton (1843).
2. 16 Aug. 1793, quoted in James Tagg, *Benjamin F. Bache and the Philadelphia "Aurora"* (Philadelphia: University of Pennsylvania Press, 1991), 142.
3. 19 Dec. 1796, ibid., 313.
4. 22 Aug. 1795, quoted in ibid., 252; 18 Sep., 16 Oct., 1 Dec. 1795, quoted in Richard Rosenfeld, *American Aurora: A Democratic-Republican Returns. The Suppressed History of Our Nation's Beginnings and the Heroic Newspaper That Tried to Report It* (New York: St. Martin's Press, 1997), 30.
5. See ibid., 29–30 for examples.
6. 11 Sep. 1795, ibid.
7. *Aurora*, 22 Oct. 1795, quoted in Tagg, *Benjamin F. Bache*, 279.
8. *Aurora*, 16, 23 Dec 1796, quoted in ibid., 282.
9. Washington to Jeremiah Wadsworth, 6 Mar. 1797, quoted in Rosenfeld, *American Aurora*, 31.
10. Rutland, *Newsmongers*, 70; Rosenfeld, *American Aurora*, 28.
11. Page Smith, *John Adams*, vol. 2 (New York: Doubleday, 1982), p. 961.

12. 16 Mar. 1798, quoted in Rosenfeld, *American Aurora*, 42.

13. 19 Mar. 1798, ibid., 44.

14. 19 Apr. 1798, quoted in ibid., 78.

15. Annette Gordon-Reed, *Thomas Jefferson and Sally Hemings: An American Controversy* (Charlottesville: University of Virginia Press, 1997), 61.

16. William Cobbett, *Peter Porcupine in America: Pamphlets on Republicanism and Revolution* (Ithaca: Cornell University Press, 1994), 3, 10.

17. 4 Mar. 1797, quoted in Rosenfeld, *American Aurora*, 25.

18. 12, 17 Mar., 21 Apr. 1798, quoted in ibid., 38, 44, 84.

19. Ibid., 29, 31.

20. John C. Miller, *Crisis in Freedom: The Alien and Sedition Acts* (Boston: Little, Brown, 1951), 44.

21. 12 Nov. 1798, quoted in Rosenfeld, *American Aurora*, 536.

22. Merrill D. Peterson, *Thomas Jefferson and the New Nation: A Biography* (New York: Oxford University Press, 1970), 604.

23. Douglas S. Freeman, *Washington: An Abridgment in One Volume by Richard Harwell* (New York: Simon & Schuster, 1968), 731.

24. Ibid., 54, quoting *Aurora*, 2 July 1798.

25. As quoted in Miller, *Crisis in Freedom*, 67, emphasis added.

26. To John Taylor, 4 June 1798, quoted in Dumas Malone, *Jefferson and the Ordeal of Liberty* (Boston: Little, Brown, 1962), 381.

27. 26 Nov. 1798, quoted in Smith, *John Adams*, vol. 2, 978.

28. Miller, *Crisis in Freedom*, 90.

29. John C. Miller, *Alexander Hamilton: Portrait in Paradox* (New York: Harper Bros., 1959), 483.

30. Miller, *Crisis in Freedom*, 113.

31. Stanley Elkins and Eric McKitrick, *The Age of Federalism: The Early American Republic, 1788–1800* (New York: Oxford University Press, 1993), 710.

32. Miller, *Crisis in Freedom*, 122, 128.

33. Ibid., 114–15.

34. *Dictionary of American Biography*, s.v. "Chase, Samuel"; also Chase in *Columbian Centinel*, 3 May 1800, quoted in ibid., 117–18.

35. Ibid., 118–19.

36. Ibid., 98, emphasis added.

37. To James Monroe, 19 Oct. 1823, quoted in Rosenfeld, *American Aurora*, 521.

38. Ralph Ketcham, *James Madison: A Biography* (Charlottesville: University of Virginia Press, 1990), 396.

39. Peterson, *Thomas Jefferson*, 614.

40. Ibid.

41. To John Taylor, 1 June 1798, quoted in Rosenfeld, *American Aurora*, 136.

42. 22 Feb. 1799, quoted in Malone, *Ordeal of Liberty*, 415.

43. To Edmund Pendleton, 14 Feb. 1799, quoted in Elkins and McKitrick, *Age of Federalism*, 723.

44. Malone, *Ordeal of Liberty*, 412.

45. Miller, *Crisis in Freedom*, 179.

CHAPTER 12: THE CLIMAX AND THE DRAWN BATTLE OF 1800

1. J. R. Pole, *Political Representation in England and the Origins of the American Republic*, appendix 2 (New York: Macmillan/St. Martin's, 1966).

2. Ketcham, *James Madison*, 356.

3. They were Georgetown, Union, Williams, Bowdoin, and Middlebury, and the state universities of Vermont and North Carolina.

4. *Aurora*, 23 Sep. 1799, quoted in Rosenfeld, *American Aurora*, 696.

5. *Aurora*, 24 Aug., 11 Sep. 1799, quoted in ibid., 687, 692.

6. *Porcupine's Gazette,* 19 Oct., quoted in ibid., 705.

7. Ibid., 698, quoting the Boston *Russel's Gazette.*

8. *Dictionary of American Biography,* s.v. "McKean, Thomas."

9. Ibid., 741.

10. *Annals of Congress,* quoted in ibid., 758.

11. Madison to Jefferson, 15 Mar. 1800, quoted in Daniel Sisson, *The American Revolution of 1800* (New York: Alfred A. Knopf, 1974), 365–66.

12. To T. M. Randolph, 2 Feb. 1800, quoted in ibid., 366.

13. Rosenfeld, *American Aurora,* 773.

14. Francis Wharton, *State Trials of the United States During the Administrations of Washington and Adams,* 638–39.

15. 4 Mar. 1800, quoted in ibid., 177.

16. Sisson, *Revolution of 1800,* 368.

17. Hamilton to Jay, 7 May 1800, quoted in Noble E. Cunningham Jr., *Jeffersonian Republicans: The Formation of Party Organization, 1789–1801* (Chapel Hill: University of North Carolina Press, 1957), 185.

18. McHenry to Adams, 31 May 1800, quoted in Page Smith, *John Adams,* vol. 2 (New York: Doubleday, 1982), 1028.

19. Pickering to McHenry, 13 Feb. 1811, quoted in ibid., 129.

20. Quoted in Ralph Adams Brown, *The Presidency of John Adams* (Lawrence: University of Kansas Press, 1996), 178.

21. James R. Sharp, *American Politics in the Early Republic: The New Nation in Crisis* (New Haven, Conn.: Yale University Press, 1993), 239.

22. To Rufus King, 15 July 1800, quoted in Cunningham, *Jeffersonian Republicans,* 186.

23. 1 Aug. 1800, quoted in Smith, *John Adams,* vol. 2, 1042.

24. James Bayard to Hamilton, 18 Aug. 1800, quoted in Brown, *Presidency,* 182.

25. Roy Robbins, *Our Landed Heritage: The Public Domain 1776–1936* (Gloucester, Mass.: Peter Smith, 1960), 16.

26. So James Callender reported to Jefferson in a letter of 13 Sep. quoted in Herbert Aptheker, *American Negro Slave Revolts* (New York: International Publishers, 1963), 219.

27. Sharp, *American Politics,* 242.

28. Thomas B. Adams to William Shaw, 8 Aug. 1800, quoted in Cunningham, *Jeffersonian Republicans,* 190.

29. Ibid., 154.

30. 26 Aug. 1800, quoted in ibid., 198.

31. 26 Oct. 1800, quoted in ibid., 188; 3 Oct. 1800, ibid., 189.

32. Quoted in *Boston Gazette,* Apr. 1799, quoted in ibid., 202.

33. Hartford *Courant,* 2 Feb. 1801, ibid., 207; Oliver Wolcott to Ames, 10 Aug. 1800, quoted in Sharp, *American Politics,* 245.

34. *Letter . . . concerning the Public Conduct and Character of John Adams, Esq., President of the United States,* quoted in Sharp, *American Politics,* 240.

35. Ibid.

36. Cabot to Hamilton, 29 Nov. 1800, quoted in Noemire Emery, *Alexander Hamilton: An Intimate Portrait* (New York: Putnam, 1982), 189.

37. Smith, *John Adams,* vol. 2, 1045.

38. Abigail Adams to Mary Cranch, 4 May 1800, quoted in ibid., 1035; to John Quincy Adams, 1 Sep. 1800, quoted in ibid., 1040.

39. Quoted in Noble E. Cunningham Jr., *The United States in 1800: Henry Adams Revisited* (Charlottesville: University of Virginia Press, 1988), 48.

40. *Gazette of the United States,* 10 Sep. 1800, quoted in Cunningham, *Jeffersonian Republicans,* 225.

41. 30 Oct. 1800, quoted in Rosenfeld, *American Aurora,* 873.

42. To William Tudor, 13 Dec. 1800, quoted in Smith, *John Adams,* vol. 2, 1034.

43. Quoted in Sisson, *Revolution of 1800*, 394.
44. Ibid., 395, 403.
45. Figure is from Stanley Elkins and Eric McKitrick, *The Age of Federalism: The Early American Republic, 1788–1800* (New York: Oxford University Press, 1993), which is also the number given in Sharp, *American Politics*, though *Historical Statistics of the United States* makes it 69–36.
46. Quoted in Rosenfeld, *American Aurora*, 890.
47. Ibid.
48. Adams to Thomas B. Adams, 17 Dec. 1800, quoted in Smith, *John Adams*, vol. 2, 1053.
49. Quoted in Rosenfeld, *American Aurora*, 894.
50. Smith, *John Adams*, vol. 2, 1053.
51. To William Tudor, 3 Feb. 1801, quoted in ibid.

CHAPTER 13: THE CROSSROADS OF FEBRUARY 1801

1. Quoted in Noble E. Cunningham Jr., *Jeffersonian Republicans: The Formation of Party Organization, 1789–1801* (Chapel Hill: University of North Carolina Press, 1957), 241.
2. Jefferson to Madison, 19, 27 Dec. 1800, quoted in Daniel Sisson, *The American Revolution of 1800*, (New York: Alfred A. Knopf, 1974), 407–8, 409–10.
3. Thornton to Lord Grenville, 27 Dec. 1800, in Public Record Office (London), FRO 115/8.
4. Jefferson to Burr, 15 Dec. 1800; Burr to Jefferson, 23 Dec. 1800, quoted in James R. Sharp, *American Politics in the Early Republic: The New Nation in Crisis* (New Haven, Conn.: Yale University Press, 1993), 254.
5. Herbert Parmet and Marie B. Hecht, *Aaron Burr: Portrait of an Ambitious Man* (New York: Macmillan, 1967), 158.
6. Quoted in Sisson, *Revolution of 1800*, 417.
7. Dumas Malone, *Jefferson and the Ordeal of Liberty* (Boston: Little, Brown, 1962), 498.
8. Parmet and Hecht, *Aaron Burr*, 162.
9. Sisson, *Revolution of 1800*, 417.
10. Quoted in ibid., 414.
11. Ibid.
12. 26 Dec. 1800, Henry C. Lodge, ed., *The Works of Alexander Hamilton*, vol. 10 (New York: G. P. Putnam's, republished by Scholarly Press, St. Clair Shores, Mich., 1971), 401.
13. 22 Dec. 1800, ibid., 397–98.
14. N.d., Dec. 1800, ibid., 404–5.
15. Dec. 27, 1800, ibid., 402–4.
16. To Morris 26 Dec. 1800, 10 Jan. 1801, ibid., 401, 407–8.
17. 16 Jan. 1801, ibid., 412–13.
18. N.d., 1801, ibid., 405–07.
19. Dumas Malone, *Jefferson the President: First Term, 1801–1805* (Boston: Little, Brown, 1970), 429.
20. Abigail Adams, 3 Feb. 1801, quoted in Page Smith, *John Adams*, vol. 2: 1784–1826 (New York: Doubleday, 1982), 1061; John Adams to Thomas, quoted in Sisson, *Revolution of 1800*, 415.
21. 22 Jan. 1801, quoted in Sharp, *American Politics*, 263.
22. Albert J. Beveridge, *The Life of John Marshall*, vol. 2 (Boston: Houghton Mifflin, 1916), 553.
23. Quoted in Merrill D. Peterson, *Thomas Jefferson and the New Nation: A Biography* (New York: Oxford University Press, 1970), 648.
24. Ibid., 537.
25. Madison to Jefferson, quoted in Sisson, *Revolution of 1800*, 419.
26. "Plan at time of Balloting for Jefferson and Burr," quoted in Sisson, *Revolution of 1800*, 421–22.
27. McKean to Jefferson, 19 Mar. 1801, quoted in Harry M. Tinkcom, *The Republicans and Federalists in Pennsylvania, 1790–1801* (Harrisburg: Pennsylvania Historical and Museum Commission, 1950), 255–56.
28. Joseph Nicholson, quoted in Sisson, *Revolution of 1800*, 420.

29. Parmet and Hecht, *Aaron Burr,* 164–65.
30. William Cooper to Thomas Morris, 13 Feb. 1801, quoted in Sharp, *American Politics,* 272.
31. To Nicholas Low, quoted in Sisson, *Revolution of 1800,* 419.
32. 11 Feb. 1801, quoted in ibid., 425–26.
33. Sharp, *American Politics,* 270.
34. Adams letter to James Lloyd, 6 Feb. 1815, quoted in Sisson, *Revolution of 1800,* 428.
35. Quoted in ibid., 429.
36. Ibid., 430.
37. Ibid., 431–32.
38. Margaret Bayard Smith, *The First Forty Years of Washington Society,* Gaillard Hunt, ed. (New York: Scribner's, 1906), 25.

CHAPTER 14: THE REPUBLICAN PRESIDENT

1. Dumas Malone, *Jefferson the President: First Term 1801–1805* (Boston: Little, Brown, 1970), 29–30.
2. To John Dickinson, 6 Mar. 1801, quoted in Joseph J. Ellis, *American Sphinx: The Character of Thomas Jefferson* (New York: Alfred A. Knopf, 1996), 220.
3. To Levi Lincoln, 25 Oct. 1802, quoted in Stanley Elkins and Eric McKitrick, *The Age of Federalism: The Early American Republic* (New York: Oxford University Press, 1998), 754.
4. *American Heritage Dictionary of American Quotations,* 433.
5. "Address to the Electors of the State of New York," 26 Mar. 1801, quoted in Ellis, *American Sphinx,* 216.
6. Malone, *Jefferson the President: First Term,* 22.
7. Merrill D. Peterson, *Thomas Jefferson and the New Nation: A Biography* (New York: Oxford University Press, 1970), 659.
8. 12 Mar. 1801, quoted in Daniel Sisson, *The American Revolution of 1800* (New York: Alfred A. Knopf, 1974), 444.
9. Quoted in Ellis, *American Sphinx,* 233.
10. Peterson, *Thomas Jefferson,* 692.
11. 7 Mar. 1801, quoted in Ellis, *American Sphinx,* 234.
12. Peterson, *Thomas Jefferson,* 667.
13. Ibid., 666.
14. Ibid., 676.
15. Malone, *Jefferson the President: First Term,* 118.
16. To Livingston, 18 Apr. 1802, quoted in Ellis, *American Sphinx,* 244.
17. All of Iowa, Missouri, Arkansas, Oklahoma, Kansas, Nebraska, and South Dakota and parts of Minnesota, Louisiana, Montana, Wyoming, Colorado, North Dakota, New Mexico, and Texas.
18. To Levi Lincoln, 30 Aug. 1803, quoted in Ellis, *American Sphinx,* 249.
19. Ibid., 250.
20. Peterson, *Thomas Jefferson,* 703.

EPILOGUE

1. For the record, the earlier five were John Tyler, Millard Fillmore, Andrew Johnson, Chester A. Arthur, and Calvin Coolidge.
2. Richard Nixon, Hubert Humphrey, Fritz Mondale, and George Bush were the four.
3. *Fletcher* v. *Peck.*
4. *Dartmouth College* v. *Woodward.*
5. *McCulloch* v. *Maryland.*
6. *Gibbons* v. *Ogden.*
7. *Cohens* v. *Virginia.*

Bibliography

The following bibliography is in no way comprehensive or exhaustive and lists only those works actually cited in the endnotes. Moreover, I have used notes only to identify the sources of direct quotations or statistics. Luckily for posterity, the letters, diaries, and papers of the major players are available in printed form and supplemented by an abundant secondary literature without which this book could not have been written, and to whose authors I am deeply grateful. Readers who wish to follow the story in more detail will find abundant direction in the bibliographies of the studies listed below.—BW

Adams, Henry. *History of the United States During the Administration of Thomas Jefferson*. 2 vols. New York: Albert and Charles Boni, 1930.

Ammon, Harry. *James Monroe: The Quest for National Identity*. New York: McGraw-Hill, 1971.

Arnebeck, Bob. *Through a Fiery Trial: Building Washington 1790–1800*. Lanham, N.Y., London: Madison Books, 1991.

Bemis, Samuel F. *Jay's Treaty: A Study in Commerce and Diplomacy*. New Haven, Conn.: Yale University Press, 1962.

Berkeley, Edmund, and Dorothy Berkeley. *John Beckley: Zealous Partisan in a Nation Divided*. Philadelphia: American Philosophical Society, 1973.

Bernstein, Richard B., with Jerome Agel. *Amending America: If We Love the Constitution So Much Why Do We Keep Trying to Change It?* New York: Times Books, 1993.

Beveridge, Albert J. *The Life of John Marshall*. 4 vols. Boston: Houghton Mifflin, 1916.

Billias, George A. *Elbridge Gerry, Founding Father and Republican Statesman*. New York: McGraw-Hill, 1976.

Boller, Paul F. *Presidential Campaigns*. Rev. ed. New York: Oxford University Press, 1996.

Brant, Irving. *James Madison, Father of the Constitution, 1787–1800*. Indianapolis, Ind.: Bobbs-Merrill, 1950.

Brown, Ralph Adams. *The Presidency of John Adams*. Lawrence: University of Kansas Press, 1975.

Cappon, Lester J., ed. *The Adams-Jefferson Letters: The Complete Correspondence Between Thomas Jefferson and Abigail and John Adams*. Vol. 1, *1774–1804*. Chapel Hill: University of North Carolina Press, 1959.

Clarfield, Gerard H. *Timothy Pickering and the American Republic*. Pittsburgh: University of Pittsburgh Press, 1980.

Cobbett, William. *Peter Porcupine in America: Pamphlets on Republicanism and Revolution.* Edited and with an introduction by David A. Wilson. Ithaca: Cornell University Press, 1994.

Cunningham, Noble E., Jr. *The United States in 1800: Henry Adams Revisited.* Charlottesville: University Press of Virginia, 1988.

———. *The Jeffersonian Republicans: The Formation of Party Organization, 1789–1801.* Chapel Hill: University of North Carolina Press, 1957.

De Conde, Alexander. *Entangling Alliance: Politics and Diplomacy Under George Washington.* Durham: Duke University Press, 1958.

Dictionary of American Biography. 10 vols. New York: Charles Scribner's Sons, 1936.

Dictionary of National Biography. New York: Macmillan, 1885–1900.

Dinkin, Robert. *Voting in Revolutionary America: A Study of Elections in the Original Thirteen States, 1776–1789.* Westport, CT: Greenwood Press, 1982.

Elkins, Stanley and Eric McKitrick. *The Age of Federalism: The Early American Republic, 1788–1800.* New York: Oxford University Press, 1993.

Ellis, Joseph J. *Passionate Sage: The Legacy and Character of John Adams.* New York: W. W. Norton, 1993.

———. *American Sphinx: The Character of Thomas Jefferson.* New York: Vintage Books, 1996.

Emery, Noemie. *Alexander Hamilton: An Intimate Portrait.* New York: Putnam, 1982.

Farrand, Max, ed. *Records of the Federal Convention of 1787.* Revised edition in four volumes. New Haven: Yale University Press, 1966.

Federal Writers Project. *WPA Guide to Washington, DC.* New York: Pantheon, 1983.

Ferling, John. *John Adams: A Life.* New York: Henry Holt & Co., 1996.

Flexner, James. *The Young Hamilton: A Biography.* Boston: Little, Brown, 1978.

Fowler, William M., Jr. *Jack Tars and Commodores: The American Navy, 1783–1815.* Boston: Houghton Mifflin, 1984.

Freeman, Douglas S. *George Washington: A Biography.* Vol. 6: *Patriot and President.* New York: Charles Scribner's Sons, 1957.

———. *Washington: An Abridgment in One Volume by Richard Harwell.* New York: Simon & Schuster, 1968.

Froncek, Thomas, ed. *An Illustrated History of the City of Washington by the Junior League of Washington.* New York: Alfred A. Knopf, 1977.

Fuller, Wayne E. *The American Mail: Enlarger of the Common Life.* Chicago: University of Chicago Press, 1972.

Furman, Bess. *White House Profile.* Indianapolis, Ind.: Bobbs-Merrill, 1951.

Gordon-Reed, Annette. *Thomas Jefferson and Sally Hemings: An American Controversy.* Charlottesville: University of Virginia Press, 1997.

Green, Constance M. *Washington, Village and Capital, 1800–1878.* Princeton, N.J.: Princeton University Press, 1962.

Hecht, Marie B. *Odd Destiny: The Life of Alexander Hamilton.* New York: Macmillan, 1981.

Henrickson, Robert A. *The Rise and Fall of Alexander Hamilton.* New York: Van Nostrand Reinhold, 1981.

Historical Statistics of the United States, 1790–1957. Washington, D.C.: Government Printing Office, 1961.

Ketcham, Ralph. *James Madison: A Biography.* Charlottesville: University of Virginia Press, 1990.

Kline, Mary Jo, ed. *Alexander Hamilton: A Biography in His Own Words.* New York: Newsweek Books, 1972.

———. *Political Correspondence and Public Papers of Aaron Burr.* Vol. 1. Princeton, N.J.: Princeton University Press, 1983.

Kohn, Richard H. *Eagle and Sword: The Federalists and the Creation of the Military Establishment in America, 1783–1802.* New York: The Free Press, 1975.

Korngold, Ralph. *Citizen Toussaint.* Boston: Little, Brown, 1944.

Kurtz, Stephen G. *The Presidency of John Adams: The Collapse of Federalism, 1795–1800.* Philadelphia: University of Pennsylvania Press, 1957.

Lankevich, George J., and Howard B. Furer. *A Brief History of New York City.* New York: Associated Faculty Press, 1984.

Lodge, Henry C., ed. *The Works of Alexander Hamilton.* New York: G. P. Putnam's Sons, republished by Scholarly Press, St. Clair Shores, Mich., 1971.

Lomask, Milton. *Aaron Burr: The Years from Princeton to President, 1756–1805.* New York: Farrar, Straus & Giroux, 1979.

Malone, Dumas. *Jefferson the President: First Term 1801–1805.* Boston: Little, Brown, 1970.

———. *Jefferson and the Ordeal of Liberty.* Boston: Little, Brown, 1962.

Marsh, Philip M. *Philip Freneau: Poet and Journalist.* Minneapolis, Minn.: Dillon Press, 1967.

Miller, John C. *Alexander Hamilton: Portrait in Paradox.* New York: Harper Bros., 1959.

———. *The Federalist Era, 1789–1801.* New York: Harper Bros., 1960.

———. *Crisis in Freedom: The Alien and Sedition Acts.* Boston: Little, Brown, 1951.

Minnigerode, Meade. *Lives and Times: Four Informal American Biographies.* New York: G. P. Putnam's Sons, 1925.

Morison, Samuel Eliot. *The Maritime History of Massachusetts 1783–1860.* Boston: Houghton Mifflin, 1941.

Morris, Gouverneur. *A Diary of the French Revolution by Gouverneur Morris, 1752–1816.* Ed. Beatrix Carey Davenport. Boston: Houghton Mifflin, 1939.

Morris, Richard B., ed. *Alexander Hamilton and the Founding of the Nation.* New York: Dial Press, 1957.

Moyers, Bill. *Report from Philadelphia.* New York: Ballantine Books, 1987.

Parmet, Herbert, and Marie B. Hecht. *Aaron Burr: Portrait of an Ambitious Man.* New York: Macmillan, 1967.

Peterson, Merrill D. *Thomas Jefferson and the New Nation: A Biography.* New York: Oxford University Press, 1970.

Pinckney, Elise, ed. *The Letterbook of Eliza Lucas Pinckney, 1739–1762.* Chapel Hill: University of North Carolina Press, 1972.

Pole, J. R. *Political Representation in England and the Origins of the American Republic.* New York: Macmillan/St. Martin's Press, 1966.

Powell, J. H. *Bring Out Your Dead: The Great Plague of Yellow Fever in Philadelphia in 1793.* Philadelphia: University of Pennsylvania Press, 1949.

Robbins, Roy. *Our Landed Heritage: The Public Domain 1776–1936.* Gloucester, Mass.: Peter Smith, 1960.

Rogers, Donald W., ed. *Voting Rights and the Spirit of American Democracy: Essays on the History of Voting and Voting Rights in America.* Urbana: University of Illinois Press, 1992.

Rogers, George C., Jr. *Charleston in the Age of the Pinckneys.* Norman: University of Oklahoma Press, 1969.

Rogow, Arnold. *A Fatal Friendship: Alexander Hamilton and Aaron Burr.* New York: Hill and Wang, 1998.

Rosenfeld, Richard. *American Aurora: A Democratic-Republican Returns. The Suppressed History of Our Nation's Beginnings and the Heroic Newspaper That Tried to Report It.* New York: St. Martin's Press, 1997.

Rossiter, Clinton. *1787: The Grand Convention.* New York: W. W. Norton, 1987.

Rutland, Robert. *The Newsmongers: Journalism in the Life of the Nation, 1690–1972.* New York: Dial Press, 1973.

Sharp, James R. *American Politics in the Early Republic: The New Nation in Crisis.* New Haven, Conn.: Yale University Press, 1993.

Silbey, Joel, ed. *The Congress of the United States: Its Origins and Early Development.* Brooklyn, N.Y.: Carlson Publishers, 1991.

Sisson, Daniel. *The American Revolution of 1800.* New York: Alfred A. Knopf, 1974.

Slaughter, Thomas. *The Whiskey Rebellion: Frontier Epilogue to the American Revolution.* New York: Oxford University Press, 1986.

Smith, James Morton, ed. *The Republic of Letters: The Correspondence between Thomas Jefferson and James Madison, 1776–1826.* Vol. 2, *1790–1804.* New York: W. W. Norton, 1995.

Smith, Margaret Bayard. *The First Forty Years of Washington Society.* Ed. Gaillard Hunt. New York: Charles Scribner's Sons, 1906.

Smith, Page. *John Adams.* Vol. 2, *1784–1826.* New York: Doubleday, 1982.

Still, Bayrd. *Mirror for Gotham: New York As Seen by Contemporaries from Dutch Days to the Present.* New York: New York University Press, 1956.

Tagg, James. *Benjamin Franklin Bache and the Philadelphia "Aurora."* Philadelphia: University of Pennsylvania Press, 1991.

Tinkcom, Harry M. *The Republicans and Federalists in Pennsylvania, 1790–1801.* Harrisburg: Pennsylvania Historical and Museum Commission, 1950.

Weise, Arthur J. *The History of the City of Albany New York from the Discovery of the Great River in 1524, by Verrazzano, to the Present Time.* Albany: E. H. Bender, 1884.

Wharton, Francis. *State Trials of the United States During the Administrations of Washington and Adams.* Philadelphia: Corey and Hart, 1849.

Zahniser, Marvin R. *Charles Cotesworth Pinckney, Founding Father.* Chapel Hill: University of North Carolina Press, 1967.

Index